The Total Quality Management Approach to IT Security

For Oscar, my son

A Quality Product of Love:

I do not love him because he is good,

but because he is my little child.

The Total Quality Management Approach to IT Security

Mario Devargas

NCC BLACKWELL

First published 1995

NCC Blackwell
108 Cowley Road
Oxford OX4 1JF
UK

Blackwell Publishers Inc.
238 Main Street, Cambridge, MA 02142
USA

ISBN 1-85554-352-4

Library of Congress data has been applied for.

Typeset in 10.5 on 12pt Times Roman by ScribeTech Ltd, Bradford
Printed in Great Britain by Hartnolls Ltd., Bodmin, Cornwall

This book is printed on acid-free paper

Contents

Preface		*vii*
1.	**Introduction**	1
2.	**What is Quality Assurance?**	5
—	History of Quality Assurance	5
—	What is Quality?	10
—	Total Quality Management	21
—	Manufacturing versus the Service Industry	41
—	Measuring Quality within the IT Industry	43
—	Cost of Quality	48
—	Management Involvement and Leadership	53
—	Quality System and Manual	62
3.	**IT Security and Quality**	65
—	Information Security	67
—	Quality IT Security Policy	68
—	Planning and Design for Quality IT Security	81
—	Risk to Information	88
—	Quality Contingency Planning	93
—	Security and Systems Audits	98
—	Managing Security within a Quality Environment	99
4.	**Quality Standards and their Association with IT**	103
—	BS5750 / ISO9000 / EN29000	104
—	Software Quality	126

5. IT Security Standards and their relation to Quality 135

— Orange Book 136

— European Security Standard (ITSEC) 140

6. Auditing IT Security in Terms of Quality 147

— Formal Quality Audits 149

— Informal Quality Reviews 157

Appendix A: Example Quality Manual 161

Appendix B: Example Security Policy / Standard 183

Appendix C: Example Disaster Recovery Plan 207

Appendix D: Glossary 231

Appendix E: References 247

Appendix F: Useful Addresses 251

Footnotes 261

Index 273

Vivimos la vida ajeno al futuro pero
debemos vivirla sin pajaritos en la mente
... Antonio Mancera

Preface

Quality and Security are intertwined to form an essential system for all areas of our industrial infra-structure. In terms of Security, it could be said that if an IT System does not function according to requirements (eg., breaks the basic rules of Security in terms of Confidentiality, Integrity or Availability — see Chapter 3 for further details), then it is obviously not a quality product and does not meet the basic Quality definition of "fit for purpose" (see Chapter 2 for further details). Each philosophy has as its premise the criteria of supplying industry as a whole with the tools for performing a superior job and producing a more cost-effective product. In the last two decades, many leading companies and public administrations have invested heavily in these philosophies providing them with that elusive competitive advantage via reducing costs and increasing sales.

This publication will describe the main management issues concerning each area and how they inextricably affect each other to the point that one cannot function without the other. It is therefore recommended that when reading this book the reader is always aware that *Quality* does not just mean Rolls Royce cars or mink coats — it is a fitness for purpose; and *Security* is not Fort Knox or having bodyguards at every door but safeguarding critical areas against both unauthorized intrusion and unexpected occurrences.

The reading of any book should always be an adventure into the unknown, where the reader is subtly guided (not led) along a maze of ideas, concepts, philosophies, theorems and solutions. At each turning point the reader is normally left with more questions than answers but with the feeling that he/she has gained some insight into the subject. In order for this adventure to be rewarding, the reader must take an active role when reading the book and share some of its protagonism.

Without the reader wanting to seek out answers this book will not be of value. Accordingly the intention of this book is not to be an oracle of quality and security philosophies but to be the instigator of change.

In order to achieve this goal the author has included within the following pages the main Quality and Security areas and describes how he sees their inter-dependencies. He has also endeavoured to identify those issues that affect most businesses. The contents are as follows:

(i) What is Quality Assurance? This is answered not in terms of the pure definition of quality but how industry sees quality. It defines the basic quality concepts from first principles, describing where quality procedures came from, how quality can be measured and where Information Technology (IT) fits in.

(ii) IT Security and Quality. Quality is part and parcel of Security procedures and vice versa, one without the other would not function, even though identifying Quality issues within IT Security may sometimes be difficult. The basis identified within this chapter is the need to recognize where things can go wrong, how to prevent things from going wrong and how to recover from disasters in the most cost-effective undisruptive manner. Quality defines the way of handling these problems in a very specific way.

(iii) Quality Standards and their association with IT. Standards are defined in all walks of life to help and protect people from any possible difficulty or danger. They provide a way of understanding how an area of work should function and hence facilitate would-be developers the tools for adhering to the norm.

IT has in the last decade or so developed and established numerous standards to cover every possible aspect of its industry; in so doing, it has formalized a dynamic environment and provided its users with a much needed controlling function. This chapter describes the most important Quality Standards and associates their contents to IT.

(iv) IT Security Standards and their relation to Quality. In a similar manner this chapter describes the existing Security Standards and associates their usage with Quality. Security Standards have been developed in isolation, originating mainly within the Military and Counter-intelligence arena. However, in the last two decades many of the criteria identified within these fields have been applied to industry to protect information resulting in obvious implications to the preservation of business.

(v) Auditing IT Security in terms of Quality criteria. In order to be able to identify all the problem areas within this arena, good traditional auditing practices must be performed. This chapter will describe the essential skills and knowledge required to performed an effective audit within Security and the application of Quality to these audits.

Intended Audience

This book is intended for a broad range of readers interested in Total Quality Management, BS5750 and IT Security.

- Managers and Business Consultants: This book provides the reader with an understanding of what features and structures are needed within a Secure Business Environment, as well as knowledge of current and evolving quality procedures.
- Security Analyst and Implementors: This book discusses the critical security design issues in a general user environment and explores approaches to meeting company-wide security and quality requirements.
- Business Managers & Advisers: This book facilitates an insight for readers into how these concepts can influence a company's profit margin. It does not matter how big the company is, every type of company irrespective of size can benefit from taking the salient points described in this book and applying them to their own environment.

Acknowledgements

This book is a direct result of feedback from numerous clients, companies and colleagues who through their enthusiasm and professionality have guided me in compiling this brief introduction to very complex topics — Quality and IT Security.

Special thanks go to Michelle for her contribution of ideas, time reviewing and proof-reading the book and giving me constructive comments.

New and stirring things are belittled, because if they are not belittled the humiliating question arises, "Why then are you not taking part in them?"

H.G. Wells

1

Introduction

IT systems are at the heart of the present Industrial Revolution — or as some call it the Information Revolution. The extent of this revolution can be easily seen within most businesses where IT occupies a central and essential part of the business function. Because of this dependency, the increasing level of IT criminal offences and loss of IT system due to 'bad' quality (reported or swept under the proverbial carpet) represents a major threat to businesses and consequently the country's economy and society as a whole.

This danger is now recognized as a vital issue to be addressed. The availability, reliability, integrity and confidentiality of IT systems are fundamental 'quality criteria' of any IT system. These quality criteria are consequently defined according to business needs and acceptability.

Clearly the meaning of Quality within IT systems can be interpreted by different people in different ways and therefore it would suffice to say that Quality is what all of us perceive a service or product to be when we are satisfied with it. However, this simple definition would not explain the distinction between bad and good quality, nor how to improve quality. Quality (or the adherence to standards like BS5750 or ISO9000) is often the hook onto which many companies hang their hat in order to achieve success or to have said to have achieved success.

However, there is more to Quality than this; for instance, the quality of life is one item that we would all agree is everyone's prime obsession or attitude of mind. This does not mean that we are all obsessed with achieving great amounts of wealth and power (although Western Society's ethos is guided in this way) but that we all aspire to something 'better'[1], — better than what we presently have, whether that be bettering a £5,000 per annum job or a £250,000 per annum one.

In each situation, irrespective of wealth, everyone wants a certain level of quality which their income can facilitate, i.e., everyone has their own individual and unique Personal Quality Criteria (PQC). This PQC is defined in terms of six basic needs:

(i) *Self Awareness* — the way we see ourselves shapes everything we do. If you are self-confident and value yourself, you will feel that you are in control of your actions and destiny. This goes beyond any personal requirement of quality since an individual has the power to change his/her own destiny. Even minor changes can help to alter your standards of living and hence the quality of life.

(ii) *Families and groups* — a close and loving relationship is the most fundamental of all human needs since our happiness and emotional security depends closely on the way we relate to others. This raises our expectations of companionship and the type and quality of relationship we want from our neighbours on this earth.

(iii) *Job satisfaction* — many different factors influence this: the degree of control you have over the way you do your job (even within company constraints and safeguards), the amount of recognition you receive, the environment you work in, the person you work for, security, money, and promotion prospects. All these issues influence the quality of the job and the work performed within that job.

(iv) *Usage of time* — of all our commodities, this is one of the most precious. There are only 24 hours in each day, and for most of us these are divided up into day-time working hours and night-time rest or play. Fitting in all one's tasks, commitments and leisure activities into one's waking hours can create time shortages, leading to an acceptance of less quality in certain areas. For example, one may feel that by spending three hours per day on a task one gains 100% satisfaction and quality. However, one knows that it cannot be given more than two hours a week, hence is satisfied with a lower level of quality.

(v) *Space and comfort* — our environment is an extension of ourselves, within it the quality and comfort of the surroundings will inevitably influence the quality of life and what is produced within it. For example, removing unpleasant smells, controlling extremes of temperature, coping with dirt and untidiness will assist your state of mind which in turn will create a quality environment.

(vi) *Nutrition and exercise* — food is the fuel that we take into our bodies and exercise creates the energy that uses up this food. However, the quality of the food ingested will inevitably need to be to a safe and palatable standard in order for the body to attain the benefits it needs from it. Similarly the type of exercise undertaken requires training and experience in order to attain the necessary level.

These personal quality goals are attainable as long as the definition of each goal is based solely on individual needs and desires plus the resources available. It is therefore easy to see that the quality of the above six PQCs depends greatly on our needs and acceptance of quality.

Similarly the quality of anything, specially IT systems is guided by the consumer — i.e., the user's perception of what quality they deem acceptable and whether it meets a level (or standard) set by industry.

The reader by now should be thinking that if quality is as simple as facilitating the end-user with what they want and need, i.e., 'a fitness for purpose', then why all the hype? Why do we need standards like BS5750/ISO9000? What makes a product or service 'better' than another? Is what they are reading in this book of the required 'quality'? How is this ethos implemented within IT Security?

Each and many more of these types of questions will be answered throughout the pages of this book. It is obvious that quality is a very personal and cultural term that can be applied to every area of society including Computers and specifically IT Security. We all have our own specific goals towards achieving quality, however, the human animal is also immensely adaptable, accepting their 'immediate surroundings' to suit their individual needs and comforts which can include accepting a lower level of quality in their life. This inevitably leads to a great amount of contentment and stability, two very sought-after human attributes.

This quest for the status quo is one of the main reasons why Total Quality Management (TQM) concepts are seen with a great deal of trepidation and in some circles contempt — even though the concept as such is a natural extension to human nature. Western Society, especially within the confines of the 'old' world, i.e. Europe, has in the past two or three centuries created and fermented a 'stable' environment for humans to live in where historic norms, fashion, ethos and morals play a major part in it. Any change to this is seen as destructive, with civilization expecting its citizens to conform to the established standard, even when the standard is wrong or restrictive.

This is why TQM has had such a mixed reception within our culture. Its effectiveness is often limited or negated by a failure to adequately consider the relationship between productivity and cultural behaviour. Therefore, in order for TQM methodologies to flourish a major investment is required in terms of achieving culture change and changing management behaviour.

This is very apparent from the Japanese culture-shock after the Second World War. The loss of their imperial identity and the humiliation of their God (Emperor) caused them to re-evaluate themselves and their heritage. By keeping the basic principles of authority and with the help of US investment[2], Japan has become the Quality Centre of the world.

The reason is simple. The Japanese examine the process of doing a job, why it is done in a certain way and then improve upon it by thinking laterally.

This change in culture and specifically within corporate culture[3], is also needed in Western Society in order for TQM to succeed. Some may say that it is a revolution (a word Western Society since the Russian Revolution has had trouble with) that is needed in order for any advance in thought and practices within our industrial world to ever occur. This 'culture-change'/revolution and its evolution since the 1950s is described in detail in Chapter 2.

Like many methods and standards and IT security procedures, TQM and its variants has its birth in the formalization of common sense. In the main, these ideas have been addressed in terms of the manufacture of products. By strictly defining work methods and instructions, safety criteria, customer needs and design methods, TQM has been 'implemented' within many organizations. However, it is obvious that this is only the foundation on which you would build culture change and a Quality Culture.

Recent studies into TQM and its application in industry have shown that the common factor in all our activities is the pursuit of excellence, reduction of costs, increase in profits and hence a more than acceptable level of Quality. This would eventually lead to gaining that elusive competitive advantage sought after by all. Then why not use these theorems in all walks of life, other than manufacturing e.g., in the Health Service, Police, IT and the Security of IT?

It is not the intention of this book to explain the concepts of IT Security[4] in great detail, although obviously some basic principles will be described in order to briefly introduce the reader to IT Security and its effect on Quality. The relationship between these two 'marketable' twenty-first century terms will become apparent as the reader thumbs through the labyrinth of this book.

As mentioned earlier, it is well known that IT has become a very important part of business life.

Business now has a requirement for up-to-date accurate information never before thought of. This requirement means a near-total dependency upon the ability to manipulate 'quality' information. Examples of this can be seen in:

- Banking
- Insurance

- Communications
- Advertising
- Merchandizing
- Product Design and Packaging
- Publishing, news-gathering
- Education
- Leisure
- Surveillance

to name but a few. IT insecurity has led to an ever-increasing credibility problem with users questioning the reliability, accuracy and currency of information and the hardware/software supplying that information. This problem leads fundamentally to questioning the fitness for purpose of the IT environment.

This obviously means that the proper use of IT is of paramount importance since its role within industry is to supply management with the right tools for reducing costs and increasing profits. This inevitably has meant that computers are now heavily relied upon for the continued success of many organizations.

This reliance means that any threat to the operation of the systems must be addressed quickly. Such threats can include partial or complete loss of computing facilities.

A couple of examples of where such IT threats are posing a serious security and quality problem include:

- Access control, where to date there is no secure and reliable 'personal' identifier. None can be said to be 'fit for their purpose' with, for example, passwords being totally unfit to secure the most simple IT systems. This problem is further compounded by the lack of IT awareness within the users, writing their personal simple passwords on pieces of paper and sticking them somewhere for everyone to see.
- Communications and networks, where the medium used can be highly subject to failure, hacking/tapping and the total denial of the service. The quality of the service provided can be highly suspect and can obviously lead to user dissatisfaction and mistrust of the IT environment. Service level agreements can reduce the level of threat to the users but its definition can be an arduous and complicated process, especially in terms of defining the 'acceptable' fitness for purpose of the service.

The reasons and types of threats are elaborated on in Chapter 3. However, the basic definition of IT Security is to have in place management controls and procedures that ensure the protection of confidentiality, integrity and availability (CIA) of the whole system, hardware, software and data/ information.

Threats to IT resources do not solely occur from malicious acts but generally occur due to lack of awareness, controls[5] and quality. Security techniques aided by quality procedures therefore attempt to reduce the level of impact[6] of these threats.

There are no facts, only interpretations
— Friedrich Nietzsche

2

What is Quality Assurance?

Quality is about survival of companies within today's highly competitive markets where the major requirement of the normal 'throw-away' customer is quality products and services — it is very much a 'hearts and minds' exercise. Western society's conscientiousness towards proof of manufacturer's commitment to quality is evident in every area of society. For instance, child-seats for cars today are rigorously tested and must adhere in the UK to BSI[7] (British Standard Institute) quality and safety standards. If they do, a BSI 'kite' mark is stuck onto them, so that customers are aware of this conformity.

As mentioned in the introduction, implementing Quality standards and procedures requires a high level of commitment to change — of both attitudes and practices. Normally those that propose the changes (e.g., senior management) are the ones who must change the most and inevitably such change can be very stressful and distressing. Such change has been evolving since the late 1940s.

The History of Quality Assurance

As already stated, quality as a concept has been around as long as mankind. However, only recently, i.e., in the last four to five decades, has quality assurance and its underlining standards been associated with improved productivity, profits and a 'better' product — fit for its purpose. If we look at these decades we see that three eras (and within these eras Quality Experts[8]) have marked the beginning of our existing Quality Ethos, namely the 1940s-50s and the USA; 1950s-70s and Japan; now and the Western World. I will describe these eras first and investigate how certain individuals have influenced the Quality cause. After this, I will describe how standards have evolved, paying special attention to the UK Market.

The choice of Quality Pioneers discussed within these pages only reflects the evolving doctrines of Quality Theory in the last five decades. Some readers may argue that I have missed several pioneers that have influenced management and quality philosophy. For instance, we could look at the work of Niccolo dei Machiavelli (1491-1527) who described a unique nature of management in the *The Prince* or Henri Fayol (1841-1925) who merged effective management theory into practice, but both individuals dealt with issues associated with industry in their times — things have changed. In the twentieth century there are other pioneers like Henry Ford I who in 1920 developed the first Just-in-Time (JIT[9]) system for the production of the Model T car; Thomas Watson Junior, creation of IBM as a truly global company; Kenichi Ohmac, a successful Japanese management expert who developed numerous 'key factors for success'; Rosabeth Moss Kanter, one of the few women management experts who revolutionized management thought towards adapting to change within the global economy.

All these (and many more) experts and pioneers are worthy of mention but it would take several books to give a just description of their work. What follows is a very brief summary of the last few decades and some influences and achievements within Quality.

1940s-50s and the USA

This first era covers the period when the US Army developed Statistical Quality Control[10] for their production of Vietnam/Korean war supplies. This was later adopted by Toyota within their production line. In this era three Quality experts stand out as the founding fathers of Quality Philosophy. These are W. Edwards Deming, Joseph M. Juran and Armand V Feigenbaum — all three were heavily associated with Japanese industries, Deming and Juran both being professionally associated with the Union of Japanese Scientists and Engineers (JUSE), lecturing and advising Japanese industry.

Deming's approach to quality lies rooted in statistical theory. His ethos on quality is simple: all processes are subject to some imperfection that reduces their quality. If these imperfections are controlled and reduced, then quality will increase. He also advised managers to take a greater responsibility in their role and encouraged them to distinguish between what he called 'special' and 'common' problems of bad quality. The first described those areas that prevented a product's performance from remaining constant, for example, changes in operator.

The second common problem was due to the design, or the operation of the process. The special problems can sometimes be solved by local operators while the common ones require management authority to change. Additionally, he also encouraged Japanese managers to use a systematic approach to problem solving based on what he termed the Plan —> Do —> Check —> Action (PDCA) Cycle, as described in Figure 2.1 below:

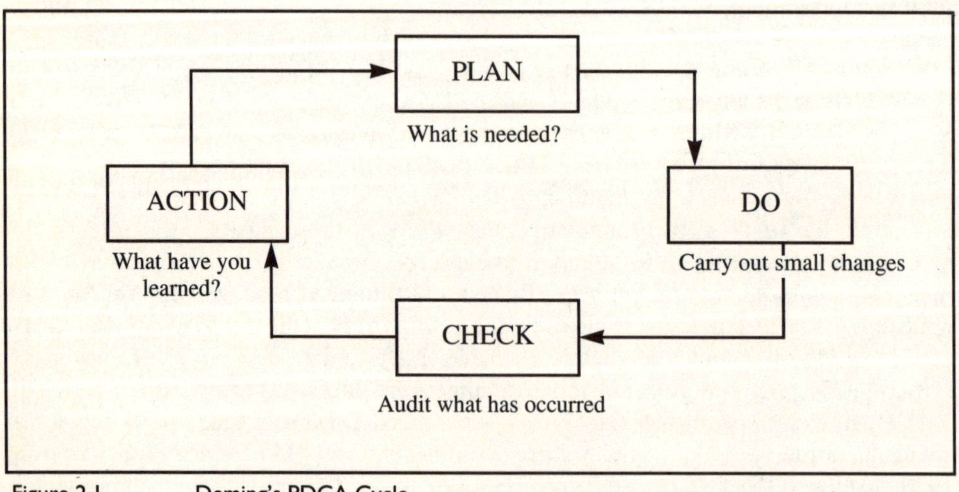

Figure 2.1 Deming's PDCA Cycle

Juran was responsible for 'Quality Control' (QC) theory publishing *The Quality Control Handbook* in 1951. In Japan he advised senior managers that QC should be an integral part of management control and therefore the impetus must come from the very top. Juran's key to quality evolved around the belief that quality does not happen by accident, it must be planned in advance. To this aim his lectures were geared towards planning, organizational issues, management's responsibility to quality and the need to set goals and targets for improvement.

Finally, Feigenbaum enhanced Juran's QC and Quality Assurance[11] (QA) and came up with Total Quality Control[12] (TQC), where he postulated that a systematic or total approach to quality requires the involvement of all functions within an organization, not only manufacturing.

1950s-70s and Japan

The second era covers the rise of Japanese initiatives and entrepreneurship. They adopted American ideas and enhanced/adapted them to suit their needs and culture. Within this era we again can highlight three Japanese experts as the prime movers within Japan of Quality initiatives. They are Kaoru Ishikawa, Genichi Taguchi and Shigeo Shingo. Between them they emphasized the need for training and education, the use of simple tools and teamwork in companies.

Taking these three individuals in turn we can see their contribution to this era as follows. Ishikawa is best known as the pioneer of Quality Circles[13] in Japan. This movement started in 1962 and with the aid of technical statistical techniques (e.g., Pareto[14] Diagrams prioritising quality improvements and cause and effect diagrams used within checking) he developed company-wide quality initiatives, where every employee in a firm is taught seven tools for ascertaining the quality of their work:

- *Pareto Analysis Chart.* This looks at determining the percentage level of errors, waste and rejections as a function of the types of causes. Typically 80% of the failures are associated with 20% of the causes;
- *Cause and Effect diagrams* (also known as the Ishikawa diagram). This looks at the problem in terms of the resources assigned to the task at hand, i.e., equipment and work methods (THE CAUSE) versus the quality attained (THE EFFECT);
- *Stratification.* This defines each element of the production cycle in layers, assigning relevant responsibilities;
- *Check Sheets.* Shingo's poka yoke;
- *Histograms.* These are used to depict the frequency with which results of quality checks occur;
- *Scatter diagrams.* These are used to depict the results of quality checks between two quality factors;
- *Shewhart's control chart and graphs.* These depict the results of quality checks.

Although the above may seem rather technical, it is really very simple, since it is based on good data collection and presentation tools. These tools are simply devices to assist the QC in establishing quality improvements.

Taguchi is famous for his methodologies for improving quality engineering within strict cost rules. His method of problem solving quantifies the total loss due to lack of quality of a performance characteristic and relates it to its deviation from the established target performance — i.e., quality and reliability are the responsibility of the design stage prior to production. This gives an indication of the 'quality loss' of a product that could be due to rework, scrap, maintenance, failure, marketing, etc. These methods are fundamentally based on 'off-line' Quality Control techniques within the design stage of products and services.

Shingo, the world's leading production management expert, is best known as the father of 'Zero Defect'. He defined the mistake proofing or Defects = 0 system; its main idea is 'stop the process whenever a defect occurs, find the cause and prevent it re-occurring' — hence defects are detected and fixed at source. This he called the poka-yoke system since he accepts that people are fallible and likely to make mistakes. Therefore he suggests the use of a simple checklist (i.e., a poka-yoke) as an aid to quality. This method is based on holistic evaluations of the whole systems, where his method looks at both the assembly processes and the sequences of assembly parts. In essence this is the principle behind JIT production.

Now and the Western World

The third era is highlighted by the re-emergence of Western quality philosophy and the extension of the first two eras. In addition to Deming[15], Feigenbaum[16], Taguchi[17], Juran[18] who developed their theories to cover our present day business requirements, we also have two further Quality Experts (although some would actually define these individuals more as Management Experts — but what is management?). These are Philip B. Crosby and Tom Peters.

Crosby is best known within the Quality arena as bringing Quality down to 'grass-roots' by effectively marketing and selling the ideas of 'do it right first time' and 'Zero Defect' within all areas of a company and the multiple customer-supplier relationships that exist in all organizations, e.g., an operator is both a supplier to the next stage and a customer of the previous one. His quality philosophy is based upon four quality absolutes. These are:

Absolute 1 Quality is defined as conformance to requirements, not as goodness nor elegance.

Absolute 2 The system for causing quality is prevention, not appraisal.

Absolute 3 The performance standard must be Zero Defects, not 'that's close enough'.

Absolute 4 The measurement of quality is the price of non-conformance, not indices.

Peters is not really directly associated with the Quality elite as such, but with the whole issue of management, leadership and the customer. By improving these concepts (the key to improving quality), he maintains that a company would succeed and beat its competitors. In addition to these axioms he investigated what the key qualities were of those companies that were consistently profitable.

In a nut-shell, he maintained that they are:

(i) A bias to action, i.e., getting the job done;

(ii) Closeness to the customers;

(iii) Autonomy and entrepreneurship encourages innovation;

(iv) Productivity through the employees;

(v) Hands-on, value-driven management;

(vi) Stick to what they know best;

(vii) Simple organizational structures leading to lean staff.

His main conclusion was that these companies were innovative and driven by market requirements. Furthermore, he argued that those that were innovative had the right type of management to succeed, e.g., they were responsible for setting the key company standards and direction that determined the corporate culture and its quality commitment. In addition, he then went on further to define the major attributes for good quality:

(i) Obsession with responsiveness to the customer;

(ii) Constant innovation;

(iii) Partnership via empowerment;

(iv) Leadership via change;

(v) Control via simple support system.

Quality Assurance Standards (a brief history)

As we have seen, since the 1940s, Quality and Quality Assurance evolved steadily reacting to the changing business world as and when it was needed. One of the first standards was adopted in the USA after the Second World War, and was followed closely by a similar standard published in Europe, called the NATO AQAP. The NATO AQAP gave birth to DEF STANS in the UK published by the Procurement Executive of the Ministry of Defence. It was not until the 1960s that major business organizations began to evaluate these Quality Standards, in order to improve their production efficiency, their control and selection of suppliers and more importantly improve the bottom-line profit margins.

As usual, (and as most IT professionals are very aware) standards are normally produced by a variety of sources to suit their own particular need. The same occurred within the Quality arena. Each organization that took DEF STANS, adapted it to suit their requirements. An example of DEF STANS is the DEF 131A which was concerned with acceptance sampling and tolerance standards. This obviously caused a great deal of concern and confusion since different auditing practices were being performed, conflicting requirements being applied to the same end product, etc. etc.

In order to stem the tide of a growing Quality conflict among major companies, the BSI published in 1972 the BS4891 — a guide to Quality Assurance. This was intended as a very basic guide to companies wanting to set up Quality systems. Its main points were:

Management Involvement and Objectives

Programming and Planning

Principles of Quality Control

Design and Specification Control

Purchasing Control and Vendor Appraisal

Production Control

Marketing and Service Quality Function

Documentation

Defect and Failure Analysis and Remedial Action

Nonconformance Control

This document helped industry to establish the ground rules for specifying contractual requirements specified in customers' standards. Since this document was simply a guide, more specific standards were still needed to accommodate the requirements of certain areas of industry, for example, in 1973 the Society of Motor Manufacturers and Traders (SMMT) published 73/851 100DC, based on the AQAP Defence Standard. This led the BSI to publish BS5179 (a three part document covering requirements and guides).

BS5179 was the catalyst amongst UK Quality Standards. It helped companies define effective vendor/supplier selection and rating schemes, but more importantly, it formed the basis for increasing the awareness level within Britain's industry. This awareness and subsequent pressure for a stronger standard led, in 1979, to the publication of BS5750 (again in three parts). See Chapter 4 for more specific details on this standard. This was later (in 1987) revised to conform to the ISO9000 series.

What is Quality?

Before we continue, let's spend a couple of minutes looking at the picture below and answer to ourselves the following questions:

How would you determine if this cup is a quality cup?

What type of questions would you need to ask to ascertain this?

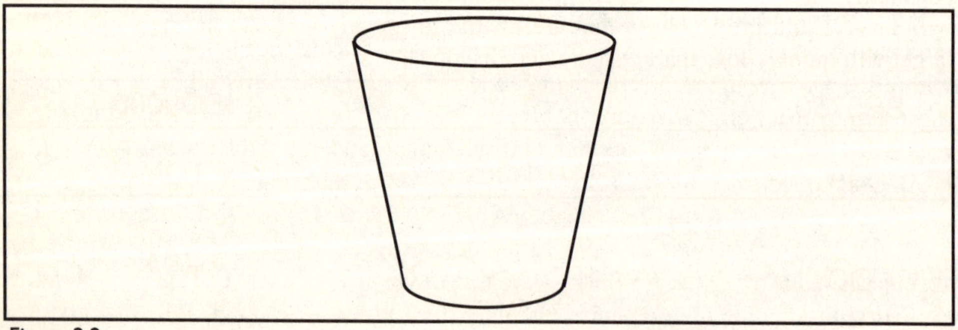

Figure 2.2

How many of you immediately decided what the cup was going to be utilized for, ascertaining whether it could hold hot or cold liquid, taste, etc?

However, I will now say that this plastic cup is specially designed and manufactured to use with washing powder in a launderette.

Is it fit for purpose now?

Boots Everyday Dictionary defines the term quality as *".. that which makes a thing what it is, nature: kind or degree of goodness or worth ..."*. This definition is fine if we all perceive quality in the same way; however, when two or more people discuss the quality of a product or service, varying degrees of quality will be established, depending upon each person's point of view and prejudices. This means that if two different people look at or use the same item, they will inevitably have different views on its quality. We therefore can expand our definition of quality simply as *"conformance with requirements"* — this definition is more apt since individual requirements of a particular item can vary but all must adhere in general to mutual criteria, hence conforming to quality criteria.

These mutual criteria can be agreed between different parties in a clear manner and hence we can then check them for conformance. For a straightforward characteristic, e.g., the minimum length of a car safety-belt, the conformance is straightforward to check. This checking process is only valid if the final customer is the one doing the checking before final despatch of the product or service. However, in our previous example, as in the majority of today's products, it is unlikely that the customer can do this, since the child-seats and belts for cars will be mass-produced.

We therefore have to further enhance our definition of quality to *"conformance with user's requirements and expectations"* as Crosby defines it, since the manufacturer must produce their product, so that they are able to sell it. This also directly influences reliability since part of the acceptability of the product or service depends heavily on it functioning satisfactorily, i.e., quality is synonymous with reliability. Furthermore, this ability of being able to sell the product makes it by definition fit for its final purpose. Hence an additional interpretation of quality would be its *"fitness for use and purpose"* as defined by Juran.

This requirement to always meet the customer's expectation and purpose of the product means that each customer's individual need will either endorse or negate the quality of a product or service, making quality a moving target — how do we meet everyone's need in an ever-changing environment? As described in the introduction, there are many influences on everyday needs and wants — fashion, hygiene, safety, statutory, competition, etc. etc.

This is the very reason why (as we shall see later), although there is a high price to pay for quality, the rewards are limitless if attained. Only companies that are able to constantly meet their customers' expectation and needs with their product and service will survive and grow. Those that are unable to quickly adapt to the moving quality target will quickly lose market share and disappear.

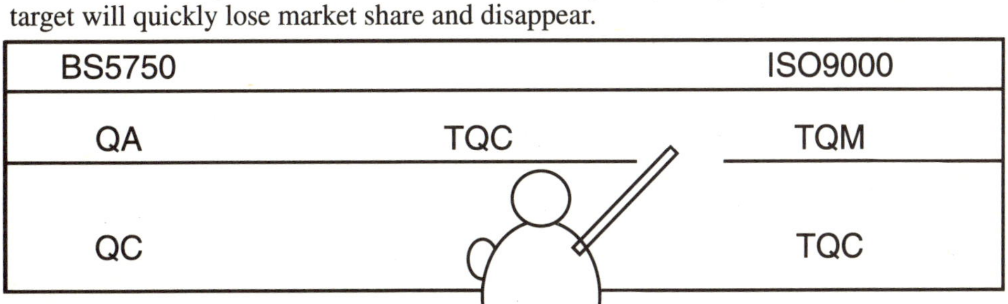

Figure 2.3 Quality Moving Target

The overall company guide to a company's commitment to quality is described in Figure 2.4 below:

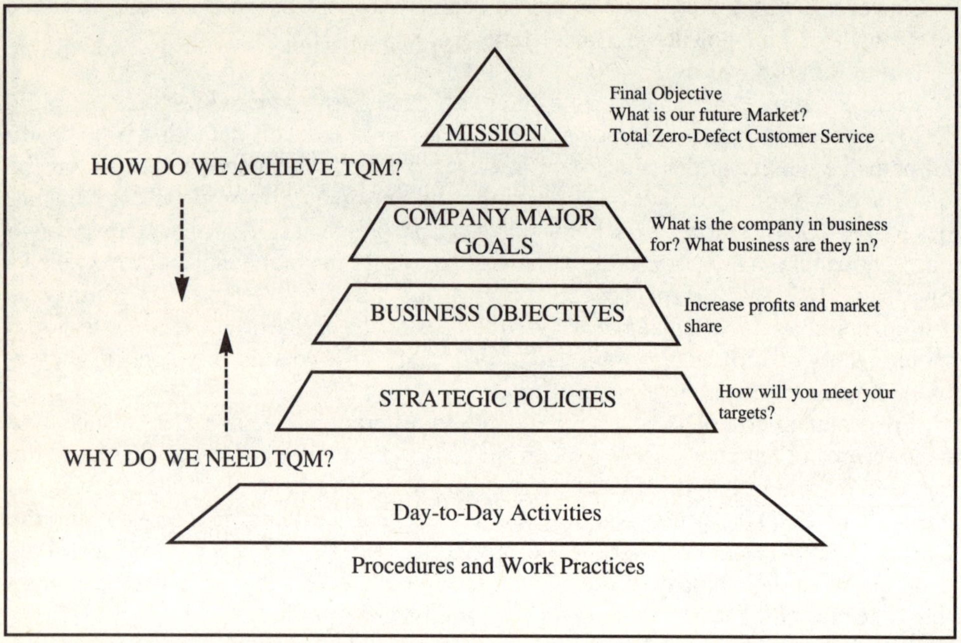

Figure 2.4 Overall Company TQM View

This overall strategy (see Figure 2.4) can be adapted to fit any organization. It describes how a company behaves and defines where it needs to instil a quality culture shock, i.e., everywhere from the shop-floor to senior management.

In order to attain that elusive competitive edge, companies must first meet their own individual company goals — be they increasing profits at any price, increasing market share, or whatever the company officers and share-holders deem important for the company at that particular point in time.

However, it is obvious that in order to meet and surpass these goals they must listen to their existing and prospective customers and find out what they really want. What makes them happy? What are their future wants and needs? How can they keep them as satisfied customers (it is a well known marketing fact that over 80% of a company's business is normally achieved through existing and returned satisfied customers — i.e., the Pareto Principle)? What gets in the way of their staff delivering good quality products and services? Why do people do business with them?

Let us assume that Figure 2.4 is the 'oracle' of a company-wide quality strategy. We can 'explode' each individual element of our model (e.g., Mission, Major Goals, Objectives, Policies and Day-to-day activities) to investigate how it affects the company, whether it will answer those vital business questions mentioned in the previous paragraph and investigate the links of each individual element of our model to IT Security.

Figures 2.4a to Figure 2.4e depict typical statements that could apply to any size and type of organization. Each figure is split into two areas — Business and IT Security. The Business side (top) represents quality statements addressing specific strategic business concerns. The bottom half of each figure depicts the same type of statement but addressing IT Security directly.

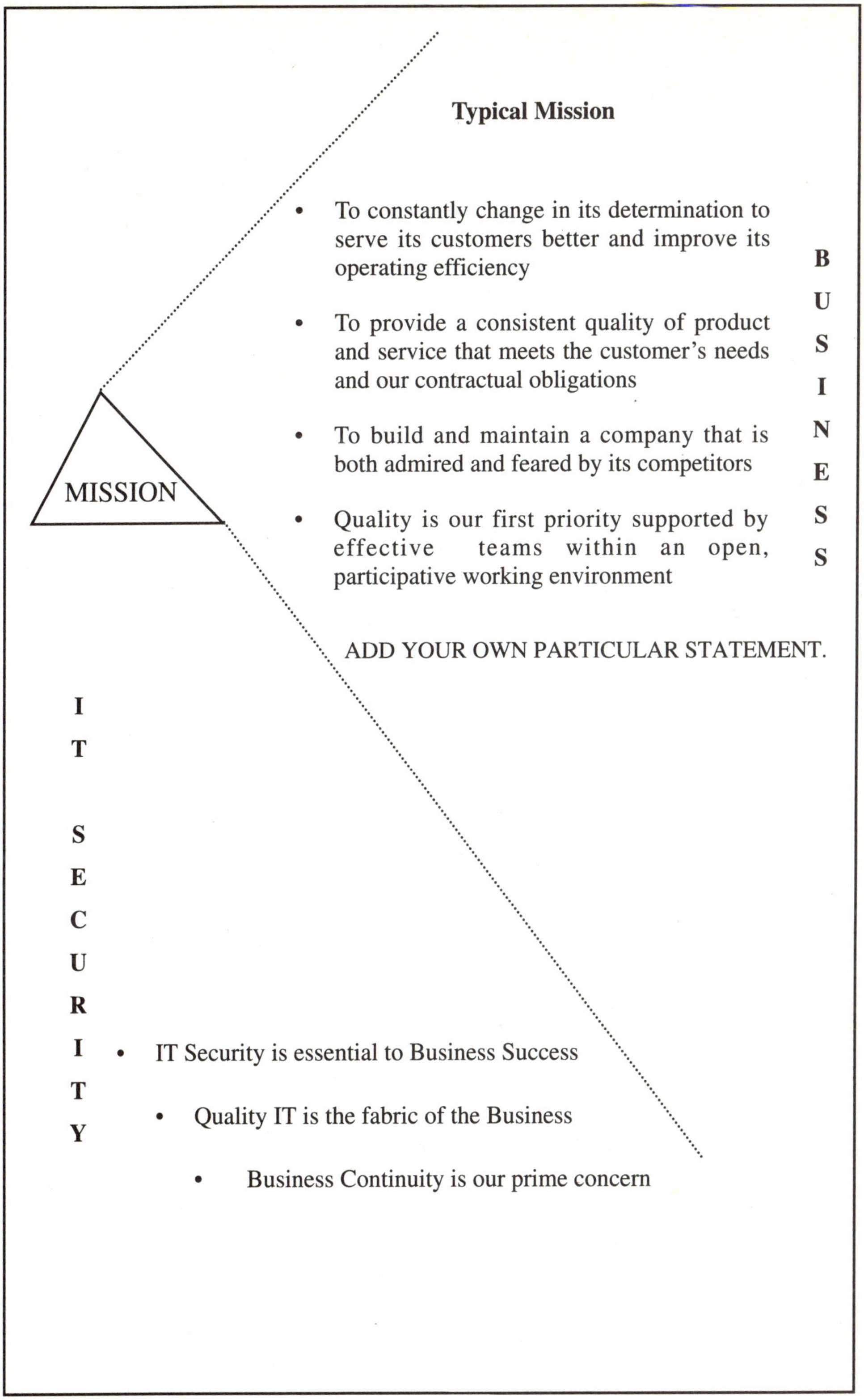

Figure 2.4a Mission Statement

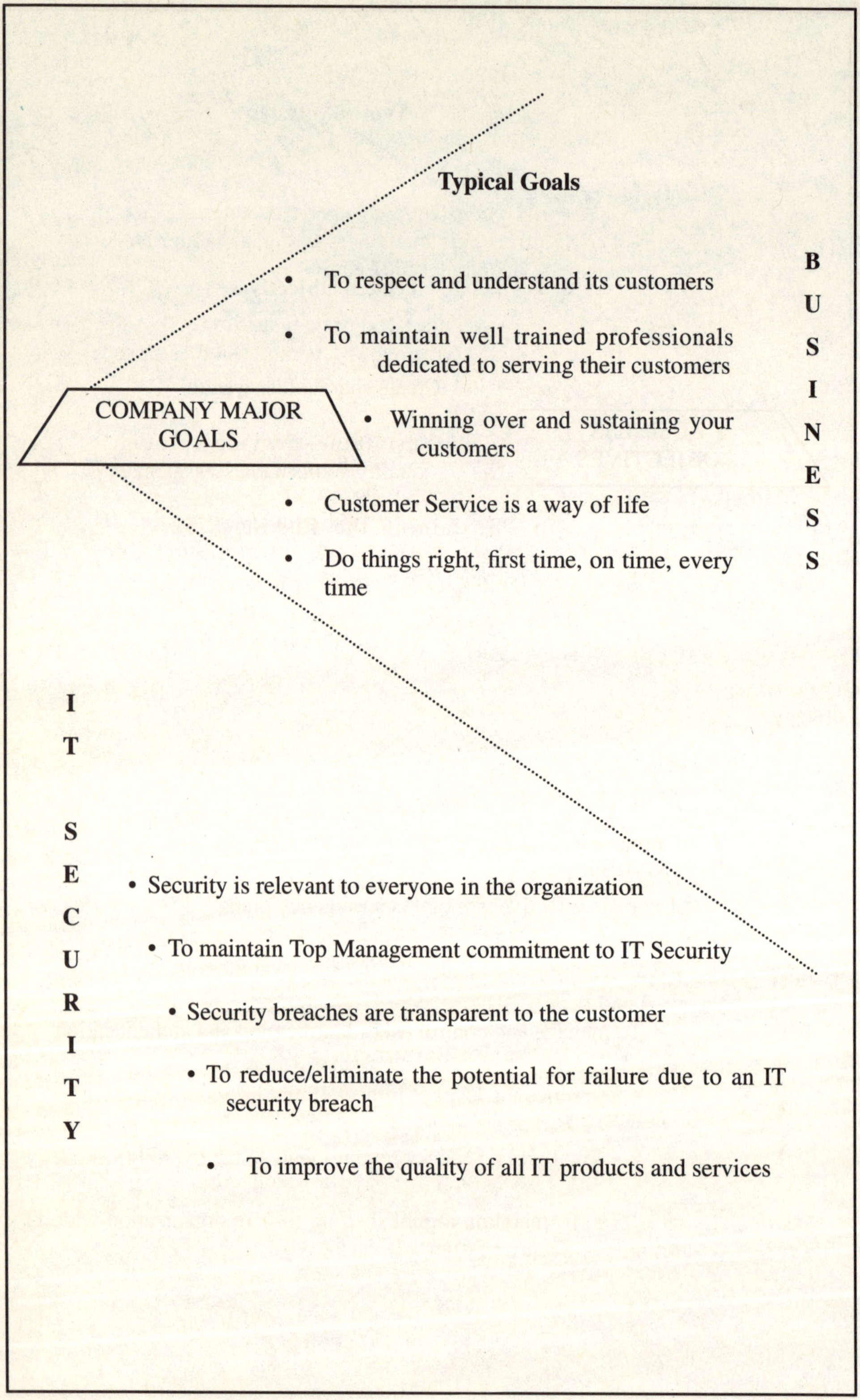

Figure 2.4b Major Goals

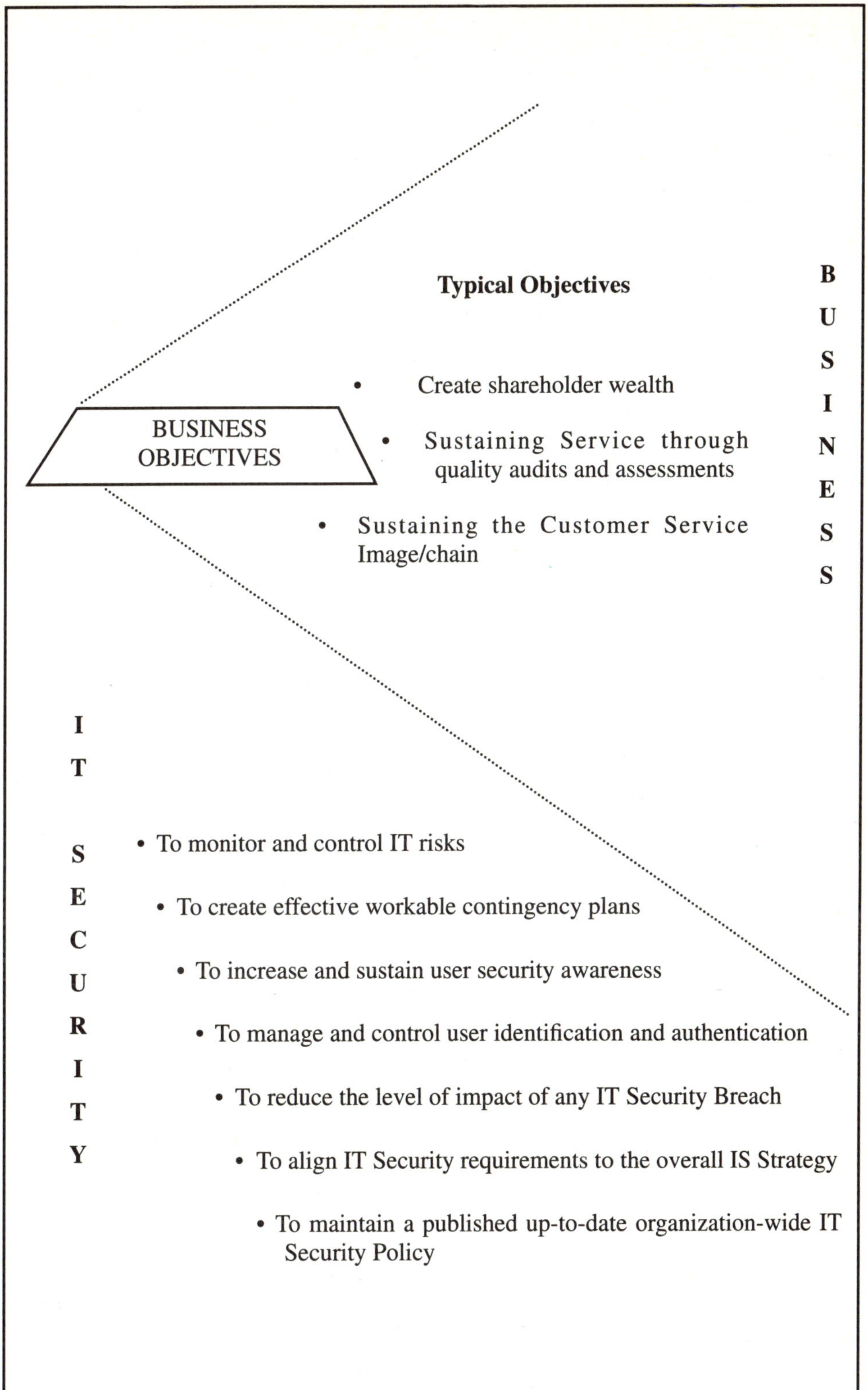

Figure 2.4c Objectives

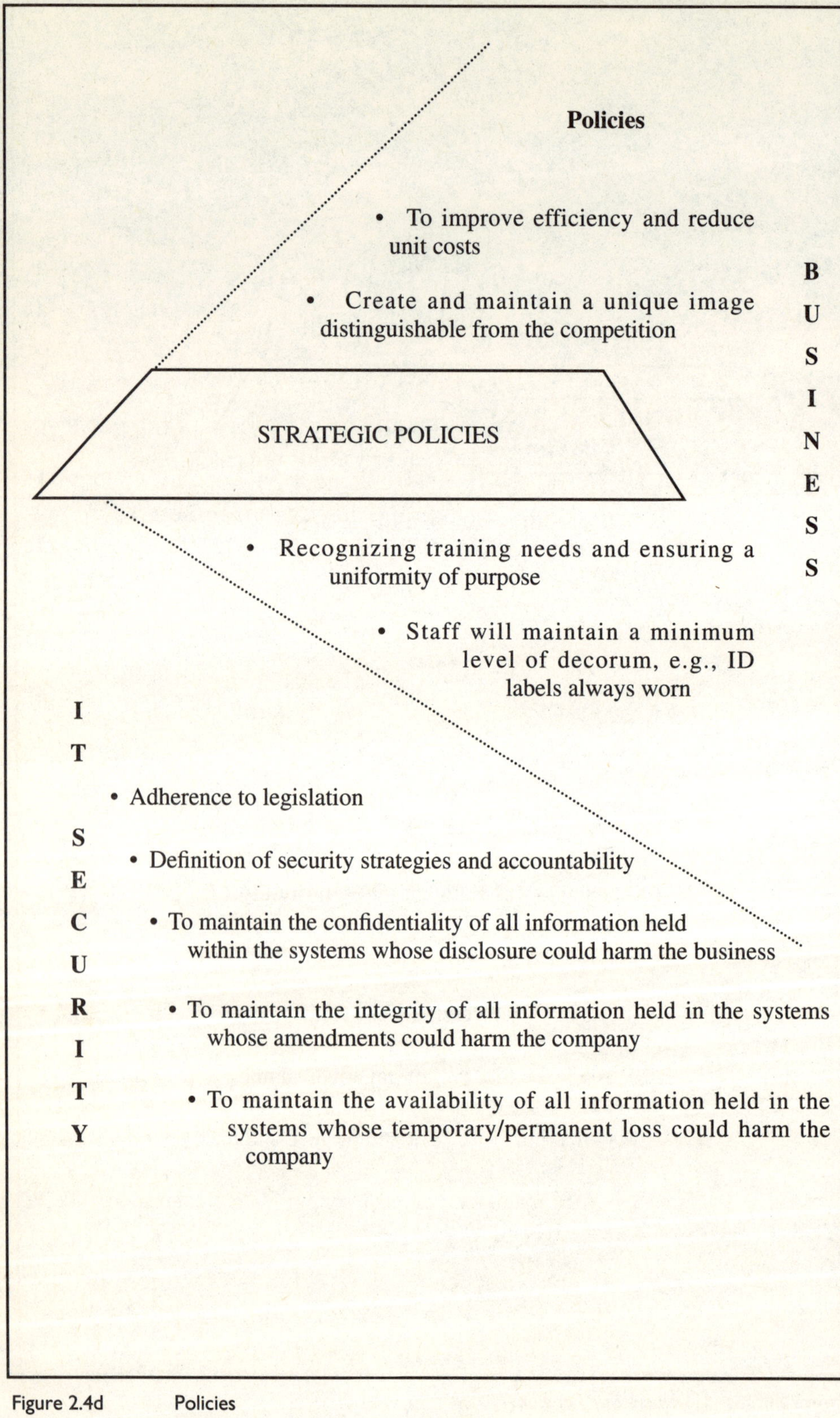

Figure 2.4d Policies

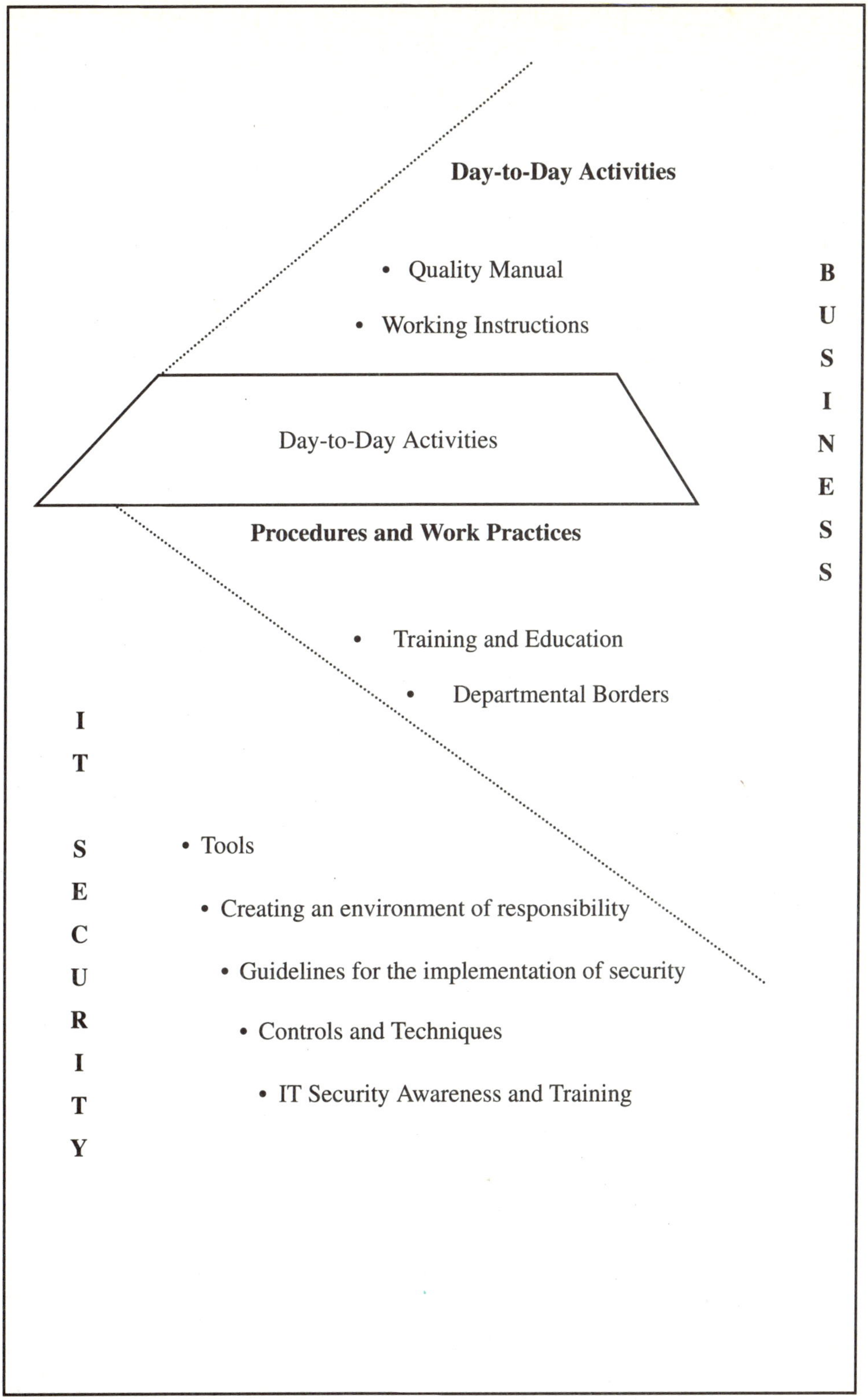

Figure 2.4e Day-to-Day Activities

Once we have identified these questions, other similar ones must also be investigated, e.g., they must also find out what their staff need and want. More importantly, they need to find the answers. This analysis supplies forward looking companies with the tools to determine their future needs as soon as possible so that at a predetermined time they can go to the market before the competition, with product, services and supporting IT tools that contain features that users have not even thought of, thereby moving the quality target again. The competition then has no alternative but to at least match that quality or improve on it in order to stay in business.

It follows then that companies must have a cohesive integrated goal with a common purpose throughout the organization. If there are areas that are not contributing towards this, then their continued existence must be looked into. So what should companies do to achieve quality?

It is important to ensure that each department, section, person, has a common understanding of the business goals and their own individual role within it.

However, each department, section or person does not work in isolation. They are dependent on others for products, services and information, each is responsible for their job and for providing an output which is normally used by another section or someone else inside or outside of the company. The company is therefore made up of numerous small links within a quality chain, where information is passed from entity to entity with possibly some processing taking place in between. This process defines the well-known quality concept of CUSTOMER--> PROCESS --> SUPPLIER (see Figure 2.5 below).

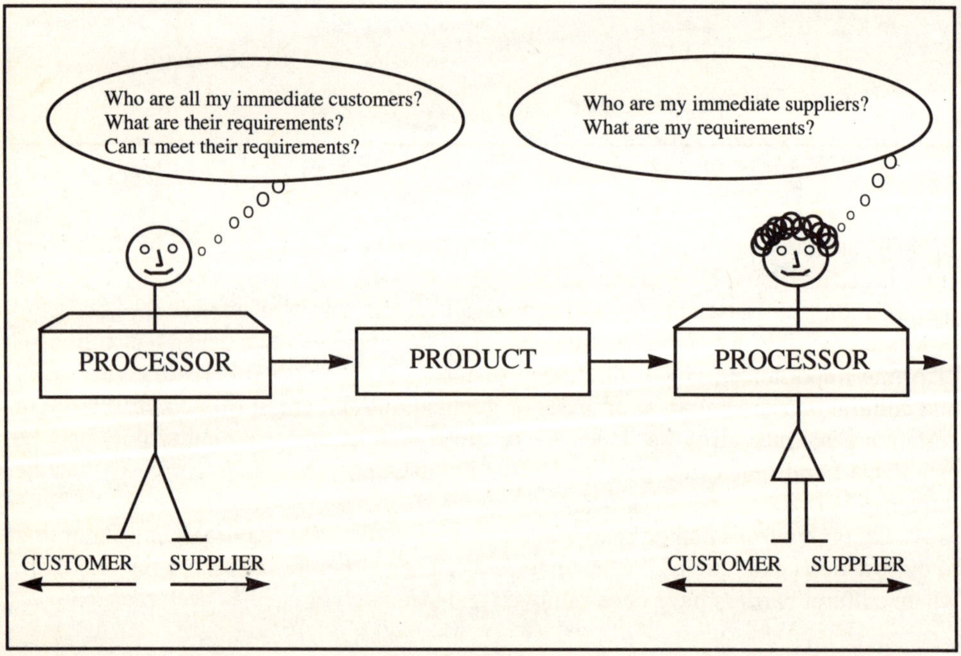

Figure 2.5 Customer — Process — Supplier Chain

As can be seen in Figure 2.5 each person is both a customer and a supplier of a product or information plus is responsible for processing its input (e.g., doing his/her task correctly, as Crosby puts it .. do it right first time, on time) and passing it to the next entity on the chain. If we look at this process a little closer, we can see that it will apply to everything we do, for instance:

(i) When a secretary produces a letter:

- MANAGER gives a SCRIPT (verbally/written) to SECRETARY
- SECRETARY PROCESSES letter and produces an OUTPUT

(ii) When a car-sheet worker produces his doors:

- RAW MATERIALS are given to the worker
- The worker PROCESSES IT and produces a door

(iii) Production of Software

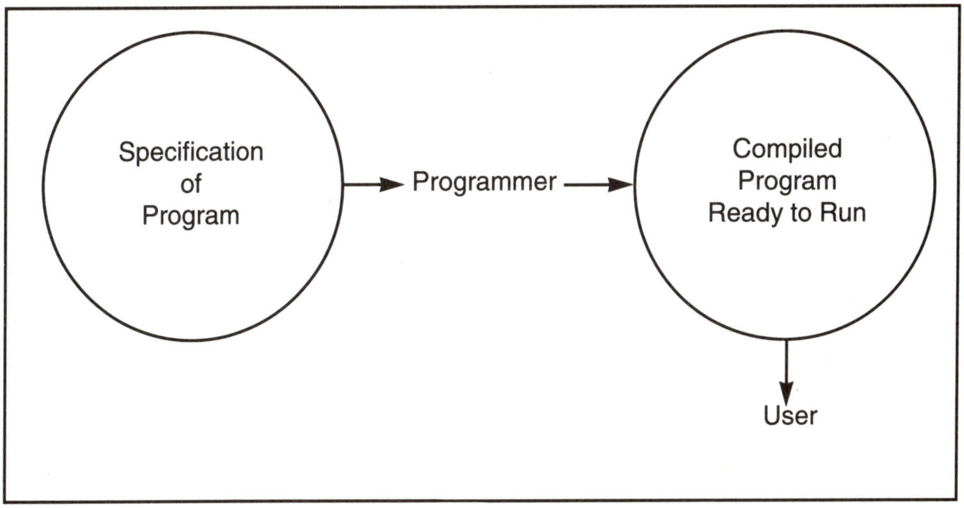

Figure 2.6

In each case there is obviously a major dependency on what is received by the worker (i.e., is it fit for use?). Having decided that it is fit for use, within any effective organization you must also try and reduce all factors that will prevent the job being processed the right way, the first time. Efficient flow between two dependent entities is of prime importance, which may mean dismantling established departmental, social and cultural barriers, removal of waste or duplications and possibly even the closure of certain areas. Once all these issues are resolved then an efficient quality flow may be established and hence the true quality or Total Quality Management ethos will be implemented.

An example of this can be seen within the traditional office environment. Returning to our previous example of the secretary we can see a 'before' and an 'after' scenario, where cultural barriers have been removed and ultimately waste has been reduced.

Before Quality Ethos

Normal office environment with a secretary working for a manager. The secretary is given specific tasks to perform with definite instructions. Ultimate responsibility lies with the manager. The secretary simply acts as a gofer and 'slave' to the manager. In a typical situation the manager gives a hand-written script to the secretary and the secretary types it according to basic office standards. This is returned to the manager for quality assurance and 'red-penning'. This activity may take several iterations before the final output is 'fit for purpose'. In the meantime the manager is getting more and more frustrated, complaining of the lack of 'good' workmanship and the secretary is getting disenchanted and bored with her/his role.

The basic problem within this situation can be summed up as follows:

(a) Manager is too 'senior' and important to use a keyboard — or so he/she believes.

(b) The secretary has only a menial unimportant job and therefore unable to take responsibility for his/her output — or so is believed by the manager.

(c) The secretary abdicates responsibility for his/her action, since his/her work is always going to be checked — and is not trusted.

(d) Each (the manager and secretary) abdicates their responsibility to the organization for working as a team.

The problem requires the dismantling of some very basic barriers. The quality ethos would promote the better use of resources by empowering each individual up to their level of competence and consequently reducing waste and cost. The new scenario could be as follows:

After Quality Ethos

Normal office environment with a secretary working for a manager, each given a well-defined specific role to play within their organization. Each possessing the right level of training and quality awareness skills to perform their job. Each given the right tools for their job. In the normal course of events, a secretary would still be required to produce a 'typed' document of a written output. However, once given to the secretary, the responsibility for the quality of the 'product' is passed onto the secretary until passed back to the manager for sign-off. In this situation we can see that:

(a) The manager trusts his/her secretary to do his/her job.

(b) The secretary takes responsibility for his/her actions.

(c) They are working as a team.

(d) Waste in time and human emotions is reduced to a minimum.

This simple example shows how a quality policy can influence day-to-day business life down to the most basic level. The length of an organization's quality chain is never-ending. At each ring a unique element of quality is established that affects the next ring in the chain and is dependent of the previous ring in the chain.

This means that the entire supply chain — supplier (external and internal), processors (everyone) and customers (external and internal) will function as one whole leading to real Just-in-Time production.

Total Quality Management

The traditional approach to quality control is to set quality standards, produce the product or service and to scrap or rework any failings to meet predetermined agreed standards — **a strategy of prevention**. However, this inspect-rectify philosophy has various disadvantages:

(i) It's wasteful because time and materials have been invested in products and services which are not usable;

(ii) It's uneconomical in terms of manpower (inspectors and/or rectifiers);

(iii) It's unreliable as standards of inspection vary from person to person and day to day;

(iv) The rectification process may itself introduce additional errors;

(v) It does nothing to improve the process that is the root cause of the problem.

On the other hand, a strategy of prevention believes that money should be spent ensuring the system and processes are right, so that the items are produced correctly in the first place. Here is where TQM comes in with its definition as 'continually satisfying customer requirements, at the lowest price'. TQM promotes a process of continuous improvements and innovation, where control is embedded within and is driven by the culture of the company as a whole (i.e., not only within the production side but also on the service side).

Quality becomes the responsibility of everyone, with senior management providing leadership and support (see Management involvement and Leadership, page 53 for a more detailed explanation concerning Management Leadership and its affect on Quality) but with the main push of quality coming from lower down the organizational ladder.

TQM therefore means the use and application of methods we have discussed so far (i.e., QC, TQC, Quality Circles, Tagushi, customer services) plus the company-wide commitment to succeed via TQM methods. This means that a clear effective quality policy must be in place and transmitted throughout the organization. In Japan they call this 'Hoshin' (Quality Policy Deployment (QPD)) in conjunction with Quality Function Deployment (QFD[19]). What this means is that QPD goes down the organization making sure that everyone is aware of their responsibility and the company's commitment to quality, while QFD goes across functions.

This does NOT mean quality functions or departments but the definition of customer needs i.e., link the customer's needs and wants with the company's resources to meet those needs. In essence QFD is an elaborate Quality Control Circle (kyü shii. säkuru) technique , which can work just as well.

Quality Circles are mainly concerned with effective teamwork and problem solving. I have already mentioned that a Quality Circle is composed of a small number of volunteering co-workers who get together to try and address and hopefully solve some work-related problem, not necessarily quality related (see Footnote number 10). The findings of these QCs should be part of an overall programme of continuous improvements. However, many QCs have failed due to their lack of preparation, knowledge and management commitment. It is worth therefore investigating two of the major components that contribute to the QC's success, namely Teamwork and Problem-Solving.

Teamwork

What is a team and how effective is it? A team can be defined as a collection of people working together for the benefit of the whole. This can be very apparent within the sporting world. In the majority of cases, when two opposing teams (it does not matter what sport, but for argument's sake, say football) meet, it is highly likely that the team that plays together normally beats the opposing team full of individual stars.

This can be graphically illustrated by looking at our picture below, where we have two very stubborn bulls, tied together trying to eat their oats. When they both go for it without cooperation, no-one gets his oats. However, a little thought and collaboration means they can first go to the left and eat and then to the right and eat — it then becomes a team effort.

It's a Team Effort

Figure 2.7 It's a Team Effort

Teams are therefore characterized by the following key points:

An effective team:

(a) has a common agreed direction and set of goals[20]. This means that its members recognize their interdependence and understand that the team goals are best achieved with mutual collaboration and support. This leads to each member 'owning' their own job output and its consequences;

(b) works together and for each other while giving individuals the necessary scope to fulfil and develop their own potential. These potential skills are supported by the whole team and guided by management;

(c) does not avoid conflict since this is a normal aspect of human nature and interaction. However, each conflict or problem is seen as an opportunity for new ideas and future development. Each member is encouraged to express openly their ideals and opinions without any fear of reprisal;

(d) practises good, open and honest communications, making sure that each member understands each other's point of view;

(e) makes better quality decisions as each member actively participates in the decision making process (knowing their own individual and team limitations and that the team leader must make the final ruling when the team cannot or requires an immediate decision in an emergency). This leads to 'self-management and empowerment';

(f) measurement of capability is owned by the team (i.e., the team knows what its customers require and are receiving plus is able to measure its capability to deliver). This will lead to the establishment of measurements that tell the team how good they are at delivering what their clients want. The types of measurements could be volumes, time, error-rate, etc.

(g) each individual member of the team has a unique ability and character psychometrics that will help the team. It is probable that the most effective team will encompass the following roles (note, one person would occupy up to two or three roles, although some are mutually exclusive — the eight 'roles' described below were first identified by Dr. Meridith Belbin in 1981 within his publication 'Management Teams: why they succeed or fail'):

Chairman (not necessarily the supervisor or manager)

Function: researches all the alternatives when solving a problem, and then takes the team's decision.

Attributes: good listener, logical and decisive; clarifies group objectives and sets its agenda-priorities.

Personality: calm and stable; extrovert.

Needs: a self-motivated team.

Shaper

Function: acts as an assertive and dynamic leader, shaping the team's efforts into a cohesive whole.

Attributes: dynamic, decisive but argumentative; can 'steamroll' the team, but gets results.

Personality: extrovert, dominant and impatient; wants action and wants it now.

Needs: an able and knowledgeable team.

Monitor / Evaluator

Function: analyses problems in a logical dispassionate manner.

Attributes: analytical and intelligent.

Personality: prudent and tenacious.

Needs: continuous feed of information.

Team Worker

Function: promotes group harmony and settles discords.

Attributes: sensitive, diplomatic, good communicator but not very decisive.

Personality: neutral — promoter of unity and harmony.

Needs: continuous access to the whole team; needs loyalty.

Finisher

Function: relentlessly makes the group achieve on time.

Attributes: professional, but apprehensive; introvert.

Personality: conscientious and perfectionist; compulsively meets deadlines.

Needs: the group's commitment.

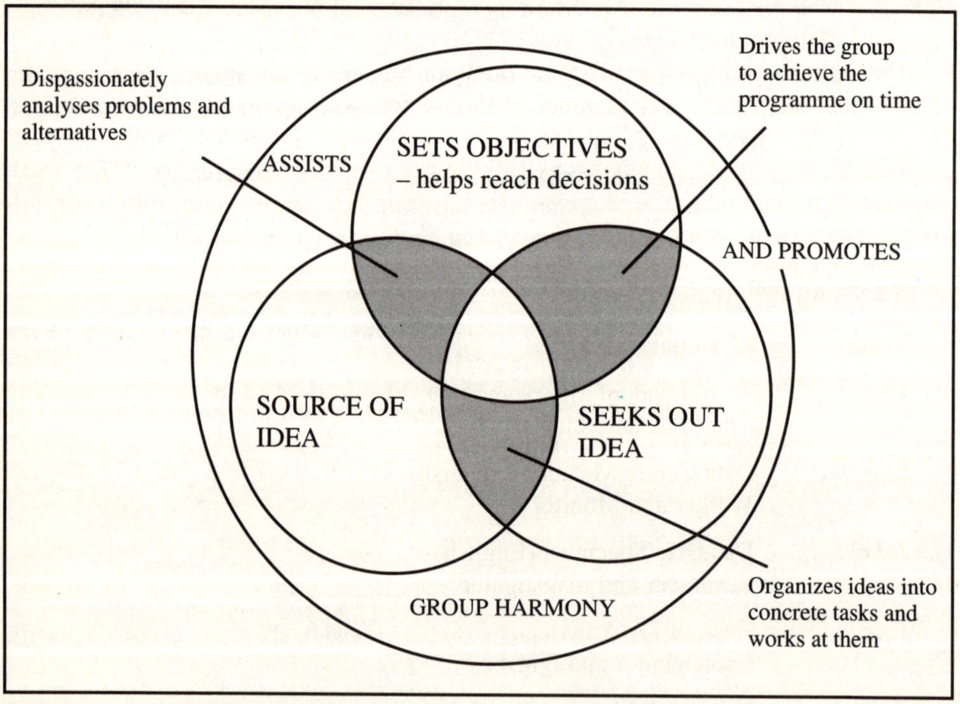

Figure 2.8 Psychometric Analysis of Team

Resourcer- Investigator

Function:	a good salesperson and liaison officer, he/she will act as the link between the team and the outside world.
Attributes:	a communicator, enthusiastic and energetic.
Personality:	extrovert and assertive.
Needs:	freedom to operate.

Worker

Function:	translates ideas into concrete tasks and performs them.
Attributes:	organizer, tenacious and logical.
Personality:	stable, cautious and analytical.
Needs:	the group's ideas and requirements.

Plant

Function:	the source of all original/radical ideas and proposals.
Attributes:	intelligent and imaginative; very original and creative.
Personality:	unorthodox, self-opinionated; may sulk if ideas are dissected or rejected.
Needs:	a motivating environment.

The effect on the team will depend on incorporating all the above roles, with the ideal falling within the shaded areas shown in Figure 2.8.

The eight roles defined above form the basic nucleus of a team, the absence of any type within the team is a good gauge of failure, whatever the intelligence, motivation, etc. of the team members.

The reader may at this stage be thinking that behavioural theory is not really applicable to the real world. An example may help. The most successful team I have been fortunate to work within was 'formed' within an American Multi-national Telecommunications Company, setting up a manufacturing plant in a foreign country. This team was as follows:

Team:	**IT Department**
Victor:	Team Leader (American/Spanish) Chairman and Shaper
Eugenio:	Data Centre Manager (Spanish) Worker and Monitor
John:	Database Specialist (English) Resourcer and Investigator
Pete:	Head of IT (American) Implementor and Finisher
Pablo:	Network Specialist (Spanish) Evaluator and Worker

Mags: External Consultant (Spanish/English)
Plant and Shaper

Paloma: Business Analyst (Spanish)
Worker

Lolin: Departmental Secretary (Spanish)
Worker and Finisher.

As can be seen above, this team had a mixture of nationalities and cultures that gelled together to form a cohesive whole. Their success stemmed from having a common sense of purpose, e.g., setting up the best IT Department. Within it, the sense of corporate achievement, supportive climate plus the breakdown of cultural barriers and differences were its main achievements.

The roles undertaken by each individual member of the team was not 'assigned' but came about by natural selection, were charactcr and personal attributes dictated the role. However, for this to occur another element of the team attributes played a major part, e.g., specialist technical knowledge and experience. This was defined as follows:

Victor: UNIX Expert and Mini Computers
> 10 years experience

Eugenio: IBM architecture Designer
> 25 years experience

John: ORACLE and Personal Computers
> 5 years experience

Pete: Various IT Environments
> 15 years experience

Pablo: Local Area Networks, Wide Area Networks (X.25)
> 5 years experience

Mags: IT Security Expert, Networks and UNIX
> 10 years experience

Paloma: MRPII
> 5 years experience

Lolin: Administration and Clerical
> 20 years

The range of specialist technical knowledge and experience worked well (and complemented) within the team because each area required to achieve the teams goals was covered. Furthermore, no team member or the team as a whole felt that they were self-sufficient. It used all the resources the organization could supply to better the team's successes. In other words technical knowledge within the team was defined by the task the team was required to perform.

This is true of all teams. For instance, if the team's objective is to investigate and support network security, it is obvious that two of the main skills/experience requirements is going to be Networking and IT Security.

Returning to our key points of effective teams, it must be made clear that if any of the team key points are missing, then normally the individuals will revert to their organizational role and hierarchical position, which is generally what occurs within a group (as in our sporting analogy previously).

It is obvious that the concept of the team is far superior to the group and therefore it is management's responsibility to always strive to create this since in this type of environment managers become more effective (in terms of managing staff) and the team becomes most productive.

It is obvious that in terms of the quality output of a team, striving to achieve this is of paramount importance, if not properly implemented, it can waste time, increase the frustration of the team members and lead to a deterioration of team performance.

As always commitment for this type of activity must come from the whole organization. Old style authoritarian management (anywhere down the management ladder) will not permit the team to evolve and in certain instances can be rather destructive of teams. Furthermore, it is not enough to try to enforce or implement the idea without management support — top-down and bottom-up. For instance, if the idea comes from senior management but the teams are ill-focused, divorced from the work processes and do not have the necessary resources (e.g., training) then it is going to fail. Conversely, if 'team-spirit' is built around a small number of individuals (including possibly lower management support) but lack senior management commitment and focus, then again it will fail. The latter case can also lead to an environment of mistrust between senior management (who see the teams working not for them but for their immediate subordinates) and lower managers who feel isolated in-between their superiors' needs and their own subordinates' demands.

Whatever the situation, it is apparent that a great deal of care is needed when setting up teams. Therefore how should we go about setting up teams? Since the key areas that a team needs to come to terms with are commitment and planning, goal setting and training, let's take these issues as our starting points.

Commitment, as I have stated, is the key to success throughout the entire organization. This starts off at the very top (the CEO or chairman) with senior management making the right noises — saying the right words. Senior management must transmit a clear and consistent quality and teamwork message down the line. This could be achieved via a clear mission statement (See Figure 2.4). But this is not enough. 'Talk is cheap', if the work force view this as a way of trying to fool the market (or more importantly the work-force themselves), then they will not participate and hence it will not work. Most staff members are 'boss watchers', they watch to see what the boss does and says, and more importantly try to catch them out in some indiscretion.

Senior management must live by their words, acting and working like a team themselves, giving the rest of the organization the lead that they are looking for. Included in this is the art of *Planning*. I am calling planning an art more than a science because planning is not simply a unilateral decision made by a senior manager who knows the company's aims and objectives and hence is able to select the correct strategies to achieve their aims by applying the necessary resources for its success. It is a two-way link between the management and the teams. The *art* of good communication and social understanding is of paramount importance if the manager is going to achieve a coherent and effective plan. The team must understand the reason for existing (why they are there?, what they are to accomplish?, etc.) and expect their leaders to know the direction they must take to achieve their team's and ultimately the company's objectives.

Planning is, therefore, the strategic thinking before the work is carried out; it will involve a large amount of information analysis and reviewing the state of the organization. Tools like SWOT[21] (strength, weaknesses, opportunities and threats) will assist in evaluating future decisions and hence setting appropriate *Goals* with the full collaboration of the teams.

Such *goals* must be achievable but also challenging enough to imbue the teams with a sense of accomplishment. Once we get into the area of goal setting it is advisable that a 'bottom-up' management approach is adhered to, with the grass-root level setting their own team-goals, which in turn is part of the whole organization's strategic goal. This is what is sometimes termed 'empowerment', where employees are given a far greater responsibility for their own actions than is normally possible through delegation, by putting decision making at the right level. It also means that management have at last become aware of the value of their employees. Each member of staff has some unique ability, it may be either manual or mental dexterity, but whatever it is, it is best put to use when the individual is allowed to express it in a free and open environment.

Empowerment of employees is seen by many managers as a dangerous ethos (even though many verbally go around saying that they do it, since it is cheep to say so and hence impress their peers — but remember that talk is cheap!) since it can radically undermine management 'control'. It states that the person at the grass-root level doing a particular job knows better than anyone else the best way of improving it. Hence you may be forgiven for believing 'what is the manager needed for, except to get in the way of progress!'

However, empowerment, like delegation, requires control otherwise the enthusiasm and naiveté of staff will create difficulties. Such controls include setting the teams terms of reference, limits, supervising performance and ensuring targets are met and most importantly, that training needs are met.

An analogy here would be the process that the American Indians undertook when training a wild stallion — a most impressive and beautiful horse. However, the stallion is more than just an impressive horse. Although its racing qualities and abilities are superior to most horses, its temperament and naiveté do not allow it to be 'king' amongst its pack. The American Indian did *not* break it, by doing so would have meant also breaking its spirit. By persistent guiding and training, the stallion became not just a slave to the Indians but their friend. In so doing, it gave the Indian its full potential. Similarly, managers must act like these knowledgeable Indians, with patience and care, they must treat their subordinates as individuals, each with an inner power that needs nurturing, guidance and training.

For the majority, working within a team is probably a new experience and hence they will need assistance in attaining their individual and team potential. *Training* will provide the necessary skills and knowledge to help the team-members be successful and will assist one of TQM's major goals — culture change, as employees are made aware that teamwork is very important to the success of the organization and ultimately the safeguarding of their jobs. Different types of training are needed. Team members need to learn how to be a team player, team leaders need basic leadership skills and conflict resolving skills, etc. and all need to learn basic problem solving techniques.

Absence of any training normally means that, despite the good intentions of the team, they fall short of meeting team goals and therefore are unable to make any real progress. Training is probably the single most important investment (apart from investment in Technology and Research) that a company will undertake in order to implement TQM and ultimately culture change. However, it is also the most difficult task to justify, especially within a recession.

The value of training is difficult to quantify in many situations and managers feel that they seem to be investing first and then having to wait for the results without any real idea when there will be a return. Furthermore, when there is a return on investment, it is normally very difficult to correlate it to investment in training.

In general any company which is truly committed to TQM will regard training as part and parcel of the TQM initiative and not only training in specific technical and professional skills (e.g., programming, use of the latest state-of-art equipment, etc.) but also all social aspects of working from management to team-interaction. This investment requires a high commitment by all and begins, in my opinion, even before the employee accepts the job offer.

The education system within Western Society (specifically within the Anglo-Saxon environment) has been evolving towards yielding individuals who are not prepared (and in some case do not wish to be) for working life. For instance, although girls are today being given the opportunity to learn and more importantly, be interested in engineering and mechanical subjects, (which is obviously a major improvement to the past since the female work-force is now firmly established as a very important part of business — gone are the days of a male dominated business environment) in some instances the manner and indoctrination of pupils in general has not changed (within some areas girls are still being treated in a Victorian manner by their parents and teachers, as second-class citizens, unable to use their brains for anything other than raising children). Add to this antiquated man/woman ethos the changing cultural environment where discipline, respect and authority have diminished to a level where the teacher or parent has lost control, we then have children being brought up without the basic understanding of life (e.g., in many instances not even the basic three Rs) and their role within society.

We therefore are left with pupils who are not being taught the basic principles of learning and how to learn. Added to this, social and environmental pressures that never existed several decades ago (for example, increase in drug-abuse, loss of parental control, lack of economic stability, etc.) has meant that students are leaving the educational system without the proper training and with the belief that society will not get better so why even try. When these individuals finally go into a work environment, they find themselves as Captain James T. Kirk did in Vulcan — in an alien world where they are expected immediately to be productive and responsible members of society within an alien culture, or so it seems. It is therefore inevitable that even when a company spends millions on training, not all of it will be profitable.

A TQM training initiative must take into account these social factors and how individuals learn. It must cater for individual strength, weakness and potential, driving away the innate feeling of mistrust of training built by the education system. How often have we heard the 30 year old shop assistant say that he or she hated mathematics at school? People do not learn if they are bullied into it or are afraid — afraid of the tutor, of failing, of making a fool of themselves, etc.; many feel as Oliver Twist did when he asked could he have more soup. The responsibility of dispelling this 'wall of silence' lies firmly on the trainer's shoulders. He or she must establish a rapport that will give the attendees a reason to be interested; this is normally achieved by making sure that the material presented is strongly participative in nature. This idea is not new, Reg Revans defined the concept of 'action training' in the late 1930s. It focused on the acquisition of a 'questioning insight', which can only be attained if the trainee is able to ask 'useful and discriminating questions in conditions of ignorance, risk and confusion'.

It is therefore apparent that effective training sessions must be a interactive 'hands-on' and customized to individual requirements, and consequently deal with specific user areas, so that the user can relate to what he or she is being taught. A Chinese proverb says:

I Hear	and	I Forget
I See	and	I Remember
I DO	and	I UNDERSTAND

This is the TQM training philosophy that TQM training sessions must try to adhere to, otherwise it is unlikely that the training will be effective.

This proverb puts the problems of learning into perspective. In order for learning to succeed, any learning difficulties that staff may have, for whatever reason, must be addressed and solved before any real training takes place. Once this has been adequately solved, it is obvious that staff's strong held negative belief about learning will change towards a more 'challenging attitude' where every individual will leave a training session with the knowledge that their learning has just begun — leaving the training session with an optimistic view of hope, enthusiasm and commitment to do things right — first time.

Therefore, in summary, the following are several conditions that are needed for effective learning/training to take place:

(i) Staff must want to be trained — what motivates them? What personal benefits are they going to attain from attending the training session? If you answer these basic questions positively then it is obvious that the staff member will be motivated to learn;

(ii) Learning is an active process as our Chinese proverb indicates;

(iii) Trainers must be adequately trained themselves in the art of participative training. Plus a certain standard of performance should be set, where the trainer must adhere to a minimum level. It is also advisable that the trainer should have a love for this work, thereby filling the trainees with his or her own enthusiasm for the subject;

(iv) Adequate time must be given to the training session for the individual to be able to assimilate the contents. Furthermore, adequate time must be given to follow-up training, with great attention being given to the individual's own personal learning-curve;

(v) Staff must receive confirmation that what they have been taught is useful and that they have achieved a certain level;

(vi) Training must be part of the work-practices of the organization, where non-attendance is unacceptable — prevention must take priority over production;

(vii) Training does NOT end in the class-room, reinforce the training message with periodic on-the-job assessments, refreshers and audits.

(viii) Learning must also question norms as opposed to trainees only learning from detecting errors, which they correct. These 'life' lessons must be absorbed into the employee's and team's experience and knowledge-base.

(ix) Quality training programmes should be established to cover the main areas of quality, e.g., Prevention, Inspection and Analysis and Rework. These programmes should be set up by line management with the help of the Quality team. The objective is to convey throughout the company the reasons for quality especially in terms of 'customer' requirements.

(x) Training programmes should distinguish between the requirements from each area of the organization, for example, does everyone need to know how Statistical Process Control (SPC) works? The answer is obviously no but another question could be, does everyone need to know who his or her client is and what their requirements are? Of course!

(xi) Specific training. Within an IT Security framework, Security Awareness is the key to good IT Security. It must cover IT Security as a whole and be given throughout the organization. The basic principle of any IT Security training is that it must meet the following requirements:

- Staff must be made aware of the need for IT Security;
- Staff must be made aware of their own legal responsibilities;
- Staff must understand how their job functions within a security framework;
- Staff must be trained to use security measures appropriate to their job and taught that circumventing them could mean, not only a loss to the business but ultimately their own job;
- Staff must be trained in emergency procedures;
- Staff must believe that security is important.

Further information on IT Security Awareness can be found in Chapter 3 under IT Security Policy.

(xii) Training records should be maintained at all times. These records will identify further training needs and highlight areas where training is lax and/or special skills/knowledge is required for the job.

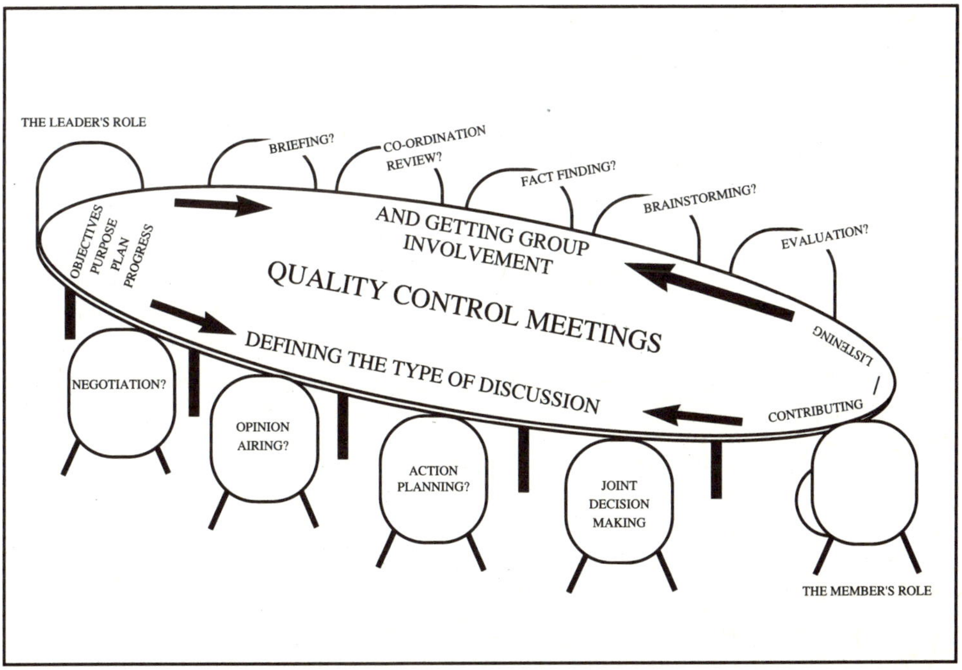

Figure 2.9 Towards Quality Improvement Teams

We have looked closely at how team dynamics can affect Quality. In any team, the interactions between the team members is vital to its success. One can add certain ingredients to assist in its development, e.g., training, and experience in specific technical issues like IT Security.

However, the 'climate' within the team must be apt for creativity and progress. Figure 2.9 summarizes the essential components required when a team gets together. The example depicts a Quality Control Meeting. Assuming that the meeting was discussing the Quality of IT Security Document, then within the figure the reader can see each 'seat' has a part to play:

- fact finding
- evaluation
- etc.

The reader will notice that if all the components described in the figure are present, then the team will inevitably become an effective Quality Improvement Team — especially if management commitment and support is also available.

It is obvious that individuals are seldom perfect but a team can sometimes come close to the company's zero-defect goal. Through proper planning, commitment and above all training, it is likely that the teams will succeed and the organization will flourish. This will inevitably lead to the success of the teams (or Quality Circles); however, there is another component to the success of QCs — the effective use of Problem Solving Techniques.

Problem Solving

Dealing with different types of problems is part and parcel of all our lives, whether on a personal or professional level. Depending on the type of problem, we normally take a different course of action in order to maximize our potential of solving the problem. This could be use of experience, intuition[22] or a logical method (we will mainly discuss the latter here, although the first two will inevitably influence the results) or simply passing the buck.

It is human nature to disown a difficult situation, shrugging off your responsibility and stating that it is up to someone else (supervisor, partner, wife, husband, etc) to solve. We all put the blame of a problem on our closest rival, blaming another department for failing and none will take the responsibility to take the 'bull by the horns' and solve it.

After this is the fact that a problem within most companies covers several functional areas; it could possibly be simply lack of communication or phantom departmental barriers. The real issue, therefore, is identifying what can be done initially at an individual level and consequently through departmental barriers, possibly via special inter-department Quality Circles.

But what is a problem? A problem is simply any situation where you do not like the result because it does not allow you to reach an objective. For instance, your objective could be to reach a zero defect production process within your team — since at the moment it has a 10% error rate. Therefore how do you eliminate the causes of the lost 10%? Attempting to solve this type of problem can sometimes feel as if you are trying to fit a quart into a pint pot — impossible. However, by answering the basic question of where the causes of the error-rate lie, you are in a better position to solve the actual problem. To answer this type of question effectively requires a two phase approach of first diagnosing the problem and then choosing the best solution.

In the first phase, we will try and identify where the problem lies. In our example, we are trying to reduce our error-rate from 10% to 0%. In Figure 2.10 we see that our team is composed of four members; a supervisor, operator-A who picks up the raw materials from the conveyor-belt and hands them to operator-B, who presses it via the door-making machine, subsequently he hands to the supervisor for checking, if the item is OK he hands the door to operator-C who places it back on the conveyor belt. In our simple example there are six possible things that could be the cause of our error-rate:

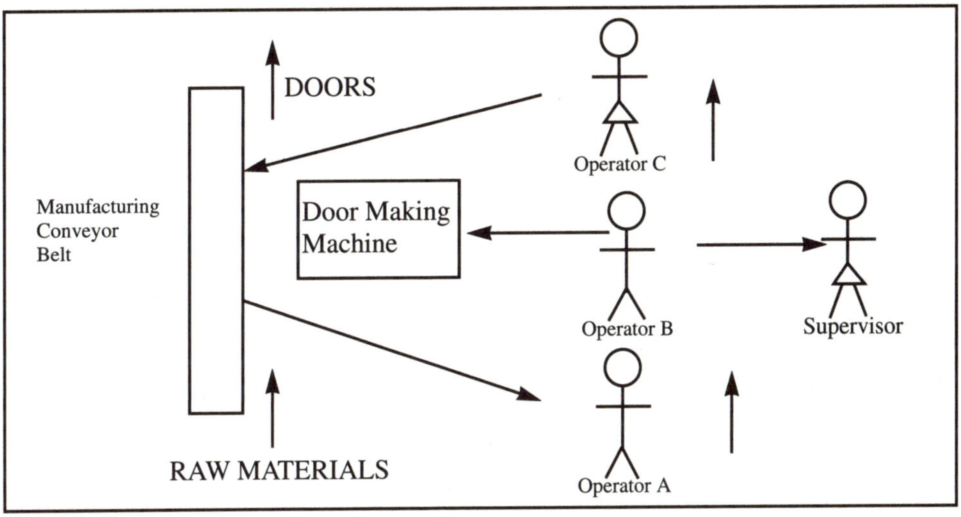

Figure 2.10 Door Assembly Team

Poor Supervisor, poor operator, no/missing operator, broken machine/conveyor belt, no/faulty raw materials and lack of training to use the machines. This situation is typical of most team-work environments and trying to identify where the problem lies can be rather difficult. Add to this other departmental interactions (see Figure 2.11 — shaded area represents team/departmental interface and consequently dependence) where the problem could affect other departments and teams or even be part of all teams, e.g., bad training processes, bad senior management, inadequate or cheap raw materials, etc., etc.

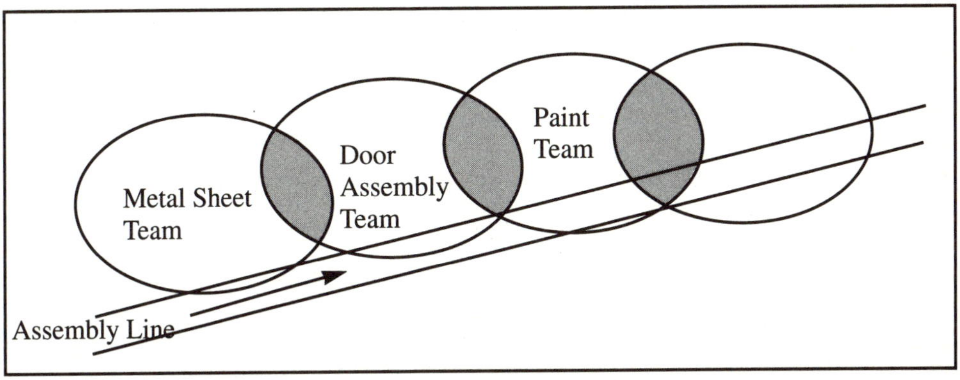

Figure 2.11 Car Manufacturing Function

In order therefore to identify where the problem lies we first need to define the problem, identifying the cause of the problem not only its effect. Then we will be able to collect information and consequently carry out a detailed examination of the processes. Within our example we have the problem of trying to reduce the error rate to zero. This analysis will continue with our cause and effect process, where we define the symptoms of the problem and the impact of the effect on the team and its work. The aim is to identify all possible items that may influence the problem. We could use simple brainstorming[23] or synetics[24] methods (see Figure 2.12 below) or questionnaires or any other information gathering tool.

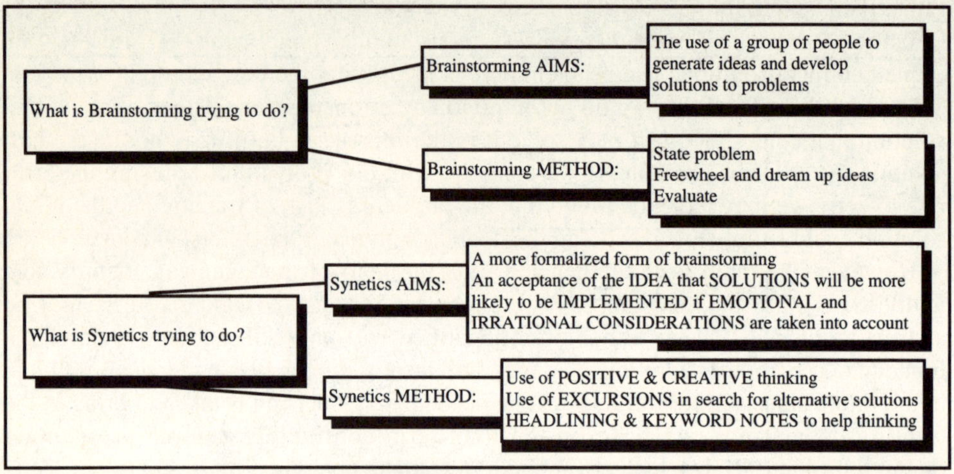

Figure 2.12 Brainstorming and Synetics

For example, we could split our causes into four areas:

- Manpower — this includes staffing skills, training attitudes, working conditions, etc.
- Machinery — this includes tools, technology, etc.
- Materials — this includes raw and factured materials, information, etc.
- Methods — this includes routine work processes, administration, etc.

In our earlier assembly example, we could then have, after a team evaluation session of the process, the following: (see Figure 2.13 below)

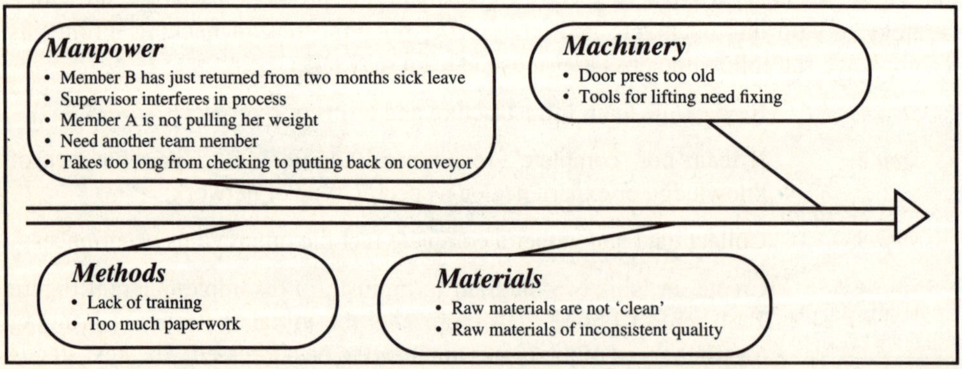

Figure 2.13 Fish-bone Cause and Effect Analysis of Door Assembly Team

This fish-bone or Ishikawa diagram will normally identify, not only the problem that we are trying to solve, but other problems (whether imagined, potential or real) that team members have identified. Subsequently it will also hopefully produce some solutions. In essence what you have done is systematically gone through all the possible logical alternatives.

However, earlier I mentioned that problem solving can also be achieved through experience and intuition. This fish-bone analysis, in conjunction with creative brainstorming, can sometimes be very fruitful, where possible future problems can be averted in advance. This makes problem solving a tool also for preventing problems rather than simply fixing existing ones (or 'fire fighting').

Once we have followed this process to its logical conclusion we are left with implementing a solution. The problem here is identifying the best solution for the job. We need to be careful that we do not jump to any erroneous conclusions or at the first solution that comes along. It may solve it in the short term but it may not be the best solution overall. For example, if we continue with our problem of reducing the error rate to zero, we may have identified that the problem is lack of training and the initial solution could simply mean sending the operators on a half day refresher course.

However, the team get together and with the help of management, identify that within six months the machinery is being replaced (or updated) and that there may be a structure change. The initial solution identified will only solve the problem of the immediate need but it is obvious that they will have a similar (if not identical) problem in the future since further training will be needed. So a decision is taken to bring in the training department to advise on the long-term continuous training programme required for their needs which covers both immediate needs and future changes.

This decision making process is part and parcel of the problem solving routine (i.e., eliminating impractical solutions and choosing the right one at the time). The impractical solution could be due, as in our example, to future organizational changes, or lack of resources, etc. etc. Such decision making process covers an evaluation of the risks associated with implementing a particular solution.

If the risks are too high, then the probability of achieving your objective is going to be minimal, the decision is erroneous and another solution must be found.

In terms of IT Security, brainstorming, synetics and the use of Ishikawa diagrams can also be valuable tools. As a group of tools they form an effective cause and effect method that can examine the inter-relationship of problems. By doing this it is hoped that they produce a list of candidate solutions for consideration. For example, incidents of unauthorized access via a corporate networked terminal can be reported to the IT Department. A team is set up to investigate the problem and come up with a strategy to stop this occurring and analyse the potential risk of hacking. From this example we can follow the possible steps the team may take:

Step 1. Review the team infrastructure and terms of reference;

Step 2. If team not 'complete', recommend additions, e.g., possible lack of knowledge or experience on a specific type of network;

Step 3. Collect date and gather a complete fact file on previous occurrences;

Step 4. Create an Ishikawa diagram to brainstorm (example diagram Figure 2.14 below) Figure 2.14 represents the initial first pass at bringing together some of the issues that need to be addressed. The next step is the most important one;

Step 5. Brainstorm the problem and produce the propose action plan. The method of brainstorming used is dependent on the group makeup and time. If the group is composed of 'creative' 'plant' like individuals (refer to discussion on teams earlier) then one of the creative synetic examples below could be used.

Step 6. Report results.

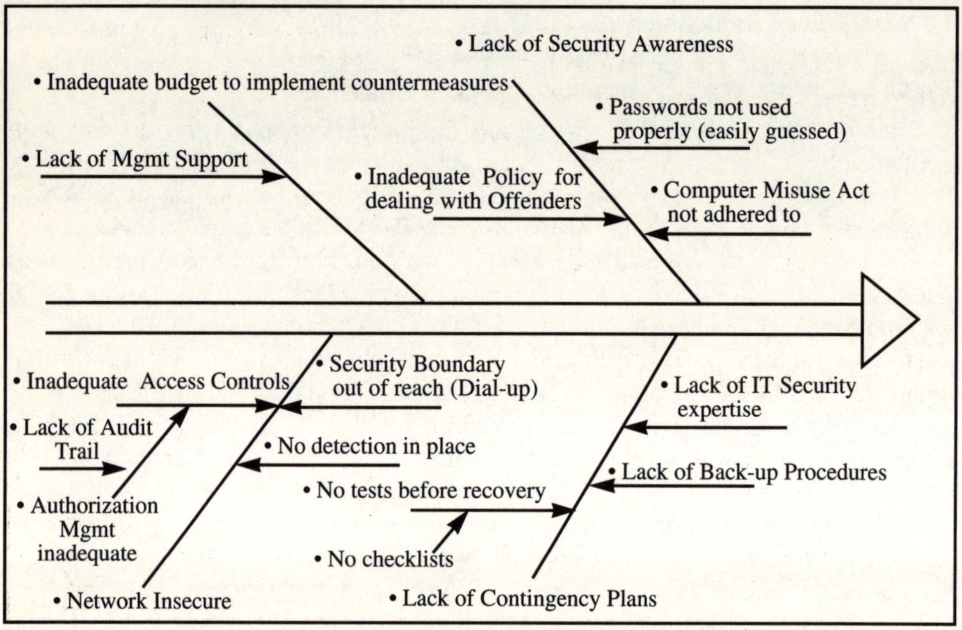

Figure 2.14 Fish-bone Cause and Effect Analysis of Hacking Prevention

Example creative synetic brainstorm Number 1.

Mnemonics

Choose a five or six letter word at random (from your head or from this book, etc.). Use each letter of the word as the initial letter of five or six words which help you:

either : define the problem more clearly
or : think of solutions to the problem.

Problem: ***IT Security not taken seriously***

Defining the problem:

	1st pass	*2nd pass*	*3rd pass*
C	Computers	Clarify	*Clear*
H	*Help*	Home	Harrass
A	*Add*	Assist	Action
N	*New*	Never	None
G	Gain	Gender	*Goal*
E	Exam	*Elevate*	Evaluate

Clear — IT Security needs are not *clearly* defined;

Help	—	*Help* is needed for everyone within the organization to comprehend the importance of IT Security;
Add	—	IT Security is *not* seen as *adding* value;
New	—	IT Security is seen as something *new*;
Goal	—	IT Security *goal* not defined;
Elevate	—	IT Security is not a *high* enough priority.

Identifying possible solutions:

	1st pass	*2nd pass*	*3rd pass*
C	Client	*Champion*	Carton
H	Horse	Hot	*Hire*
A	*Awareness*	Advert	Add
N	NO!	Need	*Nurse*
G	Grow	Gradual	*Guerrilla*
E	*Elevate*	Entise	Experience

Champion	—	Needs a 'champion' to promote;
Hire	—	Hire outside expert assistance;
Awareness	—	IT Security Awareness Campaign throughout organization;
Nurse	—	Define prescriptive type of solutions;
Guerrilla	—	It's a guerrilla war against IT Security Crime;
Elevate	—	Elevate the IT Security Problem to the highest level of management.

Example creative synetic brainstorm Number 2.

Forced Comparison

Compare your problem subject-topic with something else which is completely different from the problem-topic, the more unrealistic the better. The purpose of the comparison is to find fresh and new ways of defining the characteristics or attributes of the problem. The comparison is a means to an end, rather than an end in itself.

Problem: ***Qualities of an IT Security Officer***

IT Security Officer	*v*	*A Television*
mobile		not mobile
flexible		not flexible
to 'fight fires'		to communicate-entertain
High tech		high Tech.
Most homes don't have one		most homes have one
Always on standby		always on standby
not a direct charge to user		direct charge to user
conservative		challenging
no consumer choice		consumer choice

This comparison highlights the basic qualities of the IT Security Officer and can now be used as a way of defining its responsibilities, for instance when defining a job description.

Example creative synetic brainstorm Number 3.

Historical Figure

Choose (at random) a historical figure, someone famous from the past — or the present. The figure should be well known to the group. Get the group to identify the attributes or characteristics associated with this figure. Then ask the group to use this list of characteristics or attributes to:

either	:	define the problem more clearly
or	:	think of solutions to the problem.

Problem: ***Lack of IT Security Awareness***

Figure: Henry VIII

fat, royal, bully, songwriter, heavyweight, powerful, dead, hard to please, southerner, extremist, confrontational, liked women, obsessive, anti-church, high profile, sex maniac, coward, philanderer, cheat, etc.
etc.

Defining the problem:

Hard to please:	can't meet everyone's needs
powerful:	training lobby isn't powerful enough

Identifying possible solutions:

High profile:	Give it a higher profile.
Heavyweight:	Get senior management commitment.

All these creative techniques rely heavily on the right-hand side of the human brain, where you would find innovation, intuition, magic, inspiration, divergence and freedom. The left hand side deals with investigation, deduction, diagnostics, analysis and structure plus is used towards the end of the creative process to structure the result.

In summary, an effective problem solving session would probably encompass the following items (this is described pictorially in Figure 2.15):

(i) Define the problem, encouraging any types of contribution, no matter how outrageous it may seem. Include in your definition ownership of the problem. Draw up an agenda and stick to it;

(ii) Encourage imaginative contributions and a positive approach; people's fears, hidden agendas, tunnel vision, status are not allowed;

(iii) Build on other people's ideas — sometimes simply re-phrasing the obvious can stimulate further solutions and ideas. Don't try to re-invent the wheel.

(iv) Identify the following questions — Where does the problem lie and why does it exist? Answering these two basic questions will give the team members an insight into how to find a solution. It may also mean redefining the problem from a different perspective. A valuable way of doing this could be to find analogies to the problem as this will assist the team members to better understand the problem and hence its possible solution.

(v) Problem solving and decision making are inextricably linked, therefore you need to approach all problem solving sessions with the view that a decision (whether negative or positive) will always be made, no matter how difficult it originally may seem. However, each decision should be chosen with care and only those that have a chance of success should be taken.

(vi) Fire-fighting has become a major role within our Western Society, where in many situations, a job (especially within a support function) is felt as being 95% fixing mistakes and problems and 5% preventing them from occurring in the first place. In order for problem solving to work effectively, the culture-shock that we discussed earlier must occur here, albeit in a different form, i.e., in terms of changing the culture from a Fixing Culture to a PREVENTATIVE one.

(vii) In many of the day-to-day meetings held throughout industry, members are expected not to rock the boat or be naive when proposing suggestions. Many view these meetings as a battle ground, where you can show-up the incompetencies of your adversaries and show how well you are performing. This behaviour must be discouraged (even though it is a human trait that sometimes comes out without much help). Sometimes what seems as wishful thinking on the part of the naive members may lead to a solution not thought of earlier. Furthermore, nobody should feel that they have nothing to contribute or that their suggestions are going to be subjected to ridicule. Everyone should support each other in making the team culture work for each other.

(viii) Every suggestion should be written down and where possible a link should be made to previous ones. If the suggestion is not a valid one, valid reasons should be given to the originator for its rejection.

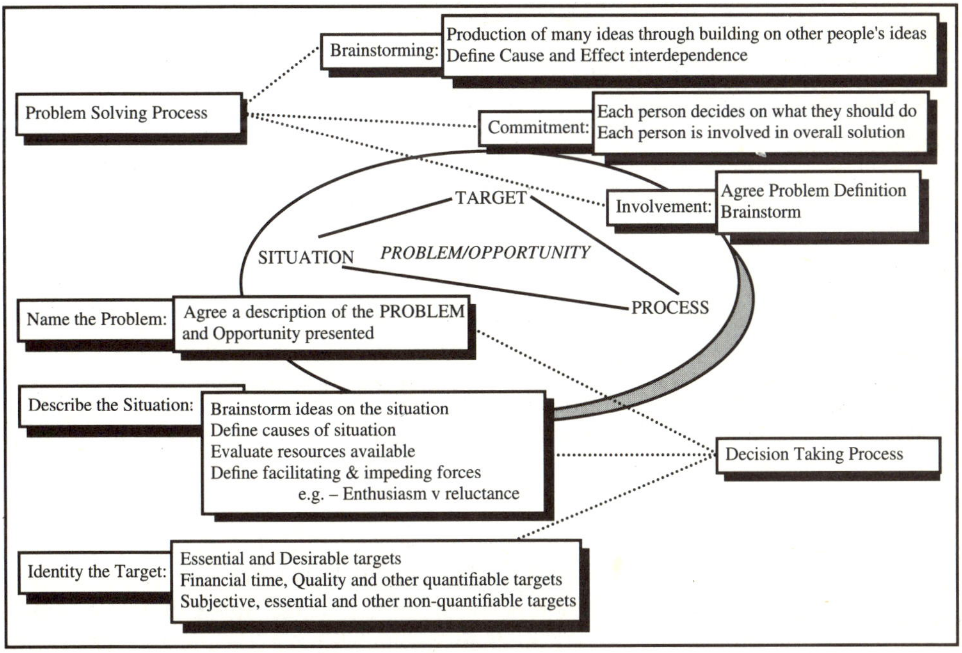

Figure 2.15 Problem Solving and Decision Taking

(ix) Use Figure 2.15 to identify the situation — target — process cycle of your problem. Identify within your problem the areas that fit within the problem solving process.

In the last few pages we have delved into three of the most important aspects of a TQM initiative — Training, Team-work and Problem-Solving. All can be applied directly to IT Security. Some early Quality drives took these three issues to heart and expected a complete change in the company — they were greatly disillusioned. TQM is more than just getting it right in these three most important areas.

Training is the essential tool equipping people with the knowledge and skills to make them aware of the company's and their own responsibility to the product or service. Problem solving techniques within teams will remedy many of the mundane problems and some of the major headaches.

However, without a passion for quality throughout the organization it will fail. The problems gathered from this failure can be very significant to the company since the workforce will consequently view any further initiatives to improve the product or service with a fair amount of suspicion. In many cases disregarding subsequent initiatives is doomed to failure.

It is therefore important that the benefits to be gained from any Total Quality initiative set by the company are achievable — both in real terms and perceived to succeed by everyone. For a Total Quality initiative to succeed it must address and change the root of most problems — human behaviour and related attitudes. A work-force and management with passion to make their company profitable, will make sure that all the tools they need are available plus every process, procedure and work-practice is 100% applicable without any waste.

This clarity in mission inevitably needs a commitment by all, but most importantly by senior management. Additionally, senior management's responsibility does not stop in coaching their employees and supplying them with the training and tools. It must also be clear how to implement and align with TQM other basic company strategies, for instance, Customer/Supplier Relationship, Management Change and Leadership Skills (see Section 7) plus the cost to a company. The costs to an organization of implementing any TQM initiative can be rather high both in terms of time and resource. The further the company goes into it the higher the cost — but also the higher the rewards.

In theory everything I have discussed so far will in the long-run bring great benefits to an organization if implemented and adapted for the needs of the organization. The art is in the adaptation process (how often have we read a best seller and then seen the movie and commented on how good or bad the adaptation was? — a badly adapted TQM drive does more harm than good) and in when to start the quality drive (like the doctor, are we going to use preventative medicine or do we have to operate?) — are we going to fix our bad quality or stop it from occurring?.

But the reader must be clear about this — the theory within these pages will bring some benefits but mainly in the long run — patience is a pre-requisite of any Quality initiative.

Most quality drives start off in an organization within small independent autonomous groups, going from QC of basic processes to QA of various processes (see Figure 2.16 below). Once this has been tried and tested and it filters both up to the senior management in terms of the financial benefits and to the work-force in terms of the team benefits, then the imposition of a Total Quality Control drive will be instigated throughout the organization. In some instances, some forward-looking companies will

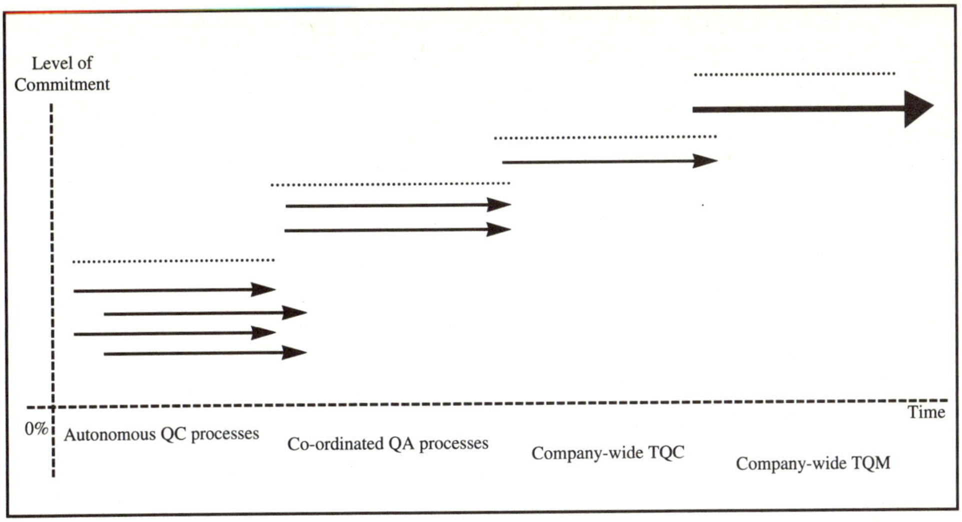

Figure 2.16 Typical Quality Growth

seek to evaluate how other similar companies have implemented TQM and will in some cases measure their own performance with the best — a form of 'Best Practice Benchmarking[25]'.

If it works (and most do), slowly but surely the culture of the organization alters towards TQM. In parallel to this QC —> QA —> TQC —> TQM sequential drive, a noticeable change in the company's commitment will be seen, with a sense of ownership of the results filtering through to everyone within the organization.

All will, with a lot of hard work, commitment and capital, bring the company that much sought after major benefit — competitive advantage.

Manufacturing versus the Service Industry

As we have already seen, the definition of quality can be a rather subjective one, depending on a variety of issues. However, within a manufacturing environment, quality can be assigned very strict criteria — be they in terms of performance, durability, aesthetics, safety, etc. Due to this it is therefore relatively easy to develop quality quantifiable measurement tools within a manufacturing environment and therefore be able to adhere to these set of rules every time, for instance, rules concerning time taken to produce a product, cost, accuracy, reliability, capability, etc. These rules are sometimes referred to as Process Quality Measures (PQMs), since they describe how the process operates (remember that a process is any continuous related work-activity that can be measured).

PQMs are indicators and controls required to ensure that an activity consistently meets the set requirements. For instance, in our simple example in the previous section, we had a team building car doors on an assembly line. The PQMs here could be the amount of heat required in the mould, the weight of the raw materials, the measurement of the door, speed of through-put, etc.

In essence, what we have is PQMs that identify the accuracy of the work (e.g., door dimensions maintained), the reliability of the product (e.g., the door will not bend or disform), the timeliness of output (e.g., each door is finished every set amount of time), volume of output (e.g., a pre-set amount is produced), ease of use (e.g., the final product is fit for its subsequent use), completeness (e.g., nothing is missing or added from the final product), efficiency (e.g., how efficient is the team producing the product?) and capability (e.g., how capable are the teams in achieving objectives?).

These eight PQMs are directly applicable to any process, no matter whether it be the production of a physical product or, as one will soon see, a service.

In the past three to four decades it has become apparent that the quality of a product does not stop at the end of a conveyor belt but a major factor is the added service offered by the company after production. Service is like quality — it is a money-maker and if effectively managed, it leads to competitive advantage. This ethos has for a long time been a major part of product-oriented organizations with the provision of an after-production service and guarantees of good working conditions.

The problem mainly lies with the pure service industry (e.g., banks, hospitals, IT consultancies, etc) where it is less likely that the necessary controls and subsequent measures exist. In many companies this goes even further in terms of identifying where exactly their costs lie, for example, costs in terms of product lines or service areas/functions or even markets. Therefore how do we best establish the necessary quality assurance criteria to produce a quality service when , in the majority of cases, a company cannot even control its main basic strategic goal — costs.

Without this a company is in danger of pumping into a service area enormous amounts of capital and effort and it will be like throwing it into a black hole. This means that they will be unable to evaluate the return on capital plus costs; therefore it is unlikely that they can effectively evaluate the return on service in terms of whether it is actually fit for purpose and customer expectations. It is hence obvious that if we control and understand costs, we will at the very least be able to measure quality in terms of cost of prevention and cost of fixing problems or defects. But this implies keeping very precise detailed records of *all* the costs.

Once you are able to measure your quality (in the company's view) at least in terms of costs, you can continue to define the quality features required for your service and ultimately your client. The art therefore is in identifying where all the costs lie and associate benefits to that cost. For instance, what is the cost of producing a product as opposed to producing a service? How do we identify these costs?

One of the main differences between providing a service and producing a product is in the way each is produced. In the service industry the customer is involved in at least part of the process of producing said service, for instance, when you go to a college to attend a course and you find the staff friendly, attentive, responsive and the teachers professional and knowledgeable, the facilities fit for your course requirements (e.g., clean, accessible, well equipped, etc). This whole environment encompasses the quality process and can directly satisfy your need for quality. Furthermore, your and other students' participation and interaction in the course may be an invaluable part of the quality service as this will assist and enhance the quality service. Additionally another facet to this service is the quality attained in the long run (e.g., after the service has finished). Do you gain knowledge and are you able to subsequently utilize it? All these and many more facets of the education industry can all be associated to a cost.

In addition to these aspects of the service industry we also have a major distinction between the service and product industries. This is the opportunity within a service to stop the service when it does not meet our expectations of its quality — in theory at any stage of the service, e.g., in our example at the registration stage or during the course. This implies that we also stop spending on said service.

Other differences between the production of a product and the provision of a service include the early stage of its design (or inception). Within any manufacturing process, various stages are executed prior to production, from product design on paper, prototyping to final specification and commissioning of the tools to build the product. This process of design prior to production is seldom utilized in a service environment. However, in order for the service to be as close to what the customer wants and be able to adhere to our zero-defect ethos, it must first be designed and prevention of defects be included within it. All too often defects[26] occur because of problems in the design and therefore are subsequently built into the product or service.

How often are service ideas executed without any real cost/benefit justification being carried out prior to their execution? The answer to this question is very easy — a great majority of the time. The reason for this is apparent and stems back to human nature and naivety to do a job. Many services start off as a 'flash of genius' in someone's mind leading heuristically to the formulation of an idea.

But like most heuristic methods it is based on past experience and trial and error. This means that within most services no real investigation is made to evaluate whether the service is even required and hence it is unlikely to take into account costs and quality of service. Those ideas that do actually get off the ground and succeed do so because of several factors which we can express in terms of our eight PQMs defined earlier. For instance, within our education example, we can evaluate:

- accuracy of work in terms of the curriculum and capability of the tutors and staff;
- reliability of the product as always meeting the the students requirements and curriculum plus the final acquisition of a certificate;
- timeliness of the output as always adhering to the time-tables and completion dates set by the curriculum;
- volume of output as adhering to the contents set in the curriculum;
- ease of use as the service provided by administration staff, library, etc.;
- completeness as adhering to curriculum;
- efficiency as tutors and staff working as a team;
- capability as the quality of tutors in terms of their qualification to teach.

These eight PQMs should always form the basis for all products and services — which also include internal services within an organization. This obviously includes the service provided by IT and its constituent parts, for instance the quality of software.

Measuring Quality within the IT Industry

It is estimated that over 50% of all investment a company normally makes goes on IT and communications. It is therefore undoubtedly a major part of many companies' business. This IT service is the cornerstone for attaining competitive advantage where in many cases any loss or corruption of this service will put the company in jeopardy. Poor or bad computer systems (and inadequate security as we will discuss later in Chapter 3) waste immeasurable amounts of time and capital, affect staff morale, damage the corporate image, lose clients and prospects, inhibit strategic vision and more importantly will always make your company second best without any measure of competitive advantage.

However, it is important to realize that not only loss of IT availability causes problems but also loss of business direction or no strategic direction at all and lack of quality.

Within most companies, the reliance on technology is steadily increasing where the utility of computer systems is not only viewed as a support function for the business but as a prime and imperative source of profit within the business.

It is essential therefore that strategic decisions are taken in the light not only of present business needs and technology but also of future company-mission and technological influences plus advances. The old ethos of only applying technology to a problem and simply expecting a return in terms of supporting the business activity is no longer acceptable or valid. Service issues within IT such as reliability, availability, Service Level Agreements[27], Help Desks, problem and change management, installation administration and how quality is attained for the whole system (service included) need to be addressed.

Systems must be 100% available not the typical 98% availability quoted in many IT SLAs, which is completely misunderstood by users, as they want the service on demand not when they are told it is available. Help Desks need to provide desired levels of support and service as perceived by the user *not* the IT boffin. A user (hence the customer) query that is left unanswered for even a couple of hours could easily be enough to prompt a loss of confidence in the service and if it is an outside client a shift of custom to your competitors. If this is multiplied by several hundreds, it could ultimately lead to loss of business.

These types of problems must be prevented from occurring in the first place and any changes must be fast and accurate. All these IT services however are all dependent on quality software — the key to IT efficiency and success.

Software quality is an integral part of the overall quality of IT services and ultimately the company. The reader is also referred to Chapter 4 where Software Quality Standards are discussed, in particular TickIT.

It is important that the cost of software (and hence its quality) is kept to realistic targets. Too often software development, like in the making of an epic Hollywood movie, falls foul of over-running targets and costing many times the original budget.

Taking our philosophy of prevention into the production of software, it is obvious that fixing something that goes wrong in the design stage will be far less costly than at the coding stage and even less than at the testing and ultimately less than when it is up and running. The cost differences between getting it right first time and fixing it later could be phenomenal.

However, the issue of software quality does not solely lie in the effective execution of the Software Production Life Cycle[28]. It is the whole process of software engineering[29] in trying to overcome what has been called the 'Software Crisis' — the production of inadequate software where the main problem lies with accurately identifying and specifying user requirements; in other words making sure that the software is 'fit for purpose'.

Software production therefore needs to be looked at in terms of what is being produced, e.g., software fit for purpose. The analogy that we could use here is in production engineering (see Figure 2.17 below) where the product is largely determined by the quality of the process plus market influences dictating what is being produced independently (but making the final product dependent on it) from the production, cost engineering and quality assurance. The problem comes when these links do not exist.

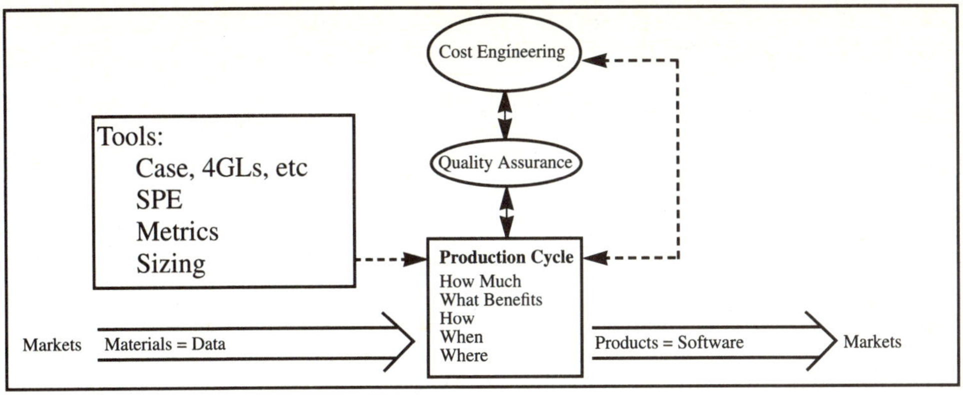

Figure 2.17 Software Production

For instance, a major omission normally found in development environments is Software Performance Engineering (SPE). SPE defines performance criteria needed from the system and this is normally done at the design stage prior to coding. This obviously prevents subsequent costly alterations and fine-tuning.

The success or failure of the development of software (as in all aspects of company life) relies on people and the culture within the organization. In order to convince the workforce that the use of standards and quality methods is beneficial you need to prove your point — software metrics can aid in this endeavour. Software metrics is based on the collection of data that is measurable, repeatable (a difficult concept within software development since there seldom exist standard units for software size and structure attributes) and comparable.

If we look closely at the Development Life Cycle of Software we can pinpoint areas where we can collect metrics. These areas we can define as inspection points were we can look at the product (i.e., the software) so that the defects can be identified and corrected. This will possibly also assist in removing the source of the defect which is a fundamental objective of quality.

> Therefore within the Software Development Life Cycle you can have a simple process of, for example:
>
> Requirements Definition —> Architecture Definition —> Design —> Code —> Test —> Implement
>
> If we stop each of these stages and add an inspection process we would have:
>
> Req.Dfn —> Inspection —> Arch.Dfn —> Inspection —> Design —> and so on

with each inspection step possibly looping back before continuing.

At these inspection points metrics would be collected within four broad areas:

(a) what the 'checkers' have found (e.g., major and minor issues-errors);

(b) what the checkers' brainstorm meeting identified;

(c) total amount of work done by the individual editing the software;

(d) time spent in administering the inspection process.

Examples of the type of data metric elements could be:

- time spent checking by an individual;

- number of 'pages' checked (e.g., a page can be defined to suit the product, but could be 50 lines of code);
- Number of 'pages' closely scrutinized;
- Number of 'pages' scanned;
- Major issues noted by each checker;
- Minor issues noted by each checker;
- Number of checkers;
- Time spent editing all issues raised;
- Brainstorming time.

Examples of the metric calculation from the data collected could be:

- Percentage of defects identified in a stage, e.g., design;
- Cost of correction:
- Average effectiveness;
- Average checking rates;
- Percentage of defects corrected after a stage.

The importance of collecting such metrics cannot be overstated, giving you a reliable picture of what exactly is happening within the software engineering environment. However, the collection of metrics (i.e., identification of defects) does not solve poor design, bad, inefficient coding or improve the quality of the software. Fixing the bugs does which in the long run reduces overall business costs. Metrics assist in pinpointing areas of lax quality that may need addressing. It also assist in justifying the inspection process and how profitable it may be.

The inspection and metric collection process fits relatively well within Crosby's five level TQM model and is applied to software engineering by the Software Engineering Institute as the Process Maturity Levels (PML):

Level 1 Initial (ad hoc/chaotic) unpredictable processes;

Level 2 Repeatable (intuitive) processes;

Level 3 Defined (qualitative) processes;

Level 4 Managed (quantitative) processes;

Level 5 Optimizing (feed-back) processes.

Within these PMLs the transition from level 1 to 2 is the most difficult one as it will require a complete change in working practices and possibly even culture. Levels 2 through to 5 cover areas of metric design and the key to its functionality lies in an effective and accurate data collection system, which in turn depends on a simplified life-cycle based on sequential attainable milestones.

All this is based on the development of new software; however, this task is normally only a small proportion of the IT department's overall work-load. Over 75% of their time is normally spent on the maintenance of existing systems. It is therefore imperative that an identical approach is undertaken when maintaining software, i.e., metrics for maintenance. In terms of metrics for maintenance the aim is to provide comparative accurate measures in terms of, for example, *capability* (the extent to which the maintenance process can change to the system), *resources used* (e.g., costs, staff, knowledge), *accuracy* (e.g., will the post-change environment behave within the operational environment as opposed to the test environment as predicted?) and *speed* (e.g., how long will it take to make the desired alterations/changes?).

Other measures like time, management, etc., may also be required to present an accurate maintenance model. The objective is to reduce trial and error maintainability and replace it with a manageable, controllable and cost-effective methodology.

In all, what comes out of that which I have discussed within this section , whether it be the development/maintenance of software, ancillary services like the help desk or the use of clever IT tools, is that the Corporate Culture of IT needs also to be 'in tune' with the Global Corporate Culture of a Company. In fact possibly more so. Most assume that because IT is 'new' and appears to be innovative, it follows that it is dynamic and has quality — how far from the truth this is.

If the old attitudes and styles of management are utilized then we have the same problems that we have in any area of industry: lax workmanship and poor products and services. IT must be used as an agent of change to the business. Its impact on organizational structures, management methods, job content and company mission can be outstanding if the right ethos is used — in this case a quality ethos.

The main role of IT should be nothing to do with technology but with the business — how many times have we heard the comment 'Those computer boffins down the corridor are always playing space invaders but what benefits do I as a user get? — none'. This is basically because IT sometimes divorces itself from the main stream of the business — the users' requirements.

Therefore in order to create the right attitude, understanding and commitment from all employees, the same culture shock that is required within all other areas of business must occur within IT. This culture change must build the appropriate environment that breeds innovation and hence facilitates the major impacts of IT — change. However, this ethos requires fundamental changes in how things have been done in the past — from a pure application of technology to the business by boffins to a business-oriented usage of the technology by users.

This inevitably will shift the emphasis of how a company functions from simply surviving and producing mediocre products and services to the entrepreneurial empowerment of the whole work-force in order to continually grow and achieve quality targets never before imagined.

The corporate culture within the IT environment has to take on board all those strategic goals that the company values and aspires to, to succeed. In a nutshell they are:

Shared vision and values throughout the company where IT is fully integrated into the overall business plan. The main aim is to harness the use of IT to improve quality and inevitably the business as a whole;

The commitment and behaviour of the whole workforce is invaluable, with everyone involved in developing and using IT systems working in harmony in order to gain any real benefits. This will mean that IT boffins must relinquish their power over systems and allow the user a more active role in the future development and usage of the systems. This will hence give the responsibility for its success or failure back where it belongs — the user and therefore ultimately the business. A user-focused culture is needed where IT becomes an enabler and facilitator of change;

Understanding and communications between IT and the business is imperative. Too often there is a general lack of business people who understand the technology and a lack of IT people who comprehend the business needs. One of the main issues in delivering quality is understanding and being able to use your knowledge and experience towards the achievement of your own goals and hence the business goals. Without the proper training in either case (IT or Business) it is obvious that a company will never achieve change and consequently any real commitment from their workforce. For example, how are line management expected to see the opportunities and benefits that can be gained from IT without any appreciation or awareness of what to expect from IT?

Confidence and success breeds confidence and success in a never ending sequential algorithm. This means that success in any area of the business will breed confidence in the future. If the use of IT is seen as beneficial to the business whether it be as a quality service or not, without any exaggerated expectations of it, then it is obvious that the future of IT as an integral part of the business is assured. In order for IT to do this, i.e., be successful, it must be managed effectively and to budget, but more importantly it must have the best people and technology.

Finally, leadership plays a primary role — we will discuss this at the end of this section. Within IT effective management leadership is an essential quality for its success as it will provide the correct impetus and support.

This all means that IT becomes a measurable entity within an organization with its strategic role within that organization strictly controlled. Any deviation, even slightly, from this definition will reduce the quality of IT and any subsequent benefits.

Cost of Quality

The Cost of Quality (CoQ) expressed as a percentage of a company's total expenditure, sales, turnover, etc. are figures normally associated with the success or failure of the TQM initiative.

Consequently a great amount of hype and misunderstanding surrounds the real CoQ of a product or service and its numerous interpretations. The CoQ to senior managers could be a 'hot button' to put a strategic action into place. To middle management it could mean a career opportunity to show what 'savings' they are achieving to senior management or just paying lip service to avoid investigation. To the workers it could mean a P.45 since not meeting unrealistic targets could make them lose their jobs.

Before I discuss how the CoQ is defined within TQM environments it is important to understand what we mean by 'cost'. Boots Everyday Dictionary defines cost as '... what is paid or suffered to obtain anything ...', which is different from the price asked or the value of anything.

Therefore, within the production of something, we can classify cost according to how much it takes to produce a 'unit' product or service. This is normally defined in terms of materials, labour and expense. This is further subdivided into whether costs are incurred as a direct result of the production of the product or service or as an indirect expense. This gives us the well known accounting principle of the prime and indirect cost associated with the production of a product or service. Prime costs are direct-material costs (e.g. any materials used in the production of the product or service), direct-labour costs (e.g., wages) and direct-expense (e.g., the extra amount required in the production of the product or service, like overtime.) Indirect costs include any overhead incurred during the production of any product or service, e.g., administration, rent, depreciation, advertising, training, research and development, service, etc.

With these definitions of cost how is the CoQ arrived at?

First of all, let's be absolutely clear about what we are trying to analyse and measure. The CoQ is a measurement that depicts the amount spent on the failure to attain a specific quality level. In other words the cost of producing products and services that do not meet the customer's expectation and hence do not conform to expected quality standards. In order to meet our quality objective, we must execute several tasks that will produce a product or service that is fit for purpose.

This initially will involve a cost of *preventing* errors occurring in the first place, then a cost of *inspecting* products and services before release to the public and if they do not pass the performance criteria, a cost of *rework* or failure.

These three costs are the basic elements of measuring how much quality is costing the company and therefore the true CoQ. It will also guide in the identification of trade-offs between quality standards and costs, i.e., how much are we willing to spend on attaining zero defects?

Taking each, let's evaluate what we mean by the three elements of CoQ:

(a) Cost of Prevention (CoP)

The CoP is normally associated with training, planning, meetings, forecasting, estimating, SWOT, etc. — in essence the design, implementation and maintenance of the Quality Management System. All those costs which indirectly influence the final quality of the product or service, the main two being training and planning.

Training, as I have already mentioned, is sometimes a difficult cost to justify since in many situations there does not exist any direct evidence of improvement. It can be like a double-edge sword. On the one hand, if you spend your budget on training and justify it in terms of expected immediate return on investment you may well fall foul of relying solely on it meeting your expectations. This is very dangerous since increases in work-related output and quality are seldom **only** associated to increase in training.

On the other hand, if you ignore the need for training, relying on individuals continuing to perform to the same standards even when changes are occurring throughout their working environment, this is very naive. How can you expect people to do their job without the proper training? Catch-22. The only thing that we can expect from training is a certain improvement in the efficiency of the worker in terms of their work-output, but we cannot expect effectiveness since obvious elements required to perform their job are still missing. (See the section on Teamwork for further information on this topic.)

Planning[30], although a costly enterprise can in the long run, eliminates a number of problems and hence avoid future errors and failures. As I have mentioned earlier (in Teamwork) planning is an art; many have tried and failed even when meticulously following all known management techniques and practices. The reasons for this failure are complex and involve various areas of the job function from management, personality, team commitment, availability of tools, etc. The aim therefore of planning is simply for managers to manage in a more methodical manner, instead of 'hoping for the best' and making corrective changes each time problems occur. Planning should be comprehensive and all-embracing where all the decisions regarding how the aims and objectives are to be carried out are fully analysed and laid down in detail.

Effective quality planning takes a lot of hard work, company commitment and good luck! This cost is the basis for the ethos 'doing it right first time'.

(b) Cost of Inspection (CoI)

Traditionally CoI was mainly associated with Statistical Quality Control and the placement of inspectors at various stages of production to catch the rejects before they progressed onto the next stage and out of the door. Areas of inspection included raw material sampling, process control, laboratory tests, calibration, life test and running test plus outgoing quality inspection and audits. However, it is now widely acknowledged that CoI is much more than this simplistic view of production.

This cost therefore is concerned with every aspect of 'checking and monitoring', whether it be carried out at the end of the production line or the time spent by every individual checking their own work.

A great amount of time is spent on checking within all organizations; most employees are either never satisfied with their work or are unsure of their ability. This leads to an ever increasing amount of wasted time spent on this activity — an activity that is seldom measured in terms of cost, simply because it is virtually impossible to do so. Within the service area this activity can be substantial, for instance, within the monitoring activity of updating an information database. The process here could be the checking of written data; transcription of the data onto coded forms; checking the codes; input onto the computer via terminal; checked by the computer; printed and checked again. In this example one activity undertook four checking processes — are all these checking activities really necessary?

It is not enough to stop bad or inadequate products and services and weed out the rejects. The cause of the rejects must be spotted quickly and the trouble put right. No amount of inspection will increase quality. In our example there may be no need to check four times but simply at the end. The quality of the output will not be changed.

(c) Cost of Rework (CoR)

This is the most misunderstood measurement within COQ and stems from the quality standards practised within manufacturing environments. Traditionally CoR has been calculated as a function of tangible measures — materials, excess inventory, scrap, re-inspection, tools failures, rework and rectification, etc. However, it is estimated that a great majority of the quality problems encountered are created by people who never touch the product (Deming). This means that the service areas like administration, sales, etc., spend a large proportion of their time on fixing errors and waste which is basically a form of rework — in other words doing unnecessary work as a result of an error etc. For instance, secretaries retyping contracts; people travelling to see clients to simply apologize for late deliveries; rework or doing the same job twice in any area whether directly involved with the product or not; handling complaints via help desks; lack of training everywhere; mis-information and bad communications between departments, between users, between the customer and the company; low morale, etc.

These individual examples by themselves may seem to be insignificant; however, when taken together they may form a very extensive loss and a high price to pay for quality.

Therefore the CoQ can be defined as Σ CoP + CoI + CoR (for i = 0 to α) with i representing the individual elements of each cost. These costs are normally split up approximately as 85% for CoR, 10% for CoI and 5% for CoP. These figures are the norm now (1994); however, this is changing with more emphasis being given to CoP and in the reduction of CoR.

The move to TQM requires that these figures are understood. This means maintaining or reducing CoR and increasing CoP to negligible limits as Figure 2.18 depicts.

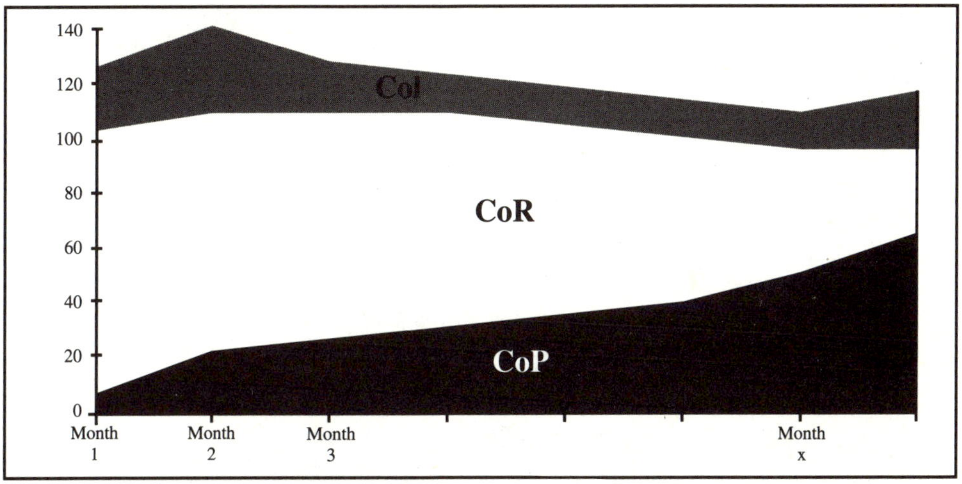

Figure 2.18 Towards TQM

In essence the road towards TQM will inevitably change the type of work that is carried out from one of fire-fighting and corrective actions to your own unique way of preventative medicine. Eventually, this means that the CoQ will shift from a high percentage of whatever figure you are measuring against and based mainly on CoR to one based on CoP. These, in the majority of cases, may always be substantially less than before. Note the road towards TQM also influences the amount spent on inspection since in theory less will be required as all workers will become their own inspector.

One of the most asked questions concerning CoQ is whether this value can be reduced, especially when every other area within an organization is under the magnifying glass? The answer to this question is a difficult pill to swallow as there is seldom a short cut to reducing CoQ. The question that should really be asked is what trade-off is there between meeting client or legal standards against a reduction in quality? If your answer is none then it is obvious that in order to keep your clients you have no choice but to continue spending to meet your quality criteria. We have discussed those direct identifiable costs but what about the costs associated with customer dissatisfaction, loss of reputation, etc.? These costs will always be incurred if quality takes second place to profit and therefore is not taken seriously.

The light at the end of the tunnel is that, as in medicine, preventative measures tend in the long run to be less expensive, even though you have to initially spend more than you would wish to.

Prevention therefore is the key and everyone must be made aware of this ethos. The cost of not conforming could be too high to even measure. In order to do this, the CoQ should be on everyone's mind; for instance, CoQ figures should be displayed for everyone to see (e.g., as a meaningful graph that everyone understands). By doing this everyone would be involved in monitoring the progress and be aware of all improvements. Remember success breeds success and if CoQ figures show a trend towards saving the company money, then this benefit should be passed back to those that deserve it. Additionally these figures can also act as a tool for management to set realistic planning goals, for instance, to reduce CoR by x%. A warning, however, should be given here. CoQ figures can sometimes be rather subjective, specially when they include cost of non-quantifiable elements. If the figures are not realistic then no one will take them seriously and the obvious consequence of this could be very detrimental to the whole Quality ethos. Furthermore, these figures should act as a way of improving team-work and act as a catalyst for improvement in general, not, as is sometimes a management trait, using them as a way of controlling and threatening the work-force. There is no way of measuring the value of inspiration and creativeness of a work force that is committed to accomplishing compelling goals. To achieve this the workforce must act in full collaboration with the management.

The bottom line is to keep the cost of quality to a minimum and in parallel reduce the cost in general through quality improvements.

Now that we have a complete picture of how CoQ can be defined and used, we can quickly associate this to the Cost of Security. As with quality, security has three basic cost elements. A cost of preventing security breaches (CoP) from occurring, a cost of inspecting (CoI) (which we can define as audit and risk analysis) and a cost of rework (CoR) (which we can define as cost of failure). Therefore,

$$\text{Cost of Security (CoS)} = \sum \text{CoP} + \text{CoI} + \text{CoR (for i} = 0 \text{ to } \alpha)$$

Looking a little closer at these elements we have:

CoP — This within the IT Security environment is hopefully the highest element. However, experience shows that this is normally the lowest since expenditure on prevention is seldom 'justified'. It can contain the cost associated with:

- definition and maintenance of a security policy;
- creation and maintenance of security awareness programmes;
- cost of specific security tools, e.g., smart cards for access control, encryption machines, physical locks, data recovery and storage, etc;
- cost of contingency plans and facilities;
- cost of security personnel;
- cost of countermeasures.

CoI — This can contain the cost associated with:

- risk analysis reviews (time);
- presence of an internal audit department;
- purchase of risk analysis tools;
- cost of maintaining accurate secure audit trails;
- cost of testing contingency plans.

CoF — This cost is normally the highest element of Cost of Security, as it is normally spent due to the impact of a breach, e.g., after the event. It can contain the cost associated with:

- recovering from fraud;
- recovering from fire, flood, lightning, hacking, tapping, theft, etc.;
- recovering from bad quality software and software viruses;
- recovering from unavailability;
- reconstruction of data and software.

Management Involvement and Leadership

Throughout this chapter a common denominator has raised its head to explain one of the main influences within any TQM drive — leadership and management's responsibility plus commitment towards this initiative. In fact, without this all TQM drives are bound for the rocks and to perish in the turmoil. In everyday life, leadership (and the power that comes with it) is one of those human traits that we all aspire to and look up to in others. Many believe that leaders are born and no amount of training can help a bad manager become a leader. Perhaps there is something in this philosophy, especially since as animals ourselves we tend to group into power-units, following the direction of the strongest viewpoint (or physical threat) simply because the individual shows his or her plumage — no real training is required. How often have we seen groups of football supporters align themselves around a team and follow the lead from the most obnoxious and aggressive individual? How often have we submitted ourselves to the suggestions (or orders) of our 'manager' only because he or she has the power to make our working life a misery or even worse lose our livelihood? How often has the individual with the power (whether it be spiritual like the Pope, monetary like a CEO of a multinational or political like the US President) used it to subjugate the people under their influence, in many instances misleading them with beguiling words and promises?

The problem, therefore, lies in using a management style and technique that will benefit the company without subjugating the employees, not only in the immediate term but in the long run. Many management initiatives are sometimes looked at by the workers as just another ploy to get that extra pound of flesh from the worker at no extra cost. The feeling of follow the leader without question mentioned earlier, like the Light Brigade in the Crimean War, is the thought uppermost in employees' minds. For this reason it is of paramount importance that the right style of leadership and management is used to attain company goal without fear.

Therefore what is Leadership as opposed to Management?

The distinction between these two concepts evolves around the requirement of the job function within specific organizational constraints. This basically means that each individual activity is a reaction to the pressures of the work process. The manager will normally work around his or her environment, concerned about day-to-day problems, trying to make the right short term decisions, avoiding conflicts and maintaining productivity, in essence focused on short term goals and objectives.

Leadership looks to the future, actively shaping ideas rather than responding to them. It covers a variety of ills (see Figure 2.19). However, its main definition is to inspire confidence and trust so that there is maximum co-operation from all. Leaders have the knack of generating enthusiasm, have a compelling vision and are able to communicate this vision to all concerned. This ethos is further described diagramatically in Figure 2.19, where you can follow within the diagram the answer to questions like:

- What is management? —> what resources does it use?
- What is leadership? —> what is an effective leader?
- Where should management merge with leadership?

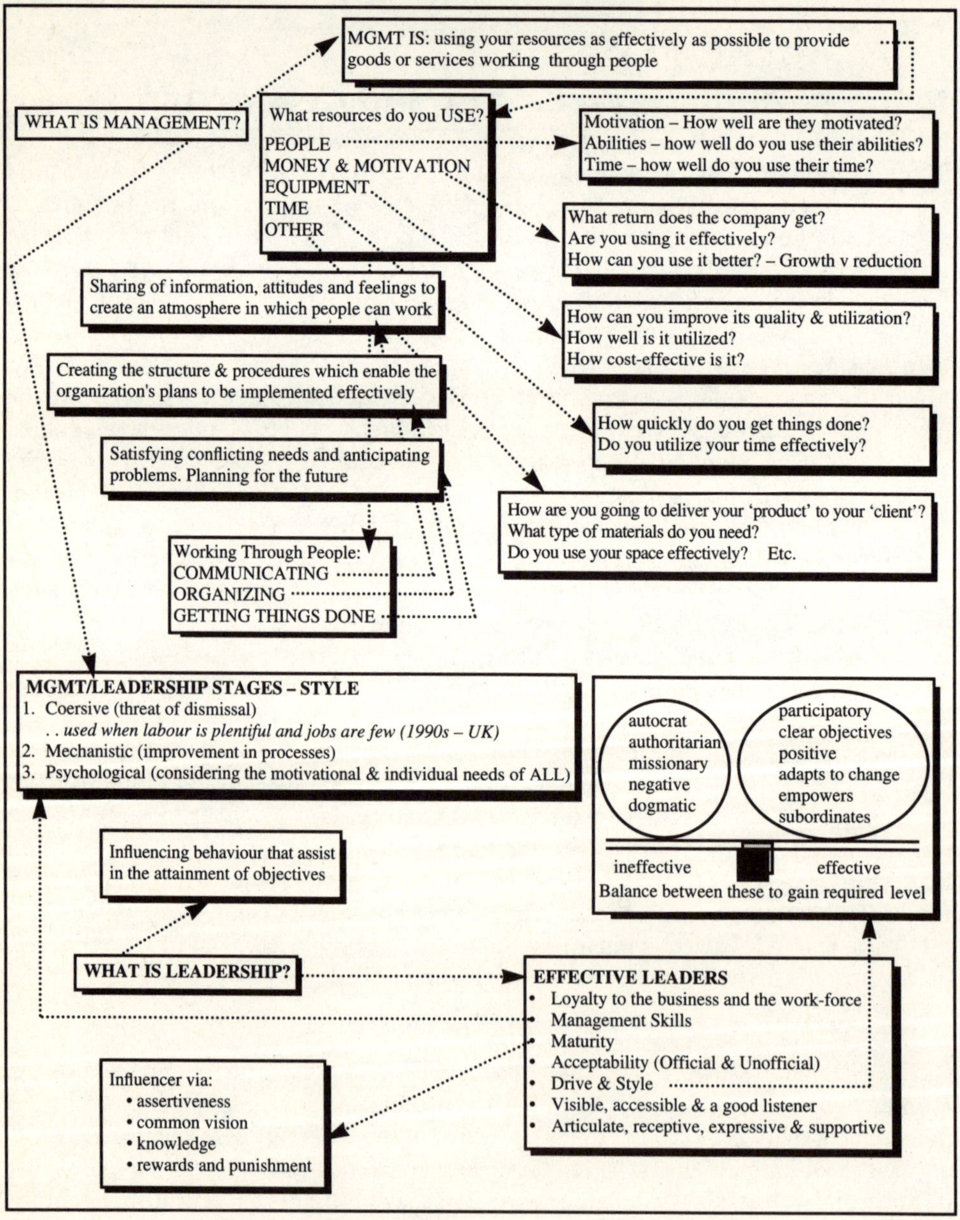

Figure 2.19 Leadership versus Management

However you will notice that there are some common areas that are required in both management and leadership in order to effectively do each. Let's also be quite clear of what management and leadership is not, described in Figure 2.20.

You will notice that management (and therefore even less for leadership) is not specific. It covers a variety of functions of which leaders require *all* of its areas in order to effectively develop their leadership skills.

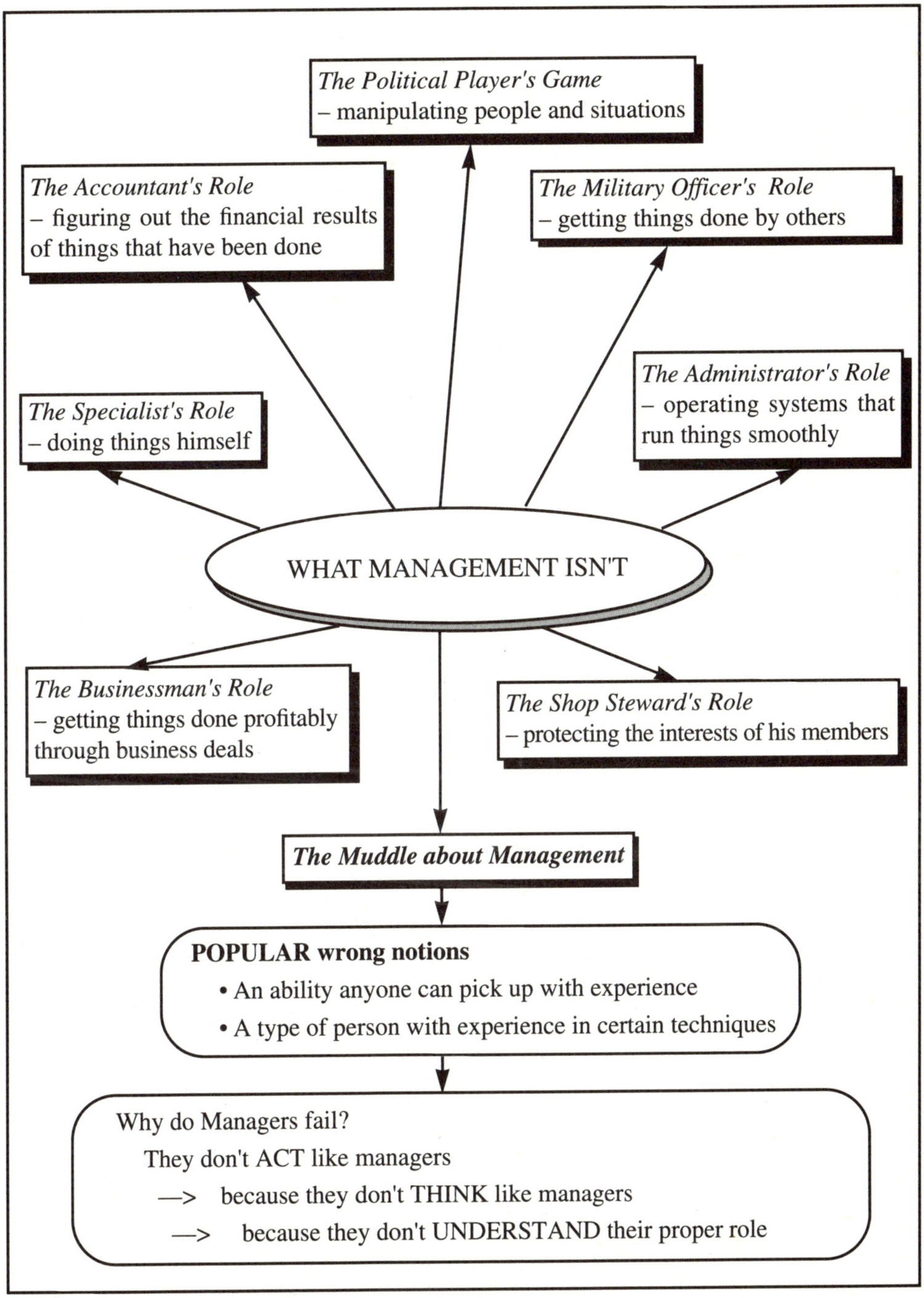

Figure 2.20 The Problem with Management

Figure 2.19 depicts the basic elements of effective management and leadership. However what are the basic skills that a manager needs to lead? Figure 2.21 below depicts the fundamental elements of effective management and leadership leading to the motivation of the workforce.

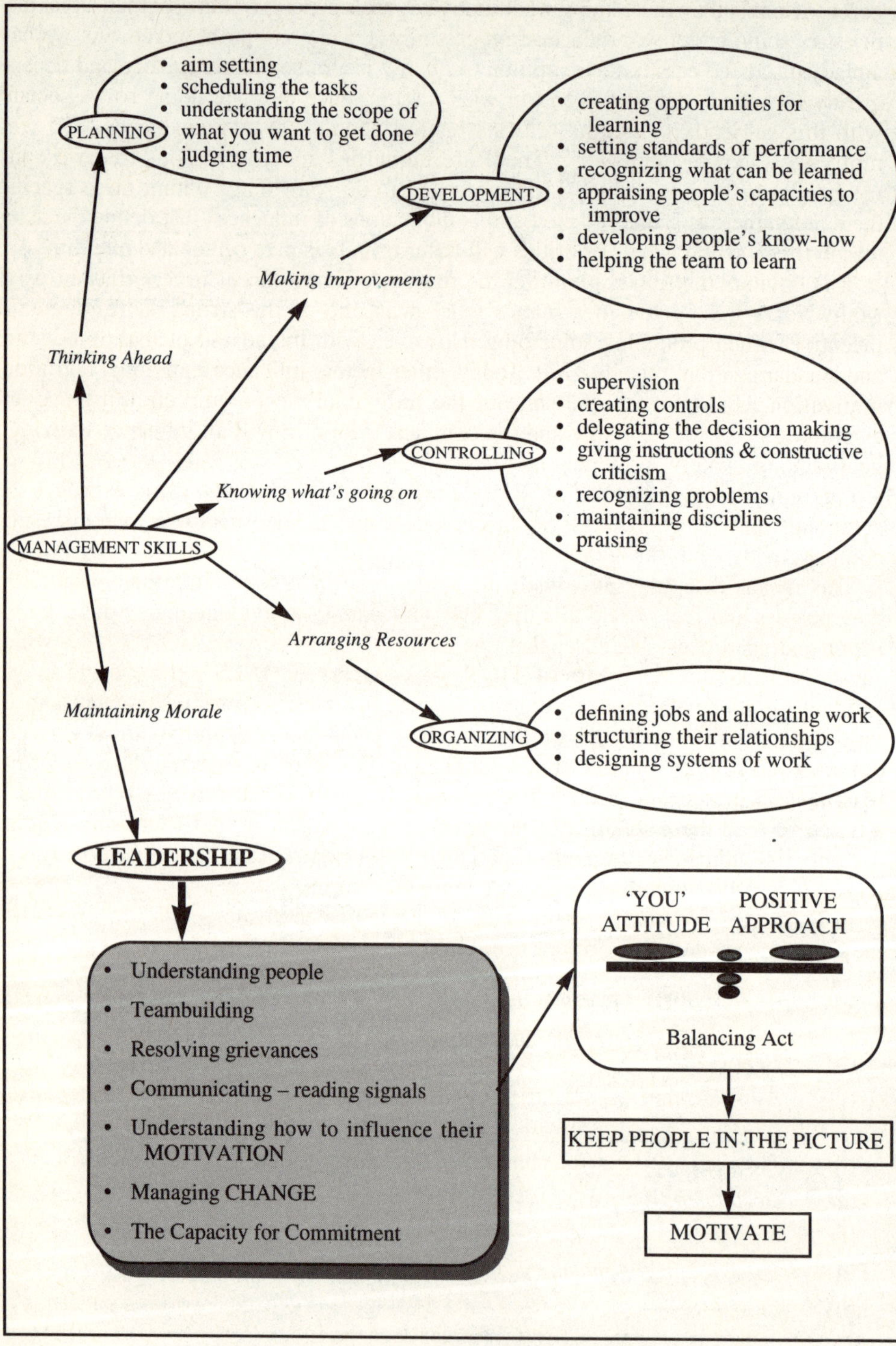

Figure 2.21 Effective Leadership leads to Motivation

As can be seen in Figure 2.21, the objective ultimately is to motivate your employees to want to do their job as effectively and proficiently as possible because they themselves want to do it in such a way. The leader needs to understand this by making work more meaningful, increasing participation and giving a sense of achievement to everyone. In order to do this they must know what motivates their people, which will then assist them in establishing effective production processes and achieving profit targets. As we have already discussed earlier, the definition of quality is a rather subjective one and depends greatly on who is defining it and in what circumstance they are doing so. Associated with this subjectivity are the reasons behind people's wants and needs, and what motivates them in their work. There are numerous specific reasons that we could mention as to why an individual is motivated to do something. Within these specifics there are numerous shades of grey and combinations of influences that define the actual reason for an action, where priorities will differ from person to person and over time.

It is obvious that motivation and the reason for it can occur in a variety of ways. Many years ago, pride in a man's work was one of the strongest fundamental incentives when producing something. However, with the advent of mass-production and standardization, this changed. Today, other factors influence individual and group motivation. Undoubtedly, the state of the individual's economic circumstance and even the state of the economy and the company within it, will all influence individual goals and, ultimately, individual motivation.

One could therefore look at motivation and the reasons for it as a process of achieving specific goals, e.g., quality. Leaders and managers must achieve specific company-wide goals through their people.

This means that they must instil the same sense of urgency into their people that they possess and feel. To do this they must first satisfy individual goals establishing a never ending process, i.e., Leaders' ACTIONS —> to achieve GOALS —> which satisfy NEEDS —> that create ACTION —> to achieve GOALS and so on and so on.

Many intellectuals have devoted their lives to investigating management and its motivational influence on the work-force. To discuss this in depth would take several volumes and is inappropriate to this publication. However, in Figure 2.22, a very brief résumé describes seven of the most well known motivational theories. The reader is advised to read these theories in terms of what management and leadership require, not only individual specific goals. Each theory has elements of reality and elements of trying to describe something intangible in tangible terms.

In Figure 2.22 you will see most of the ideas that motivate people. In a nut-shell they are (in no order of priority or need):

(a) *Achievement* — most people want the satisfaction of making a meaningful contribution;

(b) *Recognition* — it is natural to want your work effort recognized;

(c) *Advancement* — most people want to move on to more challenging situations, acquiring knowledge and skills;

(d) *Interest* — the chance to practice new skills;

(e) *Responsibility*

(f) *Security* — fear of being out of work;

(g) *Esteem / protagonism*;

(h) *Stimulation* — the need for a person to vary his/her working pattern is an essential element against frustration;

(i) *Creative ability and self-expression.*

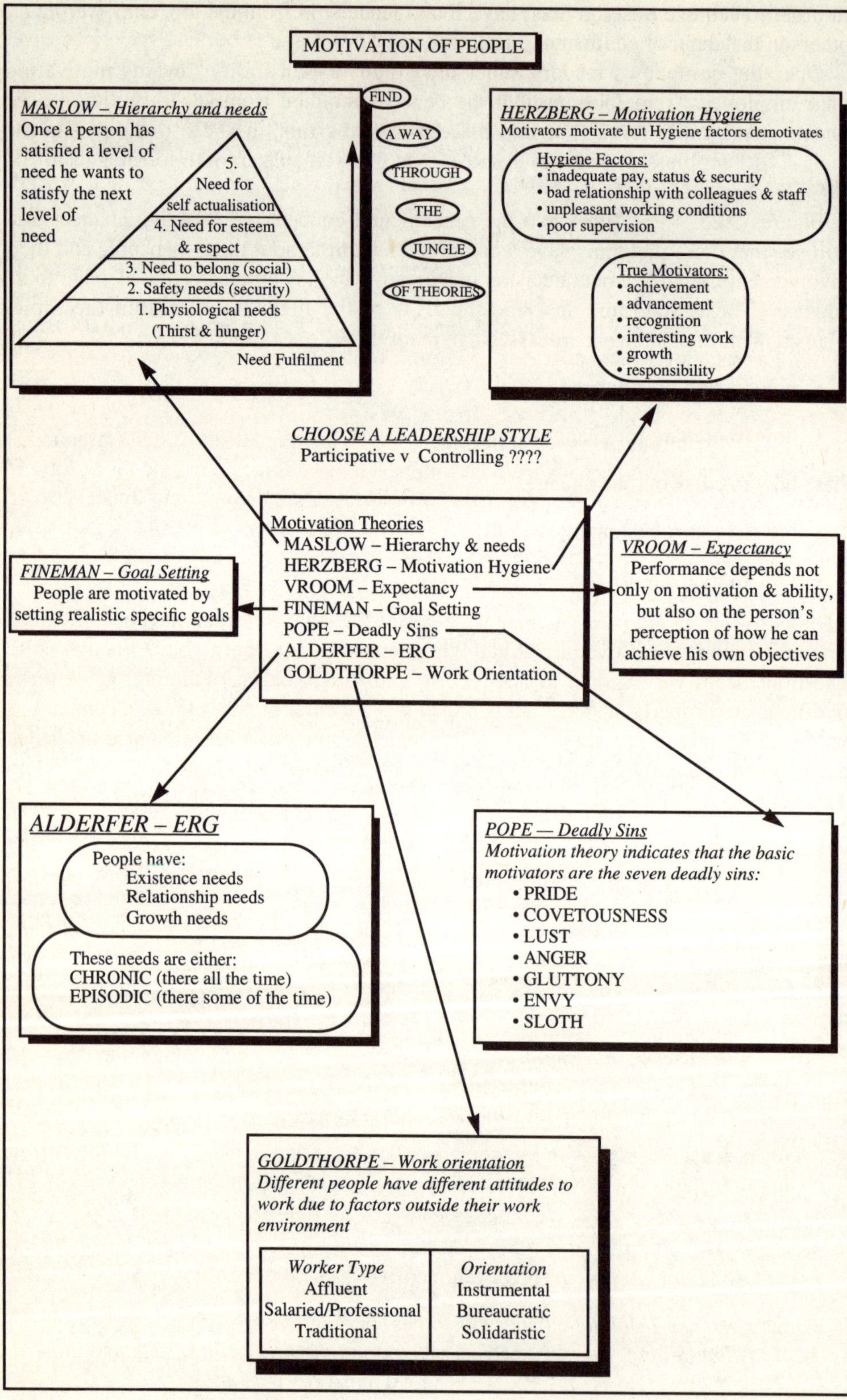

Figures 2.22 Jungle of Theories

In order to achieve this you must have sound leadership from the top, empowering all others in the chain of command to follow.

Once the company's leaders understand their responsibility towards motivating their employees (remembering that the benefits attained from such a policy can be phenomenal) and effort is put into place to achieve this, they can then go onto the main TQM problem of culture change or, as many managers like to refer to it, the Management of Change.

Figures 2.23 — 2.24 describe the fundamental concept of managing change. You will see that these diagrams have a common idea throughout them — people and their involvement in management decision making — which is a fundamental element to its success. These diagrams describe the flow of the main issues within the topic. Management of change encompasses five main 'hows' (see Figure 2.23):

- how to plan the change;
- how to prepare for change;
- how to carry out the change;
- how to control change;
- how to manage the change.

In order to effectively manage change the senior manager or leader of a company must first understand where they are at and where exactly they want to be. Although these questions seem very simple to answer, in reality they can be daunting. Once these questions are properly answered, it is hoped that a clearer picture of how a company is will emerge. Within this scenario a clearer understanding of what resistance to change exists will be identified (as described in Figure 2.24 — Objections to Change Box). This resistance could be (list not exhaustive):

- lack of information;
- historical factors;
- fear of failure;
- fear of the unknown;
- misinformation;
- threat to core skills and competence;
- no perceived benefits;
- threat to status or power base;
- reluctance to experiment;
- lack of Senior Management commitment;
- managers not listening either to customers or employees;
- etc.

Once these resistances are identified we then have the opportunity to deal with them.

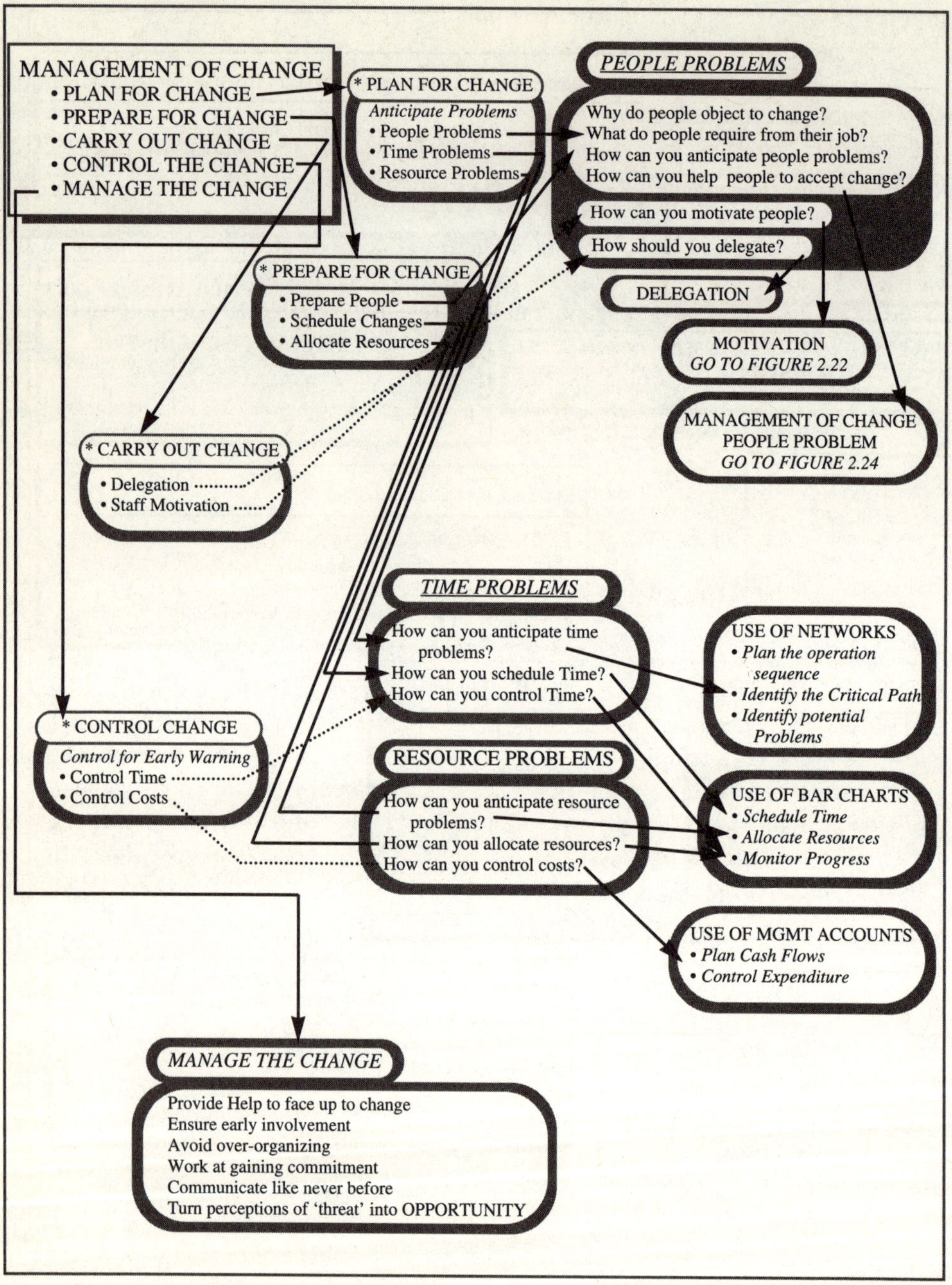

Figure 2.23 Management of Change — Part I

In essence what we have here is an amalgamation of leadership techniques that are essential to the implementation of any TQM drive. Leaders must be excellent managers capable of managing the situation (as described in Figures 2.19 – 2.20), able to instil that much needed sense of urgency in their people (Figure 2.20) together with coping with change (Figures 2.23 – 2.24).

This leads to a fundamental change in behaviour across the organization, from senior management downwards, since without change in culture nothing changes.

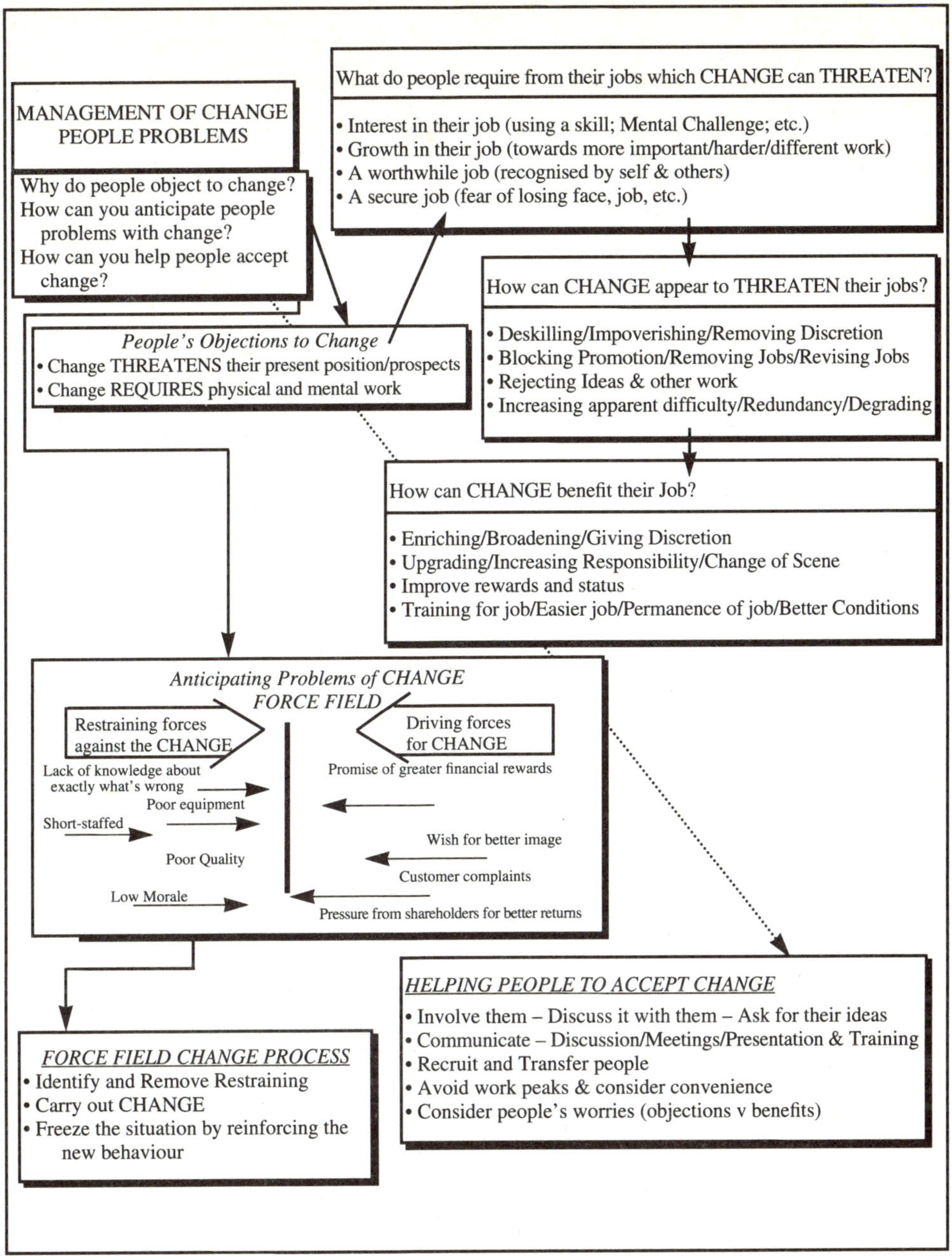

Figure 2.24 Management of Change — Part II

Applying Management of Change techniques to TQM initiatives is obvious. The basic reason being that TQM identifies areas within an organization that require a more dynamic 'empowered' environment. This philosophy is normally alien to most organizations, especially those with well established autocratic management.

The approach to move away from such an autocratic environment should start at the top with the mission statement. This is followed by analysing the company's critical success factors and consequently understanding the critical or key processes within the organization. To do this, commitment, teamwork and knowledge of the business is of paramount importance. These three are also the foundation stones of an effective IT Security Strategy.

Within IT Security, the basic requirement is to protect the business (which incidentally is part of any TQM drive). Commitment for IT Security throughout the organization is unlikely unless there is total commitment at the top of the organization. Senior management must believe (or at least appear to) in the importance of IT Security and must make sure that all staff follow suit. This evangelical belief must become part of the culture of the organization and will probably require a phenomenal amount of change. For example, the change from believing that 'security is not my problem' to 'security is up to me'.

However, like religion, evangelical belief can only grow when general and specific knowledge is acquired about the belief that confirms your faith. IT security awareness and its influence on the business requires training that will arm the individuals with the required knowledge and a 'bible of security guidelines' to enable staff to secure the environment.

Again a change in many organizations' philosophy towards training is needed — from one of 'training is a waste of time' to 'training can benefit the organization'.

Finally, without teamwork, IT Security problems will always occur. A change in the mind-set of all staff must be achieved. This change must bring about the concept/reality that 'no man is an island'. Whatever one person does will affect (in a bad or good way) another person. If due to incompetence/laziness, etc. you jeopardize the integrity of the IT Systems, this will not only affect the company but your fellow workers. This must be 'burnt into' each staff member's innermost long-term memory.

Quality System and Manual

In order to effectively implement a Quality System you must first understand fully your organizational needs and requirements. Without this understanding it is obvious that you are unlikely to produce relevant Quality Manuals that can be used to implement, monitor or enhance the Quality System. This is one of the most important areas of any Quality drive but is also the one that most professionals neglect to effectively implement. There are many reasons for this inability to produce useful Quality Manuals, from lack of Quality understanding and knowledge, lack of training within Senior Management, the use of an outsider who does not understand the industry, inexperienced Quality Manager, and so on.

Therefore let's start by defining what we mean by a Quality System. This chapter has, in its totality, described various elements of a Quality System, where we begin with the identification of the requirements and finish by satisfying those requirements. It is obvious that the Quality System is by definition those activities performed within an organization that conform to Quality Standards. This will cover areas such as Marketing, Operational Research, Design, Development, Procurement, Planning, Testing, Packaging, Storage, Sales, Maintenance, etc. etc. Therefore the Quality System is the system used to produce a product or service.

To describe this system we use the Quality Manual and associated procedures and work-instructions documentation. Hence the Quality Manual is where we start with the description of quality requirements within an organization. The creation of this document will need the help of many different responsible individuals within an organization.

One man's perception of what quality means for a company will not provide a true picture of a company's real quality requirement. Normally what tends to happen when one individual alone develops this documentation is that he describes how he would wish things to happen or thought they happened — not the reality.

Therefore what is an effective and useful Quality Manual? There are widespread differences within industry about what exactly it is or should be. In essence, it is simply a document that describes in a straightforward way how a company has implemented its quality policy. For this reason Quality Manuals are going to differ in content from industry to industry and even within the same industry, from company to company.

The contents, if they wish to adhere to a Governing Standard, must cover certain functional areas. For instance in BS5750/ISO 9000, a quality system should be 'documented' and 'established and maintained' and may cover twenty sections, from management responsibility to statistical techniques. If one of the sections defined in the standard is not relevant to the company, then only a note of 'non-relevance' suffices. The convention for the format and shape of the Quality System is therefore defined as:

Level 1	POLICY	——> Quality Manual
Level 2	DEPARTMENTAL PROCEDURES	——> Procedures Manual
Level 3	WORK PROCEDURES	——> Instructions Manual
Level 4	FORMS, LABELS, TAGS	——> Instructions Manual

This definition assumes that an organization is big enough to separate each level according to functional and organizational requirements. However, the smaller a company is the more likely that Level 4 will merge into Level 3, which in turn could merge into Level 2. Note that the more we merge these levels, the more likely it is that the size of the Quality Manual will increase and hence become unmanageable and unmaintainable. Any quality document that is more than 30 pages in length is likely to be cumbersome and contain irrelevant or unnecessary information. Likewise with the Quality Manual, since in essence all it should cover should be a brief 'Executive Summary' of the organization's management system and how it functions to achieve the general policies, referring where necessary to more detailed procedures elsewhere. Furthermore and most importantly, within it will be a clear statement of policy giving authority to the Quality drive, its procedures and instructions. Convention guides us to a Quality Manual not dissimilar in contents to the following:

Example Quality Manual — Contents

(i) Distribution list and Confidentiality of the Quality Manual;

(ii) Responsibility of the Manual holders to update and record changes;

(iii) Terms and Definitions.

1 Policy Statement [Signed and approved by the CEO or equivalent].

2 Brief Summary of products, services, facilities, organization, the business, organizational chart.

3 Brief Summary of how things are done, standards adhered to, cross reference to each clause and how compliance is achieved. (See Figure 2.25 for an

example of contents of this section and Chapter 4 for further information on adhering to a Standard.)

4 Cross reference to detailed procedures and work-instructions.

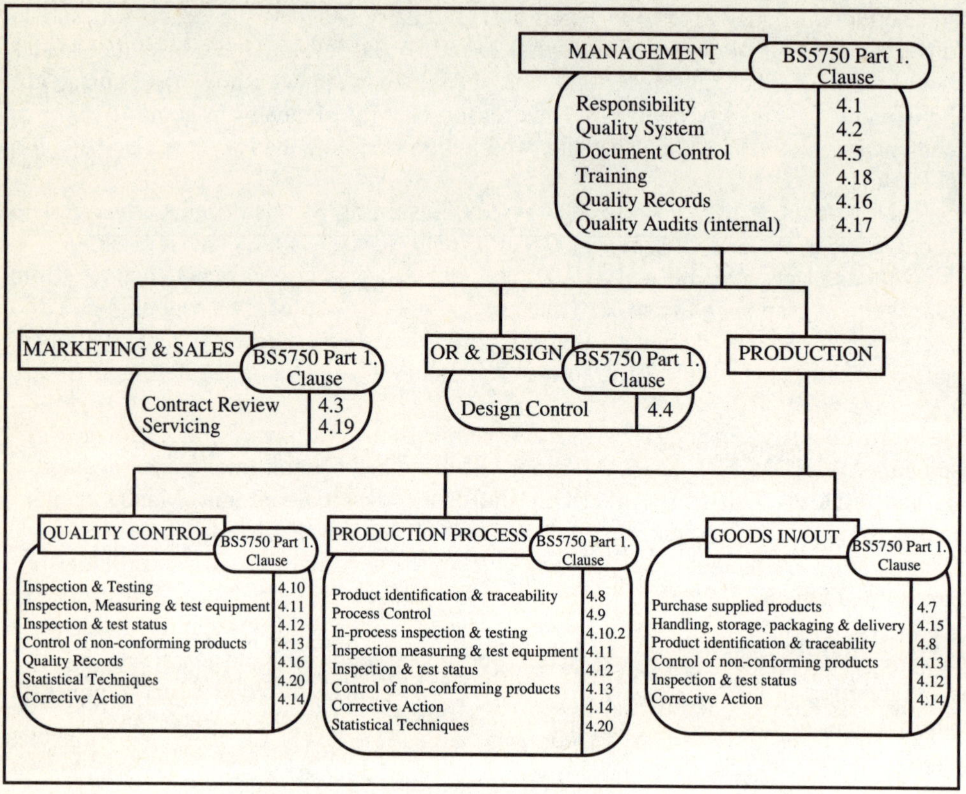

Figure 2.25 Example Section 3 Contents — Quality Manual

The contents list described above is typical of a Quality Manual, giving a guide to how to proceed in the implementation of TQM, but remember that this manual must be useful and understandable. The Quality Manual is a 'living', dynamic, current document, that should describe how things are, not how they should be. Its flexibility is of paramount importance and therefore the way it is written should aid a clearer understanding of it. If it is written in general and vague terms (similar to marketing jargon), this will only mean that it will be interpreted in the same way.

Additionally the Quality Manual must be:

(i) an aid to the audit process (both internal and external — see Chapter 7 for further information on auditing);

(ii) of benefit to users by giving them clear guidelines;

(iii) kept up to date as things change, any alteration to a procedure, work instruction, etc., should be reflected in the manual;

(iv) contain a good cross-reference to written procedures, avoiding the inclusion of any company confidential material;

(v) under strict Quality Document Control to ensure that only the most up-to-date issues are used and referred to everywhere within an organization.

O to be self-balanced for contingencies, to confront night, storms, hunger, ridicule, accidents, rebuffs, as the trees and animals do.
... Walt Whitman

3

IT Security and Quality

The word Security, a very precarious and subjective term, always raises images of espionage, the CIA, FBI, KGB, MI5, and all the other counter-intelligence agencies you can think of. This image of deceit and danger is promoted and sold by agents provocateurs within governments, multinational companies, Hollywood, etc. as a way of subjugating and keeping out the masses from the security elite. It also promotes a sense of mystery and the untouchable around the subject.

This type of promotion, although warranted in some areas, means that the public see it as something beyond their 'real' world and hence inevitably and justifiably do not associate themselves to it. How often have we seen Hollywood films depicting criminal acts of hacking[31] as an easy way of getting rich or acquiring power? — *Fantasy mixed with touches of reality.* How many times have we seen glamorous press coverage of virus attacks without any real indication of the damage caused? — *Reality with a touch of glamour.*

However, it would be very naive to believe that security is just these portraits of illusion with a touch of reality. Security is much, much more. For instance, how does one behave and trust an unknown individual when we first meet them? Imagine yourself on a train or plane. You are randomly seated next to someone you have never met before but out of boredom you start a conversation with each other. How much of your personal life are you willing and prepared to discuss? Even further, how much of your hard-earned money would you trust this person with, as an unsecured loan? How much credence would you give any advice you receive? Would you buy a car from this person? Would you tell them exactly where you lived and that you will be going on holiday for a month leaving your home unattended without any protection?

All these questions raise the issue of whether one is able to trust anyone we meet and even further how secure one feels. Security within this scenario is simply an attitude of mind, where we realize that something could go wrong and that the effects could be disastrous if we do not protect ourselves. Similarly the need for basic security within an organization is obvious, since without it the company could literally go out of business.

Since the first computer was developed, man has found numerous ways of using it to improve work activities and for the production of new products and services. Information Technology (IT) has literally taken over many processes, with many companies depending totally on IT systems to function and survive. Success in many organizations now depends on how well they can use their staff and information to make their services and products more competitive than those of their competitors. Any loss of the IT system would inevitably lead to a loss of business or, even worse, the complete closure of the company.

We therefore need to be aware of the consequences of lax IT security (as we are with our own personal belongings) and this realization will then guide us to identifying the threat to our business leading to doing something about it, i.e., establishing countermeasures[32] to avoid disaster. However, as with life itself and accounting for Murphy's Law ('.. anything that can go wrong, will go wrong..') countermeasures by themselves will not safeguard everything, especially without the co-operation of everyone committed to IT security. As discussed in the previous chapter, cultural influences will dictate how IT Security is undertaken within an organization. One of its prime influences (similar to TQM) comes from the need to safeguard the company from failure. We therefore have an issue of making everyone aware of their responsibility towards IT Security. This awareness will inevitably create commitment in the right areas, which in turn means that security policies and procedures will be implemented and followed, leading consequently to a reduction of the level of impact[33] a breach could mean.

It can be seen that the importance of IT Security is paramount. The risks associated with inadequate or inappropriate protection of IT resources could be disclosure of business secrets to unauthorized parties leading to loss of business to competitors, inaccurate/incomplete information leading to erroneous decisions and subsequently loss of business and unavailability of the IT service when required, again leading to loss of business, or even worse, a loss of that elusive competitive advantage.

These risks are even greater when the information used across the IT resources is compromised in some way without the knowledge of the user. This type of problem is inherent within IT, where evidence of intrusion is sometimes difficult to attain.

TQM philosophy defines as one of its main premises the concept of zero defects. This is normally applied to production goals, whether that be a product or service. Within it, everyone is in control of the quality of their work and is dependent on others (see Figure 2.5) — the Quality Chain. This ethos has a direct bearing on IT Security as it goes straight to the heart of IT Security — the prevention of threats, whether they be accidental or deliberate. The majority of IT Security problems stem from some accidental nature (e.g., fire, flood, etc.); however, many stem from lack of understanding, bad (error-ridden) software, lack of procedures and working practices, inadequate auditing plus inadequate disaster recovery procedures.

The latter types of security problems can in the majority of cases be avoided if care and attention is taken. Zero-defect development, quality-responsibility and procedures will reduce the level of threat. All this gives us a management problem (similar to TQM implementation). Without management commitment and acknowledgement of the problems, it would be like the three monkeys — '... See no evil, hear no evil, speak no evil —- therefore no evil exists ...'. However, all around you, chaos dominates.

Security is therefore a Management problem not a technology problem! A lack of direction and commitment from the top will create uncertainty leading to lax and inconsistent security measures. As with our Quality Chain, each ring is dependent on the previous one, which means that within security, the whole is only as good as the weakest link.

Information Security

Of prime importance within the protection of IT is information. Information can be accidentally or maliciously destroyed, modified or stolen.

As a simplistic definition, information security could be defined as:

> The protection of *information* assets from *accidental* or *malicious* unauthorized disclosure, modification, or destruction, or the inability to process that information.

The basic objective of trying to secure IT information can be explained in terms of loss of *Confidentiality, Integrity and Availability (CIA). Confidentiality* (or more strictly speaking a loss of it) defines the need for restricting information (or access to information) from prying eyes and systems resources from unauthorized users. Examples of types of objects that you would wish to restrict access to could be financial plans, production estimates, design drawings, personnel records, etc.

Integrity determines how systems resources are supposed to behave and also that information has not been altered or damaged by an un-authorized source. If information is in any way 'damaged' causing it to be unreliable, inaccurate or incomplete, then at best it becomes useless and at worst could lead to damaging the business. *Availability* means that a resource is accessible to an authorized user whenever it is required and on demand without delay.

This CIA model, when applied in a consistent manner, can be very helpful in determining threats. In order to effectively do so, you would need to measure IT systems in terms of *Authentication*[34] (the assurance that the identity of a user is ascertained and confirmed before the user is granted access to the system, for example, via passwords[35]), *Authorization* (what actions and access is allowed to the user), *Accountability* (the recording of events via, for example, an audit trail — this is a major area of business control as it facilitates *Proof* and *Evidence*, allowing for the establishment of non-repudiation and trace procedures) and *Assurance* (what level of confidence does the system have? The system must provide mechanisms that guarantee IT Security requirements.)

In order to safeguard these four 'A's of privacy we need to maintain and preserve the CIA of information and of the system as a whole. CIA can be enforced by using *physical*[36] (this aims to ensure that the systems resources and information are neither removed or physically damaged), procedural (this provides clear methods of how employees should do their work) and *logical*[37] (this is concerned with the use of software mechanisms for the provision of security) methods.

However, as already stated, even with numerous and expensive security precautions (normally addressing a business problem within a technical framework), it is still up to the user himself to enforce them and to consider how much security he really requires. It is important *not* to fall into the misconception that you can protect IT by the use of more IT — this is known as the technology trap. This situation occurs when too much emphasis is placed upon technology, e.g., the use of technology without giving complete consideration to its implications. For instance, how user acceptable are access control mechanisms? If users are going to circumvent them because they seem to be a nuisance, then obviously they lose their effectiveness.

You therefore require an effective Quality IT Security Policy that is both clear, concise and useful. It must be explicit, well defined and most importantly, enforceable.

Quality IT Security Policy

The *IT Security Policy Document* (normally a short document which contains a set of principles or rules stating how the protection of IT assets[38] should be specified and managed consistently and effectively) should be supported by the highest levels of management and should encompass the whole organization. As with a Quality statement, a written Quality IT Security Policy, signed again by the CEO or equivalent, provides the authority to establish IT security procedures and protective measures. The IT Security Policy fits very well within the overall Quality Policy of an organization as described in Figure 3.1. For example, how quality *values* creates a *vision* of excellence which in turn forms a *mission* to succeed that requires a strategy that needs an *implementation* plan.

Figure 3.2 describes where the IT Security Policy fits in the overall picture by placing itself within the strategic IT Framework. In other words it facilitates the tools, procedures and methods to protect the business.

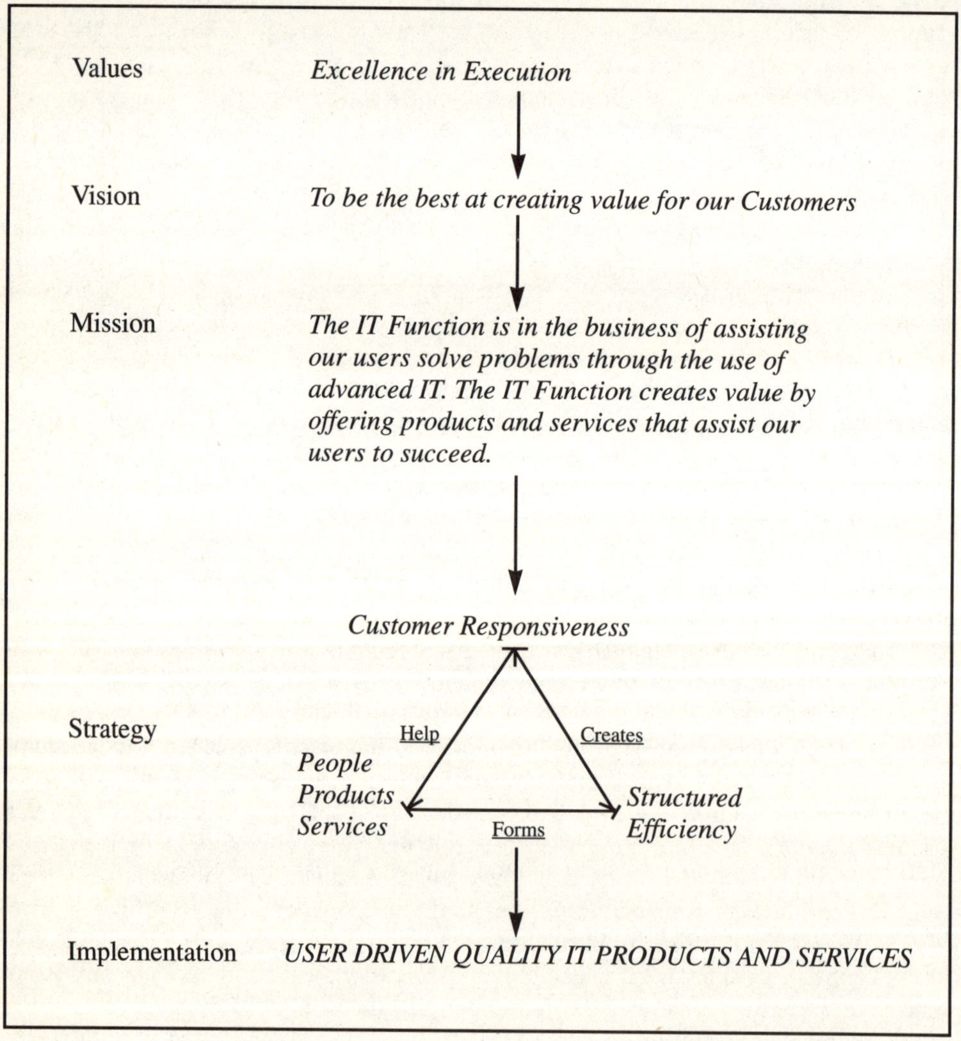

Figure 3.1 Strategic IT Framework

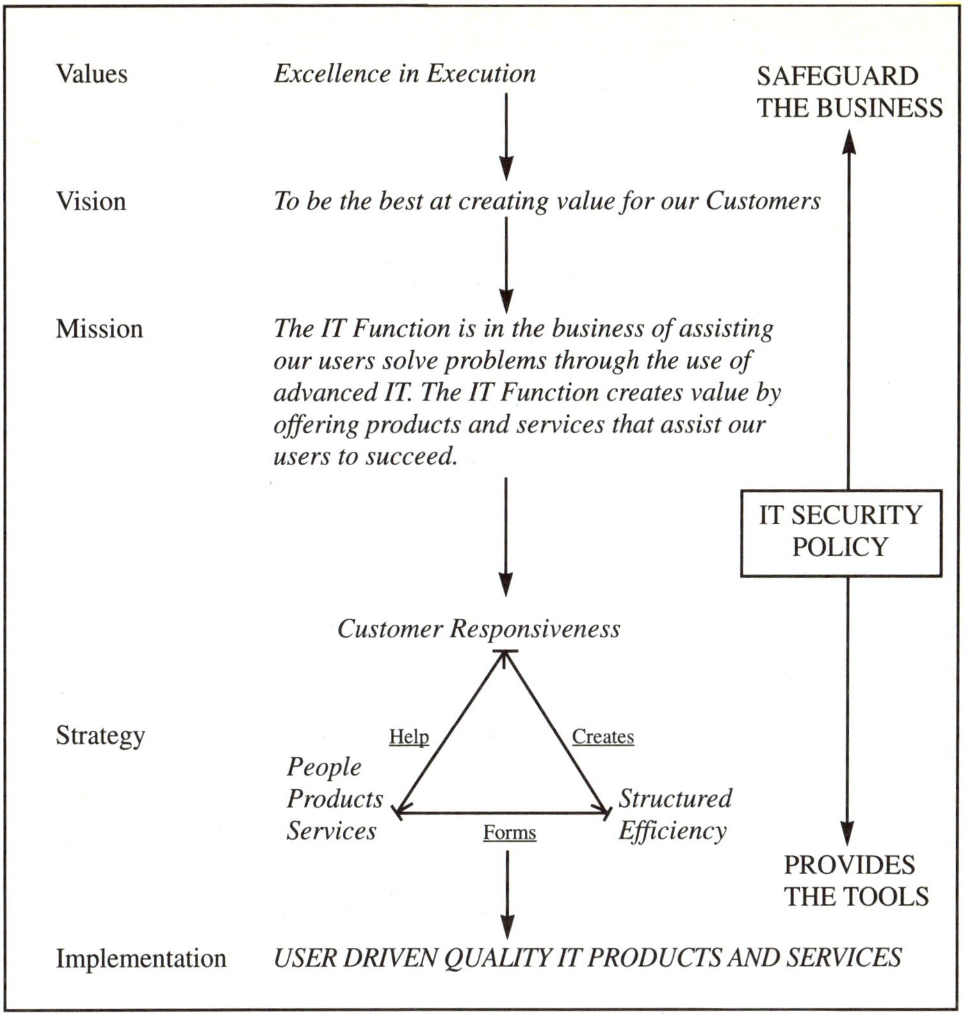

Figure 3.2 Strategic IT Framework and IT Security Policy

This policy must describe the directions for IT security and give guidance where appropriate. Supporting documents should identify the risks, explain any technical and management policies that together with the company's IS Strategy, describe cost-effective measures and how they should be implemented — making sure that it is consistent with departmental IT security policies, since many threats (for example, fire) are common to all areas of the organization. Users, management and IT personnel responsibilities should be clearly defined and described in these documents.

In essence, in a similar way to the Quality Manual, one of its main functions is to confirm management's commitment and make everyone aware of the company policy. It therefore will also be used as an auditor's tool to identify areas of concern or failure.

The likelihood of an organization having a *formal* Security Policy depends on its size, with the larger organizations being more likely to have one. The contents of these policies are generally centred on the following Strategic Areas. (The reader is also referred to Appendix B — Example IT Security Policy and Standard for further information on the contents of such a document. In this appendix an IT Security Policy and Standard Manual for a fictitious company Ibertalia is described):

- **Backup** (both of data and hardware) This is an essential part of IT Security. Its main aim is to take a copy of whatever is held on the IT system and store it in a safe place, sometimes away from the IT system itself. This activity safeguards the quality of the system by taking a 'snap-shot' if an 'assured' system, i.e., a copy of a system that we know with confidence is 'correct' and possesses quality.
- **Mission**. A clear mission statement should be defined setting out:
  - the importance and commitment of the organization to achieving and maintaining a high level of security;
  - the need to achieve full compliance with all relevant legislation including the Data Protection Act;
  - a reporting structure for dealing with breaches of security and an assurance that all deliberate breaches of security will be investigated.
- **Management**. A data protection and audit section must be in place that would be responsible for carrying out security reviews, inspection and audits plus the policing and enforcement of security procedures. Note, some companies would define this as the role of a Security Manager. Other duties could include:
  - Contingency Planning;
  - Monitoring, tuning and reviewing policy;
  - Risk Analysis and Management;
  - Incident Reporting and Investigation;
  - Policy exemptions;
  - Provision of a central point of contact;
  - Advise and Consultancy;
  - Training and awareness.
- **Access Control** (both logical and physical). This is normally achieved within IT systems via the use of passwords; however, these tend to be undermined very easily. Within other areas, i.e., physical access, this is achieved by the use of locked doors, barbed wires, video cameras, numeric keypads, biometric-controls, etc. It is however important to note that no access control mechanism is 100% secure. Even biometric fingerprint readers can be defeated by amputating the fingers of authorized users. An element of quality is to stop any 'alien' interference in a system, since by definition said alien can 'infect' the system in some way. Consequently, access control protects the quality of the system from damage.
- **PC Security** (both physical, i.e., bolted to the desk and logical, i.e. software tools). PCs can be moved, taken home or to other premises with relative ease, e.g., the laptop PC has been designed with this in mind. Due to this and the 'personal' nature of the systems, special consideration should be placed on these IT systems. A clear overall IT Security policy should be in place in terms of PCs, noting that some systems cannot be made secure. By acknowledging this threat, sensitive information should not be placed on these systems.

- **Storage and disposal of sensitive data** (e.g. a shredder). It is often the case that correct storage and disposal of information is neglected within IT environments, mainly due to the ease of accessing this information. However, Document Control is a fundamental necessity, not only in terms of IT security but also for auditing purposes. BS5750 part 1, Clause 4.5 clearly defines a co-ordinated system that ensures that documents are available and that changes are authorized, it states that we should *'... establish and maintain procedures to control all documents and data ...'*.

- **System Development Procedures** (e.g. formal use of Structured Systems Analysis and Design Methodology (SSADM), Computer Aided System Engineering (CASE), PRINCE, etc.). Formalized structural methodologies (covering analysis, design, testing, implementation and maintenance) assist in the development of quality software (refer to 'Measuring Quality within IT Systems' for further information) in turn reduce the level of risk and hence improven security. This means that there must be strict quality control procedures in place when developing and maintaining software (whether in-house or written by an outside software house to specification). Maintenance is one of the key vulnerable areas of software, specially when no control is in place. For this reason, any maintenance (whether it be due to an error or enhancement) must be justified and then effectively managed.

  Many believe that security within software is simply the use of 'access control mechanism', a rather naive view, since this is seldom the main problem with software, as access control security mechanisms (which adhere to a required security kernel[39] within the business) can be designed in or added at a later stage. Security within this environment must also address availability and integrity. Integrity can be addressed by strict control of development, demarcation of operational and test versions, consistent and complete test routines, control of backups (both of software and its associated data) and audit trail maintenance. Availability should be addressed by planning cut-over from different versions of software and reducing the level of failure by the production of quality error-free software.

- **Personnel Controls** (e.g. physical access and badge identification). Personnel controls go beyond controlling physical (e.g., access control methods to buildings, etc.) and logical (e.g., access control mechanisms to IT Systems) security within IT Systems. They mainly encompass some way of stopping the breaking of the rules or gaining some advantage, whether that be via pilfering, i.e., the unlawful possession of workplace property; non-co-operation due to low morale and inappropriate management practices; destructive practices, e.g., getting even via wilfully destroying and damaging the work environment in some way; disruptive practices which are usually done to relieve boredom but can also lead to strikes and loss of business; or simply misuse (e.g., using equipment for your own personal gain). It is inevitable that where man (or woman) is given the opportunity to gain some advantage by breaking the rules, he/she will try his/her hardest to attain it — it's human nature!. It is therefore obvious that no matter how well an IT Security Policy is implemented and managed, its realization depends to a large extent on the people.

  Staff must appreciate and understand the need for security (both against accidental and intentional security breaches), be co-operative with the company (through good morale and awareness of each person's responsibility towards maintaining security and quality standards) and therefore be persuaded (not coerced, as this normally leads to revolt which in turn will lead to some type of breach in security) into abiding by the requirements of IT Security.

- **Legal Obligations**. IT, for many years, was the poor relation of other areas of industry in terms of adequate and binding legislative positive laws[40]. It lacked completeness, direction and IT knowledge, with very few legal wizards understanding the impact of IT on industry and its ramifications across all area of business. This situation has changed for the better, with various Acts[41], Legislation[42], Bills[43], Codes[44] and Conventions[45] being implemented that protect businesses as a whole, with many of these rules addressing the protection of IT directly. In fact legislation is a vital consideration in any analysis of IT Security and Quality. It complements security mechanisms, specifying what legal matters should be attended to and when they should be implemented. This in itself can be a security strategy, providing a powerful technique for managing commercial risks and minimising exposure to liability.

  This does not mean, by any quirk of the imagination, that we have a body of legislation that adequately protects all parties. What it does mean is that, to date (1994), we have a fair amount of guidelines and procedures that, if strictly followed, can lead to prosecution of criminal activities and more importantly in terms of business needs, act as a strong preventative pill, stopping would-be hackers, pilferers, etc.

The reader is reminded that within our Quality ethos, prevention is part of the cure and is the basic necessity of maintaining Quality, which incidentally is also a prime criteria for IT security.

Many would disagree with this statement, as to date there has been few prosecutions. Needless to say, many cases do not even get to the courts for a variety of reasons (e.g., company embarrassment, lack of evidence, etc.). However, I maintain that the law is only as effective as those willing and able to police it (which does not mean just policing by external forces but by everyone). Within business this inevitably means that companies must take full responsibility for what happens within their boundaries and not get 'cold feet' when the going gets tough.

In order for this to happen, employees across the whole structure of an organization need to be aware of the legislation affecting them. Most apply within general boundaries of business areas. For example, the *Health and Safety at Work Act (1974)* requires employers to ensure, as far as reasonably practicable, that their working methods, equipment, premises, and environment are safe and to give such training, information, and supervision as will ensure their employee's health and safety; or the *Consumer Protection Act (1989)* where the producer of a defective product which causes death or personal injury or damage to property is strictly liable for the damage. Some laws, although still general in nature can be viewed as directly affecting IT, for instance, under the *Companies Act (1985)*, it is assumed that registered companies keep auditable records, where this may be achieved via a computer but it must have '... adequate precautions ... against falsification, and adequate means for detecting falsification if it occurs'.

However, even though these are general laws, they obviously affect the working environment and the work carried out within it (whether it be in a secure and quality manner or not). In terms of quality, it is apparent that these types of legislation will safeguard both the workers and the consumers and consequently make the producer adhere to a minimal level of quality. Similarly, in IT security, it again safeguards in terms of integrity and availability of the IT environment but demands a minimal level of safety, good working conditions, etc.

Nevertheless, these laws do not go far enough in protecting industry against computer crimes, specifically software piracy, data theft and computer misuse. To this aim, several laws and guidelines have been established throughout the world that cope with the growing level of computer crime.

Before discussing these laws, what do we actually mean by the term 'computer crime'? A crime, any crime, is defined as an act (or even sometimes a failure to act) that is deemed by statute or by the common law to be a public wrong and is therefore punishable by the state by criminal proceedings. This definition clearly states that criminal behaviour, no matter within what environment is punishable within law. When we refer to 'computer crime', all we are doing is pinpointing a specific area and tool by which a crime is committed. This could mean that a computer system has been used in perpetrating a crime (whether that be fraud, stealing, etc.) or that software/hardware has actually been stolen or damaged, or simply an IT system has been 'violated' via a hack. Each of these refers to a computer crime but for each you can apply a different law.

With this in mind, one can now return to identifying the available legislation:

(i) **Software Copyright;** The applicability of copyright law to software has been a burning issue for the last thirty years. In order to avoid legal misunderstandings and ambiguity, a number of countries have explicitly defined copyright protection for software within their legislation. This includes the USA (1980), where Section 101 within their Act declares computer programs to be literary works protected by copyright. Software protections is addressed in the UK by the 'Copyright, Design and Patents Law (1988)'. This supersedes the Penal Provision of the Copyright (Computer Software) Amendment Act 1985). This civil act make specific provision for the protection of software in Section 3. It basically protects unauthorized software copying without the consent of its creator (or owner). The distinction is however made when software has already been illicitly copied and is re-sold(or loaned) as an original — this is termed as software piracy. By applying piracy laws, the owner can obtain an injunction to end the infringement.

    Additional legislation covering the European Community was established in 1991, with the European Software Directive which went a little further in defining when software was legally copiable, i.e., ' ..the making of a backup copy by a person having a right to use the computer program may not be prevented by contract in so far as it is necessary for that use...'. This builds upon other European efforts like West Germany's Penal provisions of the Copyright Amendment Act (1985), Section 108a and 109 or France's Penal provisions of the Law on authors' rights and on the rights of performers, producers of phonograms and videograms and audio-visual communications enterprises No. 85-660 of 3 July 1985.

(ii) **Data Protection;** This has been an issue for a long time now, with varying attempts at implementing legislature as far back as 1975 with the European Parliament. However, it was not until 1981 that the Council of Europe Convention on Data Protection (see below) put forward its guidelines on the subject.

Council of Europe
Convention of Data Protection
1981

Article 2: *Scope*

The Convention applies to all public and privately owned automated personal data files and may be extended by any State to manual files.

Article 5: *Quality of Data*

Personal data shall be:

- obtained and processed fairly and lawfully;
- stored for specified and legitimate purposes and not used in a way incompatible with those purposes;
- adequate, relevant and not excessive in relation to the purposes for which they are stored;
- accurate and, where necessary, kept up-to-date;
- preserved in a form which permits identification of the Data Subjects for no longer than is required for the purposes for which this data is stored.

Article 6: *Special categories of data*

Personal data revealing racial origin, political opinions, religious or other beliefs, health or sexual life, as well as personal data relating to criminal convictions, may not be processed automatically unless domestic law provides appropriate safeguards.

Article 7: *Data Security*

Appropriate security measures for personal data shall be taken against accidental or unauthorized destruction or accidental loss as well as against unauthorized access, alteration or dissemination.

Article 8: *Additional safeguards for the Data Subject*

Any person has a right to:-

- establish the existence of an automated personal data file, its main purposes, and the name and address of the controller of the file;
- know whether a data file has information relating to that person and obtain the contents of that information at reasonable intervals and without excessive delay or expense;
- obtain the rectification or erasure of such data if these have been processed contrary to a basic set of data protection principles.

Article 9: *Exceptions and restrictions*

Exceptions from the provisions listed above are allowed in order to:-

- protect public safety, State security or monetary interests of the State, or the suppression of criminal offences;
- protect the Data Subject or the right and freedoms of others.

Based on this various convention within various European countries have implemented their own unique law. In the UK, the treatment of personal data is set forth in the Data Protection Act, 1984 (see below).

UK Data Protection Act 1984

1 The information to be contained in personal data shall be obtained, and personal data processed, fairly and lawfully.

2 Personal data shall be held only for one or more specified and lawful purposes.

3 Personal data held for any purpose or purposes shall not be used or disclosed in any manner incompatible with that purpose or purposes.

4 Personal data held for any purposes shall be adequate, relevant and not excessive in relation to that purpose or purposes.

5 Personal data shall be accurate and, where necessary, kept up-to-date.

6 Personal data held for any purpose or purposes shall not be kept for longer than is necessary for that purpose or those purposes.

7 An individual shall be entitled:

(a) at reasonable intervals and without delay or expense — to be informed by any data user whether he holds personal data of which that individual is the subject; and — to access any such data held by a data user; and

(b) where appropriate, to have such data corrected or erased.

8 Appropriate security measures shall be taken against unauthorized access to, or alteration, disclosure or destruction of, personal data and against accidental loss or destruction of personal data.

These principles are defined in general terms and obviously the interpretation placed on them must depend on the circumstance and the purpose for which the data was utilized. In essence the definition states:

UK Data Protection 1984
Definitions

Data: Data means information recorded in a form in which it can be processed automatically in response to instructions given for that purpose.

Personal Data: Personal data means data consisting of information which relates to a living individual who can be identified from that information (or from that and other information in the possession of the Data User), including any expression of opinion of the intentions of the Data user in respect of that individual.

Data Subject: Data Subject means an individual who is the subject of Personal Data.

Data User: Data User means a person who holds data, and a person 'holds' data if:

(i) The data form part of a collection of data processed or intended to be processed by or on behalf of that person; and
(ii) That person (either alone or jointly or in common with other persons) controls the contents and use of the data comprised in the collection; and

(iii) The data is in a form in which it has been or is intended to be processed as mentioned in (i) above or (though not for the time being in that form) in a form into which they have been converted after being so processed and with a view to being further so processed on a subsequent occasion.

This Act must be abided by all users of IT systems that contain or use personal data. This is done by registering the company's usage and abiding by the rules stipulated in the Act. It is however, interesting to note that under English Law, there is no automatic right of privacy.

Information cannot be 'stolen' like money or hardware can. Information disclosed in confidence will not of itself determine its protection at law. This Act simply protects the confidentiality of personal information from error or misuse which is further protected by the UK Computer Misuse Act.

(iii) **Computer Misuse;** This is the major area which has had a substantial increase in types of crimes and how to stop them. Legislation that deals with this dilemma is still in its infancy and the only regulation that directly addresses the misuse of computers in the UK is the *Computer Misuse Act (1990)* and in the US the *Computer Fraud and Abuse Act (1986)*. These acts both go a fair way towards safeguarding against hacking and unauthorized access. The US version however falls short in terms of dealing with viruses and similar threats which is why the UK version has such a deliberately wide interpretation within its sections. Note the US Act is now being supported by the *Computer Virus Eradication Bill* and the *Computer Protection Bill;* both are to date (1993) under ratification procedure within the US Congress.

US Computer Fraud and Abuse Act 1986

1030(a)(1) .. ' knowingly ... obtains information that has been determined by the US government .. to require protection against unauthorized disclosure for reasons of national defence or foreign relations, ... or any restricted data as defined in .. the Atomic Energy Act of 1954';

1030(a)(2) .. ' intentionally ... obtains information contained in a financial record of a financial institution ... or contained in a file of a consumer reporting agency on a consumer, as such terms are defined in the Fair Credit Reporting Act .... ';

1030(a)(3) .. ' ... intentionally accesses a computer without authorization if such computer is exclusively for the use of the Government of the US or, in the case of a computer not exclusively for such use, if such computer is used by or for the Government of the US and such conduct affects such use';

1030(a)(4) .. 'knowingly and with intent to defraud, accesses a Federal interest computer without authorization, or exceeds authorized access, and by means of such conduct furthers the intended fraud and obtains anything of value, unless the object of the fraud and the thing obtained consists only of the use of the computer';

1030(a)(5) .. ' intentionally accesses a Federal interest computer without authorization, and by means of one or more instances of such conduct alters information in the computer, or prevents authorized use of that computer, and thereby causes loss to one or more others of a value aggregating $1,000 or more during any one year period';

1030(a)(6) .. 'knowingly and with intent to defraud traffic (as defined in section 1029) in any passwords or similar information through which a computer may be accessed without authorization, if (a) such trafficking affects interstate or foreign commerce; or (b) such computer is used by or for the Government of the US'.

UK Computer Misuse Act 1990

This Act defines three criminal offences:

(i) Unauthorized access to a computer program or data;

(ii) Unauthorized access to a computer program or data with intent to commit a further crime;

(iii) Unauthorized modification of a computer program or data held on a computer.

Section 1 — defines the simple hacking offence, in terms of 'unauthorized access to computer material', i.e., causing a computer to perform any function with intent to secure access to any program or data held in any computer. This offence can be committed by anyone without the proper access authorization. It also covers even failed attempts at hacking into the systems provided the computer does something in response to an input from the hacker. On conviction an offender faces a possible prison sentence of up to 6 months and/or a fine up to £2000.

This section excludes any accidental access (e.g., dialling a wrong number) since no intent is proved. It also excludes anyone passively eavesdropping or gaining physical access to a computer room, since neither action 'causes the computer to perform a function'.

Section 2 — is concerned with the 'ulterior intent offence', in terms of 'unauthorized access with the intent to commit or facilitate the commission of another offence', e.g., where an unauthorized access is made with the intention of carrying out a serious crime, e.g., fraud. On conviction an offender faces a possible prison sentence of up to 5 years and/or an unlimited fine.

The prime factor within this section is the intent to commit the crime. Consequently, in order to prove the crime it is necessary to prove unauthorized access.

Section 3 — identifies an unauthorized modification as one where the contents of any computer are modified without authority and with the requisite intent and the knowledge. This covers the case of a hacker entering a virus into a system by whatever means. On conviction an offender faces a possible prison sentence of up to 5 years and/or an unlimited fine.

This section excludes any users or programmers who while working within their authority make a mistake since there is no intent. Similarly anyone causing direct physical damage through their actions are not covered by the Act. However, they may be liable under the Criminal Offence Act 1971.

In summary this Act covers three criminal offences. The Act in itself will not prevent or detect crimes that it covers, but should provide some deterrent.

These examples of legislative procedures in the UK and US give a brief guide to the extent to which IT Security can be dependent on the law of the day. However, to date

(1994), more computer related legislation is required to cover systems which are mission critical in order to protect the business as a whole, these will inevitably be developed in years to come.

The use of legislation by a company demonstrates the importance placed on its IT systems, however this must be supported by the use of effective record-keeping, personnel disciplinary measures and a clear policy statement. All this will help to enforce confidentiality in an employee's approach to their work and also provide evidence to a Court when needed. Law therefore must be regarded as intrinsic to security to limit exposure.

These IT Strategic areas within a normal IT Security Policy Statement only cover the basic prerequisites for an effective policy. Its relation with a Quality ethos and other areas of the organization depends on how much importance is given to IT, for instance, how the IT Security Policy relates to Planning — see Figure 3.3.

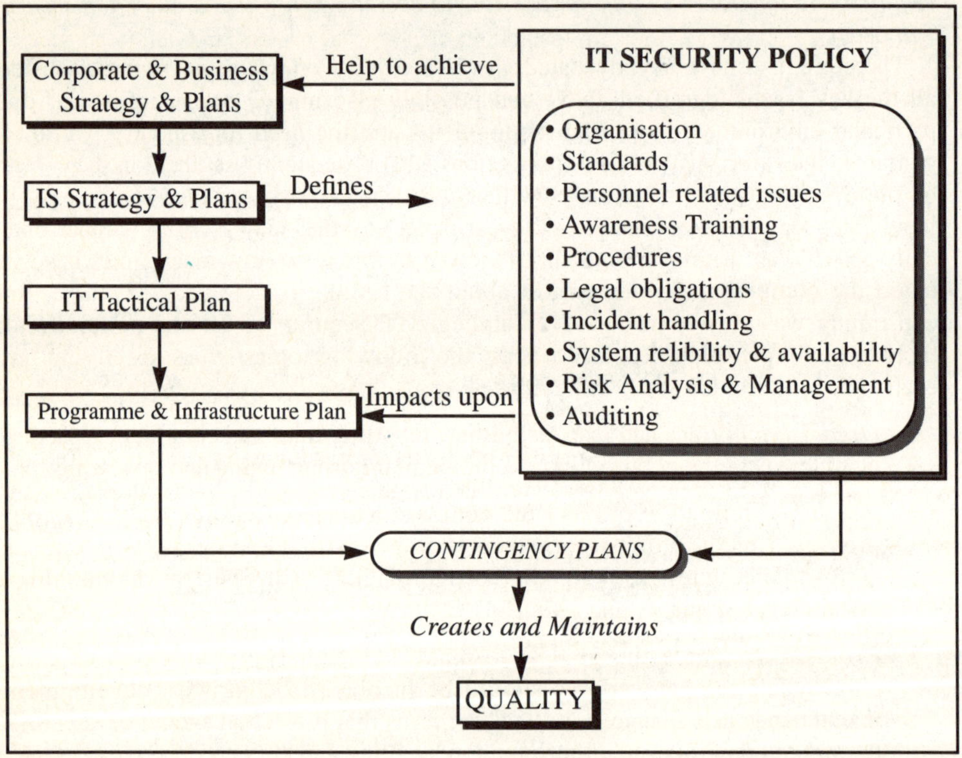

Figure 3.3 Relationship between IT Security Policy and Planning

The higher the level of dependence on IT by the business, the more likely that these areas within the IT Security Policy will become increasingly more important to safeguarding the company and ultimately the success of the business. It is therefore apparent that a full analysis of the situation should be carried out before embarking upon the formulation of any Policy that will affect the running of the business. In summary, the key issues therefore to be considered when determining a Quality IT Security Policy (covering all these seven areas and any other unique area specific to the business) for the whole organization include:

- Degree of company's dependence on IT systems plus how quality is affected by this dependence;

- Level of investment in IT as a whole [present and predicted future];
- Value of the information held [to the organization and to the outside world];
- Threats to security [both internally and from external sources];
- Vulnerabilities of IT systems within the organization. We all have them, e.g., how many PCs do you lose control of and are you prepared to accept this risk?;
- Cost of Security/Insecurity;
- The need for a planned approach.

Without a formal IT Security Policy, individual measures may be introduced in a haphazard and ineffective manner, often producing within the organization a misplaced confidence — *without a security policy, there is no definition of the security required and theoretically it is not possible to decide when/where a breach of security will occur.*

Therefore, as I have already stated, the *IT Security Policy Document* must consider all the key issues identified above and possibly also unique ones within your own particular environment, e.g., EDI requirements and the need for a notary public[46] to guarantee the safety of your EDI transactions and consequently set them in the context of the organization's culture. As with Quality, a possible culture shock may be inevitable. No one likes change, and least of all any that may seem to hamper one's daily activity, as security is sometimes viewed in this way. How many times have we heard the computer operator protest about the levels of access controls as a time consuming waste? Within our seven strategic IT Security areas, this policy should include in simple, plain English at least the following topics/issues specifying how each topic will be addressed:

- *Organization:* roles and responsibilities, reporting lines and committee structures at all levels of the organization, including monitoring, tuning and reviewing;
- *Standards:* how to implement the policy in a standard fashion and in so doing provide a method of conformance testing for the IT systems. For instance, conformance with BS5750, ISO9001 or TickIT will assist in maintaining a certain level of quality and ultimately security;
- *Procedures:* since the goal is to make IT security a major part of every employee's job, procedures should be in place to cope with development, maintenance and change control. This means that protection should be supported throughout the life cycle of information handling and systems design and usage.

  Included within these procedures, the Security Policy should also identify and define procedures for detecting authorized/unauthorized access, audit trails, etc.;
- *Risk Analysis and Management:* a method should be chosen to assess the risks to IT assets against both physical and logical security threats and manage their security in a consistent and acceptable way.

  The risk analysis process applies a series of criteria to the use of IT systems to determine which are at greatest risk. Within this IT Security Policy Document it should also clearly identify what procedures/methodology will be used, e.g., MARION, [47]CRAMM, etc.;
- *System Reliability and Availability:* business needs should define the levels of reliability and availability required for the whole system;

- *Personnel Related Issues:* staff vetting (enquiries about prospective employees should be undertaken in confidence and should be aimed at verifying the past employment/educational history of the individual) and the treatment of security violations, together with policies on recruitment and retention of staff plus the use of external consultants.

  A possible inclusion within this category would be the procedures to undertake to avoid and find 'hackers'. The policy should state the company's response to a hacker intrusion, how intruders would be tracked and apprehended, how legal evidence will be produced, in order to prosecute the hacker and the role of the police/judicial bodies;
- *Awareness and Training:* good training and awareness-raising campaigns should reduce the level of 'accidental' threats to a manageable level. The IT Security Policy Document should state explicitly the level of awareness required to meet the Policy's objective and mission. For further information the reader is referred to the section on this topic later in this chapter;
- *Incident Handling:* all security breaches and incidents should be logged. If the incidents are judged to be criminal, then the policy should clearly state the procedures to be followed on such occurrences — i.e., should the authorities be notified and legal action taken? All incidents should be analysed for trends and 'loop-holes' within organizational procedures — this should indicate where guidance and training is required and possibly where further investment is needed to protect the asset. Once an incident has been identified, what action is likely to be taken against staff or outsiders who commit or attempt to perpetrate a computer related crime? It is important to understand any legislation that could help in the definition of legal responsibility;
- *Contingency Plans:* to fail to ensure the safety of the system in the event of a disaster is, quite simply, a failure of senior management. For this fundamental reason at least, a clear statement of what level of contingency the organization is adopting will suffice and guide the contingency implementors. An example Disaster Recovery Plan is presented in Appendix C.;
- *Auditing:* periodically internal audits should be undertaken in order to check compliance with policy, standards and procedures. The IT Security Policy Document should state who is responsible for initiating and controlling the Audit. Furthermore, it should identify what types of audits will be undertaken (i.e., an abbreviated audit carried out by an in-house team versus a full audit carried out by a professional organization).

The rate at which an IT Security Policy Document and the Policy as a whole should be formally reviewed and updated should be governed by the business objectives and the level of vulnerabilities. However, a simple statement of direction should be made at the outset which defines how and when the policy will be reviewed/updated. Generally most organizations would review their policy every two years, although some do it every year and even every six months.

Furthermore, most security-conscious businesses will review their policy on an ad-hoc basis, identifying areas that need addressing as and when the vulnerability is identified or breached.

Planning and Design for Quality IT Security

In order to effectively implement a comprehensive Quality IT Security Policy, you need to systematically plan or examine the process of securing the business against any breach of CIA within all areas. To do this effectively, you will have to record the series of events and activities, stages and decisions in a form that can be easily understood by everyone. If your main objective is to improve your present conditions, you must first understand the existing environment and how it functions. From this, you can then formulate a quality strategy, where continuous reviews that are based on zero-errors become a strategy of never-ending improvements. The quality plan within a secure IT environment has therefore to focus on providing preventative action (and mechanisms) that will stop any breach of security occurring (irrespective of it being accidental or malicious). The whole approach therefore must be methodical, systematic and designed to function irrespective of changes in management style of personnel.

This IT Security Plan must also define how the following basic security principles are going to be addressed within a Quality environment:

(i) Security Responsibility

(ii) Classification of levels of Information

(iii) IT Security and Quality Awareness

(iv) Disciplinary measures to cope with malicious breaches

(v) Risk analysis methodology and identification of each area of risk

(vi) Contingency Plans

(i) *Security Responsibility*:

Our Quality ethos defines that everyone is responsible for their own actions, especially in terms of a quality output. It is obvious that security must follow the same principle. Security is relevant to everyone within the organization. This means that in principle the responsibility is shared across the whole organization. Furthermore, security is really a management issue, not a technology problem. This means that the right level of management commitment and structure should be in place in order to have an effective organizational security policy.

However, in order to effectively promote this philosophy it is important that momentum is maintained by formally assigning the promotion and management of this security responsibility to one individual. This individual should be a high-level security manager with authority to act for the entire company. He/she would be responsible for directing and co-ordinating implementation of security policy and procedures.

It is management's responsibility to identify the policy required, reduce risks to an acceptable level, comply with applicable laws and regulations, and assure the confidentiality, integrity and availability of information processed via its IT systems. Therefore, it should:

- consider IT Security as a key issue in Information Systems Strategic Planning;

- develop policy and implement a co-ordinated IT Security Programme;
- demonstrate commitment to IT Security by showing continued support for the structures and procedures that have been set up;
- assess the risks to information and IT systems;
- provide the resources to implement appropriate and justified countermeasures without incurring unnecessary costs, impact on services or inconvenience to users of the IT systems.

(ii) *Classification of levels of Information*

Classify all levels of information — which by definition also means *implement a personnel clearance procedure.* Ownership should be assigned to different types of information, which ensures that all information is accounted for and therefore receives the required protection. Furthermore, by applying ownership to information, it is far easier to define who is authorized to do what with certain types of information.

The classification of information must be easily understood and could simply be viewed as GENERAL (i.e. everyone is able to read, copy and alter), CONFIDENTIAL (i.e. can only be viewed by the owner or creator of the information plus who ever he/she allows access to) and RESTRICTED (i.e. can only be viewed by the owner of the information and any authorized officers of the company — even though an individual may have created or assisted in the creation of the information, he/she will still require the proper authority to be able to alter).

Therefore applying this simple classification to information could define the following:

CLEARANCE	DATA EXAMPLES
GENERAL	• Departmental minutes of meeting • Transfer of personnel • Overall productivity figures
CONFIDENTIAL	• Software Design Documents • Personnel Information (Level 1) — Department — Name
RESTRICTED	• Corporate Banking Details • Personnel Information (Level 2) — Wages — Address • Job Role Specifics

These classification levels must apply throughout an organization, not only within the IT systems. For example, there is no point in assigning something as 'restricted' within the IT system if when printed out is 'public property'.

(iii) *IT Security and Quality Awareness*

User Security and Quality Awareness needs to be taken seriously. All employees must comprehend the importance of security and quality and therefore be alert to the need for it. This IT Security and Quality Awareness Programme[48] must come from top management and through the proper training of all employees. Unless staff are persuaded to use the appropriate security precautions, security measures are unlikely to be effective. Training and awareness will convince the users that security is not an obstacle or inconvenience to their daily work. On the contrary, it can help them, for example, in the recovery of lost work.

Furthermore, once users are properly trained you can then formally proceed into creating a clear statement of accountability, where everyone will have some level of responsibility assigned to them.

Therefore, in summary an IT Security and Quality Awareness programme is a continuing (never- ending) series of activities that improves the effectiveness and quality of security. It does this by:

- keeping staff aware of their responsibilities and their role within a secure environment;
- gaining and maintaining staff commitment and acceptance of their responsibilities and actions;
- treating security and quality as part of their everyday activities rather than an optional extra or relying on someone else to do it;
- defining a security awareness plan and a quality awareness plan.

To effectively establish such a programme the following example project plan could be used as a model. The reader is also referred back to Chapter 2 within the Training discussion.

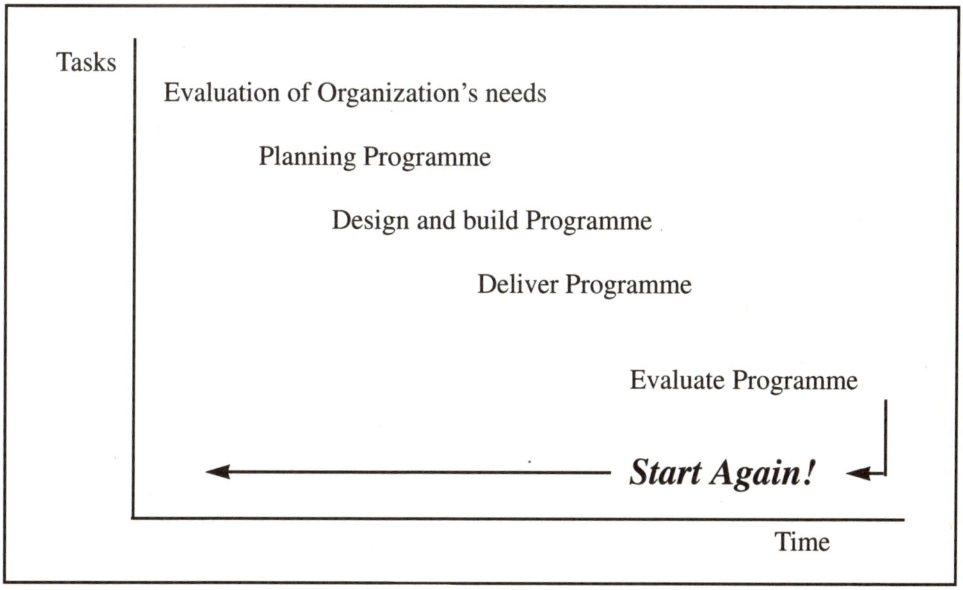

Figure 3.4

Each task feeds and is dependent on each other for their success. Looking at each one a little closer, we have:

- **Evaluation of Organization's needs** — This task will involve the definition of the current state of IT Security Awareness within your organization and the proposed target state. You need to establish the security awareness needs of all staff at all levels. Different staff will require different levels of awareness ranging from senior management, middle managers (technical and non-technical) through to general IT users.
- **Planning the Programme** — This task will involve the definition and specification of how your programme will be implemented. To do this you will need to:
  - establish short and long terms aims and objectives;
  - define a Quality Plan and quality criteria for the programme and all the stages, e.g., a quality criteria for this project as a whole could be the desired level of effectiveness of the programme. The quality criteria could also be based upon specific stages of the project addressing specific products developed within the stage, e.g., the contents of a Security Manual;
  - base your Quality Plan on the overall quality criteria defined within your TQM initiative;
  - establish the resource requirements for the project in terms of people, capital, materials, etc.;
  - create the awareness programme plans. Within this you would describe individual tasks to be performed, the audience your programme is addressing, control and management tools to be used and most importantly the deliverable to be produced;
  - get senior management approval to proceed.
- **Design and Build Programme** — This task will involve the definition of the following points:
  - *audience*. Further define the audience you are addressing, identifying needs, types and motivation. In terms of audience needs you will need to understand the structure and culture of your audience and evaluate how acceptable your message will be to them. In terms of types you need to establish how many of each group you are 'hitting', e.g., managers, etc. Finally, in terms of motivation, you need to understand individual and collective worries. Staff can only be motivated to be aware of security if they understand what security risks are, their relevance to them and how they can affect those risks.
  - *definition of your Security Awareness Curriculum*. This could include:

    IT Security Principles

    - Definitions (threats, vulnerabilities, risks, etc.)
    - Threats in detail
    - Impact
    - Specific topics (viruses, theft, accidents. etc.)

IT Security Requirements

- Corporate Policy and Procedures
- Legislation
- Risks and Responsibilities
- Monitor and Review

- *identification of Available Resources.* This could include the utilization of existing departmental courses, staff induction, Total Quality courses, specific user training, etc. Also the use of corporate and departmental means of communications, e.g., magazines, newsletters, circulars, e-mail, posters, stickers, videos, etc.
- *identification of how your message will be presented.* This is a horses for courses approach, each method and tool may convey a particular issue effectively or fall on deaf ears. The choice is yours. Examples of medium that can be used could include:

Conferences — advantages include

: large scales dissemination

: uses economies of scale

: suite for basic awareness

— disadvantages include

: cannot convey detail information

: can take a long time to set up

Workshops/Seminars — advantages include

: small workshops can be quickly set up

: deals with specific detail issues

: cheap

: brings similar minded people together

: deals with individual worries

— disadvantages include

: need many sessions to cover all staff

Passive Communications:

- Circulars / Internal Memos
- Screen Displays
- Electronic Bulletin Boards

- Newsletters
- Video
- Staff letters
- Wages attachments
- Notice Boards
- Posters
- Stick-on labels
- CBT

- produce your 'products' and materials and make sure they adhere to your Quality Standards/Criteria. To do this it is recommended that specific Quality Reviews be conducted to evaluate each product (see Chapter 6 for further information).

- **Deliver your Programme** — Before you proceed with the delivery of your Programme you need to decide whether you are going for a 'big bang' effect or a collection of little bangs. This will indicate the level of promotion of your programme you need and how to launch your programme, e.g., via your annual Marketing jamboree or via the use of Quality Improvement Team Meetings. Once this is decided you can go ahead and schedule your programme. Scheduling is not only fixing dates but making sure that staff are available to attend seminars, etc. and that the production and delivery of any material coincide with your plan of activities.

- **Evaluate Programme.** This is fundamental to the success of your programme. It should evaluate:

  - audience needs (are they being met?)
  - content (is it up to your quality criteria?)
  - resources (is it adequate to do the job?)
  - should you change anything?

(iv) *Disciplinary measures to cope with malicious breaches*

Formally implement *Disciplinary Measures* and if someone is found to breach security act on them. A statement of discipline which is not used will be taken for granted.

This statement can take the form, for example, of any of the following Policy Declarations:

- Written warning to staff that unauthorized access and disclosure of company-confidential information may lead to dismissal;
- Written warning to staff reference the existing National Legislation, for example, the Computer Misuse Act. Noting how this will be utilized to prosecute the would-be criminal;
- Instruction that all breaches of security will be recorded and possibly used against the culprits;
- Clear guidelines on prosecuting malicious offenders.

Legislation can be used to enforce your measures, for example, the Computer Misuse Act defines three offences — unauthorized entry to an IT system; unauthorized entry to an IT system with the intent to commit an offence and unauthorized entry to an IT system with unauthorized alteration of the contents of the system. However, successful prosecution under this Act will only be possible if proper security measures and identification have been taken by the company.

(v) *Risk analysis methodology and identification of each area of risk*

Risk Analysis, although in many areas a difficult concept to implement, it is imperative. Vulnerabilities and hazards will differ from one organization to another and hence it is advisable to perform your own individual risk analysis to analyse your own unique exposures to loss. A policy of 'it won't happen to me' can be a rather naive and is a careless attitude, which, if the worst did happen, would probably damage not only the system but the whole company.

This analysis should help you implement point (vi) below. Further information is given in 'Risk to Information'.

(vi) *Contingency Plans*

Your *Contingency Plan* (also known as [49]Disaster [50]Recovery Plan) must cover every conceivable loss that you think could affect your business. Loss of power, fire, theft and many others can have disastrous effects on your network systems. The Contingency Plan is a document which gives clear detailed information to all relevant staff to enable them to keep at least the essential system running. Contingency Planning ensures a continued processing capability for systems in the event of an unexpected computer or network failure.

A vital part of a Contingency Plan is the testing and reviewing of it — this should be carried out periodically. An untested plan will probably not work when needed and usually causes an unjustified complacency in the IT installation — *An untested plan is worse than no plan at all.*

A Contingency Plan depends normally on some sort of stand-by facility. In terms of classifying the types of contingency plans, normally this can be done in terms of the following criteria:

- HOT SITE (a duplicate processing facility at a separate site, normally at a safe distance that is available immediately);
- WARM SITE (a fully equipped installation available for use within a few hours);
- COLD SITE (an empty installation [building] available as soon as the required equipment can be delivered);
- SPARE CAPACITY (the use of internal spare resources);
- SHARED FACILITIES (the use of another organization's facility — at a price!).

The reader is referred to Appendix C — Example IT Disaster Recovery Plan, for further information on the contents of such a document. In this appendix an IT Disaster Recovery Plan for a fictitious company Ibertalia is described.

The example in Appendix C covers the IT elements of a business in the unlikely event of a disaster. However the issue of disaster recovery is whether your business will be able to continue in an orderly manner or will complete chaos take over?

To answer this question you need to address the recovery of the Business as a whole. Our discussion has centred around IT disaster recovery alone. Business Recovery is the recovery of all business functions, from IT systems to telephones, faxes, coffee machines, etc. This makes IT disaster recovery a mere subset of Business recovery.

Therefore business recovery should be the goal of all organizations, only by recovering core business activities and facilities can an organization expect to survive.

Risk to Information

The need for security in general is obvious. However, the need for securing IT information depends on whether that information is of any use and value to the would be criminal or not. We therefore have to look at a 'perceived' need that in general is governed by the level of awareness and understanding in IT and the belief that a threat may exist. Most such 'perceived' threats could come from the misled knowledge that only computer-based information is at threat i.e., more at threat than other information holders — when in reality it is normally the insecure disposal of printed information and word of mouth where the real risk lies.

For example, what was at risk in the following scenario?

> At 10.30am on Saturday 24th April 1993, a three tonne bomb exploded in Bishopgate in the City of London. The damage from this explosion affected 2 million square feet of office space across 40 acres.

Obviously in this real disaster, everything from the office premises to the scribbled Post-it note with your password was at risk and consequently destroyed. It would have been pointless to simply recover the IT systems when the rest of the business was still not up and running to deal with customers.

It is therefore important when evaluating risks that we first evaluate the real value of our asset to the company. Such assets could be hardware, software, documentation, building, people or of course information. This risk analysis will enable management to make objective decisions on the risks to its IT systems. It will also identify the required countermeasures where there is apparently the greatest need and consequently maintain the CIA of the whole IT system.

So what is a Risk?

Risk is defined as the chance or likelihood of injury, damage or loss. Therefore when it comes to the risks to information, one needs to view the environment as a whole, identifying the threats and then determining their impact and severity. We must evaluate the probability of anything affecting said information and its associated cost. This could be a 'finger in the air' approach where we only depend on our experience and judgement to evaluate the likely dangers, or we could implement and use a rigorous risk management methodology like CRAMM (CCTA Risk Assessment and Management Method). See Figure 3.5 below for a description of CRAMM.

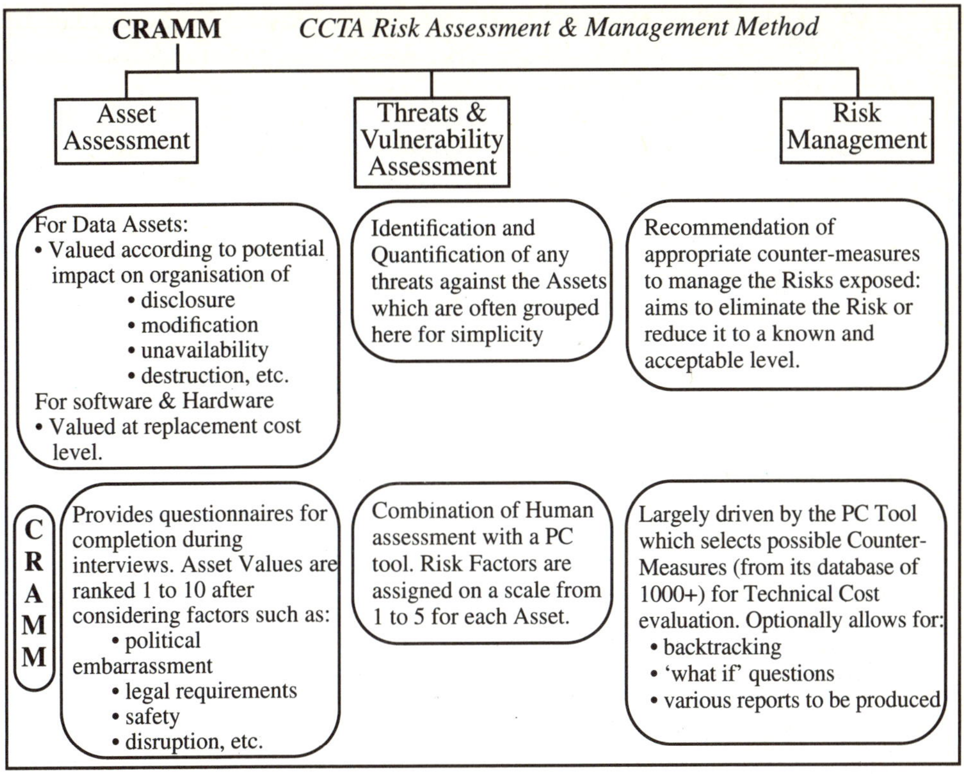

Figure 3.5 CRAMM

The general concept of security risk analysis and management can be illustrated by a simple diagram shown in Figure 3.6 below.

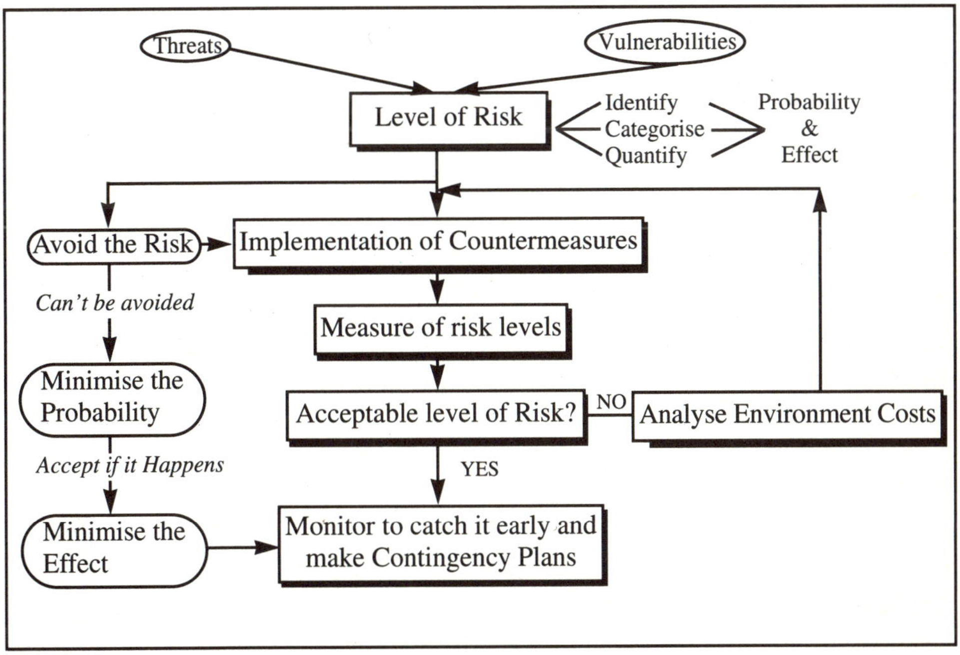

Figure 3.6 Risk Analysis Process

Risk analysis is a method of identifying the risks and applying countermeasures and therefore establishing a cost-effective risk management programme. It is a pragmatic approach, employing a series of value judgements based on the investigators experience within a strict procedural environment and taking into account the length of time that the organization could continue to operate without a particular asset, e.g., the computer system. It seeks to achieve the most cost-effective safeguards against accidental and deliberate [51] attacks against the whole or part of the IT system.

In order to do this it must first identify the threats and evaluate the loss associated with each threat. The types of loss that we should be concerned with include:

Qualitative Losses:

- destruction;
- unavailability;
- disclosure (staff and outsiders);
- modification (accidental and deliberate).

Quantitative Losses:

- financial loss;
- legal repercussions;
- commercial and political embarrassment;
- personal safety;
- disruption.

With this in mind we can then progress in analysing and identifying the probable threats to our assets and how they create a loss.

Threats can be executed against either physical (e.g., fire, theft, failure, power loss, etc.) or logical (e.g., errors, fraud, viruses, disclosure, etc.) assets. Therefore with the knowledge of where a threat may be perpetrated, how vulnerable a situation is and an evaluation of the loss (or impact) if threat is perpetrated, we can calculate our risk as follows:

RISK = (Possibility of threat succeeding) x (Impact if it does succeed)

This subsequently will guide us into implementing the most cost-effective safeguards by putting together the investigator's experience and, for example, the following list of counter-measures. This will probably identify nearly 100% of all the possible vulnerable areas within most IT system.

The types of countermeasures can be classified as follows:

- *Avoidance*: this is where the data or physical resource is not to be removed or used by any entity.
- *Transfer*: this is where the asset or assets at risk is/are transferred outside the security boundary. For instance, a highly sensitive program could be executed on an entirely separate IT environment, hence transferring the risk or alternatively, insurance against failure or loss can be attained.
- *Reduction of Threat*: this is where a barrier of some type is placed between the threat and the asset, for example, an accidental threat to information can be

reduced by better training of staff and hence reducing the level of error. A deliberate threat from an outside source can be eliminated if for instance the use of dial-up services are prohibited.

- *Reduction of Vulnerability*: this makes it more difficult for a vulnerability to be exploited by a threat, for example, within a wide area network, reducing the ability of dialling into the system from an external source by introducing dial-in protection of some type, i.e., dial-back facilities.
- *Reduction of Impact*: this lessens the effect of an impact on an asset where a threat has exploited a vulnerability, for instance, the use of fire extinguishers.
- *Detection*: this detects the evidence of a threat which has exploited a vulnerability, for example, error-logs and traceable journals.
- *Recover*: this assists in the recovery from the impact of a threat exploiting a vulnerability, examples of this include contingency plans and back-up procedures.

The use of these broad countermeasures against an organization's vulnerabilities should be reviewed in light of the overall objectives of risk analysis. It will thereby enable the Risk Analyst to maintain his main objective, which is:

- to outline the key risk areas which could expose the company to loss of business, assets and/or public embarrassment.

There are various software packages (mostly for the Personal Computer) available to help the investigator evaluate their environment. Some examples include CRAMM (a qualitative methodology, developed by the Central Computer and Telecommunications Agency (CCTA)), MARION (both a qualitative and quantitative methodology, developed by a French Insurance Group), RISKPAC (a qualitative methodology, produced by Profile Analysis of America), SIVOR (both a qualitative and quantitative methodology, produced by Siemens), RiskWatch (both a qualitative and quantitative methodology, developed by Expert Systems Software in the USA) and LAVA (both a qualitative and quantitative methodology, developed by Los Alamos National Labs, USA). Note this is *not* an exhaustive list with many more coming onto the market every day.

However, before any of these software packages can be effectively used, the investigator must first understand the business basics and where things can go wrong. The list of countermeasures and threats described above can only guide the risk-investigator.

Certain threats, such as viruses and other glamorous computer crimes, have been highlighted through extensive press coverage, causing too many safeguards to be implemented in some areas. On the other hand, within non-quality oriented organizations, repeated errors by employees may receive only minor consideration. Yet, statistics reveal that errors and omissions generally cause more harm (and obviously cost more) than virus attacks.

This means that safeguard selection must be taken very seriously as it may not be simply applying a mechanical safeguard and increasing quality in all areas. Furthermore, each safeguard must be analysed in terms of the specific security requirements of the environment. It is an important function of risk management and normally works in several ways:

- to reduce the likelihood of the occurrence of threats;
- to reduce the impact of threats occurrences;
- to facilitate recovery from threats occurrences.

Remember that the principle purpose is to reduce the risk to information, and thereby reduce the level of impact of:

- loss of confidentiality (i.e., disclosure to unauthorized parties);
- loss of integrity (i.e., inaccuracy /incompleteness /alteration /destruction of information);
- non-availability (i.e., not accessible when it is required).

These risks are particularly great when the information is compromised without the knowledge of the owner or user. This basic problem is inherent within IT, where evidence of such an occurrence is often difficult (if not impossible) to discover.

In summary, risk analysis normally provides management with the level of 'proof' required to justify the necessary expenditure in security mechanisms and procedures. This investment in security can then be evaluated in terms of the level of loss that the organization could have incurred without it.

Furthermore, if management decide that security is too expensive or they do not have the budget for it, then they have to assume a level of 'self-insurance' accepting the risks and losses if they occur. Hence this supplies management with the necessary information to effectively manage their organization's security requirements.

However, all the safeguards that you can imagine from card keys, encryption, smart cards, etc. will *not* stop all the threats from occurring. In the majority of cases, threats are allowed to happen, simply because of lack of awareness and training. Added to this, many organizations do not promote any form of Quality ethos and hence inevitably cannot expect their people to be responsible for their actions.

Quality promotes the concept of zero-error (see Chapter 2 *et al*). However, the majority of security breaches occur due to this philosophy being broken at every level. Bad workmanship in the production of hardware and software causes an enormous amount of failures; inadequate training promotes an increase in errors and in some cases can promote complacency in the existing knowledge (e.g., thinking that you know enough to get by); inadequate security plans and strategy sometimes neglect the basic of good common sense security measures.

In essence, what is required is a quality management risk program that ensures that reasonable steps are taken that prevent threats to interfere with the accomplishment of the company's mission. This requires that a company:

- has top management commitment (via a policy statement);
- identifies problem areas;
- introduces checking procedures;
- introduces error detection measures;
- cultivates a 'Quality' culture;
- aims for 'Zero Defects'.

By doing this it will develop a strategy that:

- supports the long term business objectives;
- ensures organizational survival following a loss situation;

- provides assurance in a cost-effective way;
- provides the optimum mix of control, retention and transfer of risks.

Quality Contingency Planning

IT Contingency Planning has already been briefly discussed in the previous three sections. In essence, it is a method of designing and developing the facilities to ensure that in the event of a failure of any or all the constituent parts of an IT environment, the business and financial risks to the organization are kept to a minimum and the business keeps going after the disaster. It does this by defining the key systems, determining the most appropriate method of stand-by and consequently ensuring that all the required back-up and any other steps are taken.

The effects on the business following a major failure can be devastating with estimates calculated by various studies concluding that after ten days approximately of failure, five days work is lost, increasing exponentially with time.

This unavailability of the IT environment and of the business as a whole can obviously have a dramatic effect on the business, with the predicted figures in some circles of 90% of companies that lose their IT systems go out of business within two years.

It is therefore obvious that contingency plans that protect the business are of paramount importance. Quality Contingency Plans bring together IT Contingency Planning and Business Recovery Planning. This covers all aspects of the business from the loss of the building to the loss of stationary. One without the other would be useless. So how do we develop a Quality Contingency Plan?

Quality Contingency Plans may seem at first glance to be a misnomer, since it is mixing Quality (a zero error ethos) with the acceptance that some failures (even disasters) may occur. However, the basic premise of Quality is prevention before problems occur and if all else fails the fixing of those problems after the event. Therefore, Quality and Contingency Planning are inextricably intertwined to form a completely secure environment.

In essence, the objective of Quality Contingency Planning is to provide a disciplined response to emergencies supplying management with the information required to determine the level of investment sufficient to reduce the impact of an IT disaster to an acceptable loss. The first step in defining any Quality Contingency Plan is to conduct a Business Impact Analysis. This is different from Risk Analysis (see previous section for further information on Risk Analysis) which assesses the probability of the occurrence of threats. Business Impact Analysis assesses only the effect if any threat has already occurred and resulted in the non-availability of the IT system. The procedure to follow therefore is:

(a) Gain commitment from all involved, moving down from Senior Management making sure that your business actually needs a Quality Contingency Plan;

(b) Develop a structured approach towards identifying the possible threats;

(c) Define existing systems (it is imperative that a complete picture is ascertained with respect to your business systems and exactly whether each system is required for the business);

(d) Identify critical areas avoiding politics and the protection of un-profitable groups;

(e) Define manual procedures (noting how the manual system integrates, and in some cases is dependent on, the IT systems);

(f) Calculate disaster effects, both within quantifiable financial criteria like failure/replacement cost and un-quantifiable aspects that may be less easy to evaluate, like cost of future trade due to dissatisfied customers going elsewhere. Note, this evaluation should also define, to the company, what exactly constitutes a disaster, for instance, loss of data host, communications facility, etc.;

(g) Examine cyclical issues, e.g., impacts on the business of holidays, temporary works, etc.

(h) Gain audit input (for further information refer to Chapter 6.);

(i) Walkthrough results and publish.

Once the Business Impact Analysis has been conducted you are subsequently armed with most of the information required to evaluate what the actual costs to the business could be after a disaster. This will assist you in choosing the type of 'stand-by' to use. CCTA's guideline on the choice of standby include the following:

(i) Do nothing. This is a valid option if it is based on a very low assessment of the impact to the business of losing the IT system. However, often doing nothing is the result of no decision at all being taken. In such a situation, this cannot be classed as a valid option;

(ii) Clerical backup. As identified within your Business Impact Analysis, manual procedures can also be important to your business but if they are dependent on the IT systems then, obviously, any IT failure will affect the manual system. Consequently any clerical backup must be independent of the IT systems your are trying to safeguard against a contingency;

(iii) Fortress approach. A rather expensive approach to safeguarding your environment and is seldom 100% secure. Murphy's Law shows its head within this environment when least expected;

(iv) Cold Start — fixed centre. This contingency is defined as an 'empty' dedicated, fixed cold stand-by. It is normally set up by organizations that do not need rapid recovery after a disaster and therefore can wait for the necessary equipment to be delivered by a supplier;

(v) Cold Start — portable centre. This contingency is defined as a dedicated, portable cold stand-by. This set-up will come with the required skeletal equipment to set up a computer room, e.g., communications lines, air-conditioning, etc. An example of this type of contingency could be a Porta-Cabin that can be moved anywhere;

(vi) Cold Start — Internal. This contingency is defined as a dedicated, fixed cold stand-by. This set-up encompasses a cold room within the building (or at close proximity) with the necessary basic skeletal equipment to set up a computer room. There is still a need to wait for the system from the supplier;

(vii) Hot Start — Fixed Centre. This contingency is defined as a dedicated, fixed warm stand-by. Being the most expensive solution, it establishes a spare, fully equipped room;

(viii) Hot Start — Internal. This contingency is defined as a dedicated, fixed, warm stand-by. By definition is the same as (vii);

(ix) Hot Start — Mobile. This contingency is defined as a dedicated, portable, warm stand-by. This is normally achieved by the supply of a complete computer room in the afflicted area within an agreed time span by a supplier.

In reality the choice of any of the above contingencies comes down to answering three basic contingency questions:

Is it going to be:

(a) Dedicated or shared?

(b) Fixed or portable?

(c) Warm or cold site?

Once you have answered these questions the application of the contingency depends on how soon it is necessary to restore the key IT systems and how much the organization is willing or can afford to spend. In essence what is required is to:

(a) Go to where the emergency has occurred obtaining the facts. Note, access to a stricken area may be denied and therefore you will need to be prepared for any eventuality.

(b) Contact key personnel required immediately, informing them of where and when to meet. This meeting should set the ground rules to follow and an initial evaluation regarding the degree of damage and impact to the business undertaken.

However, in order to be able to do this effectively and without any undue loss of time, and therefore business, a Quality Contingency Plan must be in place. Such a plan could be to:

(i) Produce a Business Impact Analysis;

(ii) Gain Senior Management Commitment;

(iii) Gain authorization to proceed with Contingency Plan. Note this is an essential step, since drawing up a workable plan involves considerable expense;

(iv) Select appropriate options, specific to the requirements of your organization;

(v) Gain authorization to proceed with the application of specific measures;

(vi) Define responsibilities. This should also include a decision on who should have copies of the Contingency Plan when it is completed. Note this is a company confidential document and may contain information on where a company is highly vulnerable by its inclusions, omissions, etc. It, however, needs to be as complete as possible. Its contents should include detailed information of how to overcome a disaster, including information on individuals responsible for the execution of the Quality Contingency Plans (including names, addresses, telephone numbers, etc.);

(vii) Prepare detailed plan(s). Any plan, once you have chosen your stand-by, should not take more than six months to complete. It should state clearly at what stage it should be invoked, for instance, if the IT system is down for more than a specific period of time, where the impact of the threat is unacceptable, then invoke the Quality Contingency Plan. This depends on the organization and can range from a matter of hours for mission critical systems to several days for administrative systems.

(viii) Produce a Quality Contingency Plan Document. This document must be comprehensive, detailed and flexible, as its main function is to tell the reader clearly and without any ambiguity exactly what he or she must do after a disaster. Remember that this document is to be read after a disaster, when the likelihood of fear and confusion is going to be extremely high and therefore it must assist as much as possible in overcoming any unforeseen problems. An example of its contents could be:

- Introduction
- Team Responsibilities
- Team Structure
- Contingency Definitions
- Preliminaries (the back-ups and other procedures that must be carried out before any contingency arises)
- Plan Initiation (a full description of the first steps to be taken to get the plan into operation)
- Team Activities (a very detailed description so that each team member knows exactly what to do)
- User Activities (this informs the user how they are expected to manage during the contingency).
- Appendices (this must include lists of names, addresses and telephone numbers of the persons to be contacted, both inside and outside the organization, plus it must also include maps and other information as to how to reach back-ups and stand-by facilities and any other unfamiliar locations. Other information within this section should be inventories of equipment, folders of plan, update procedures, audit procedures, etc.)

(ix) Test and maintain the Quality Contingency Plan. Note, some disasters are less than total and subsequently the Quality Contingency Plan must be designed so that parts of it can be brought into operation without the whole. An example of this process can be seen in the Figure 3.7 below. You will notice that this simple flow chart shows a number of steps that needs to be executed in order for the Quality Contingency Plan to be effectively invoked. Testing is of paramount importance as an untested Quality Contingency Plan could appear capable of implementation, but, until it is put to the test, no one knows for sure. Obviously it will be tested if a contingency arises, but, at that stage, any errors that are detected will be impossible to correct. An untested Quality Contingency Plan is worse than no plan at all, since its existence gives a false sense of security.

(x) Revise Quality Contingency Plans after loss, disaster or change in the organization's needs. It is essential that your Quality Contingency Plan does not

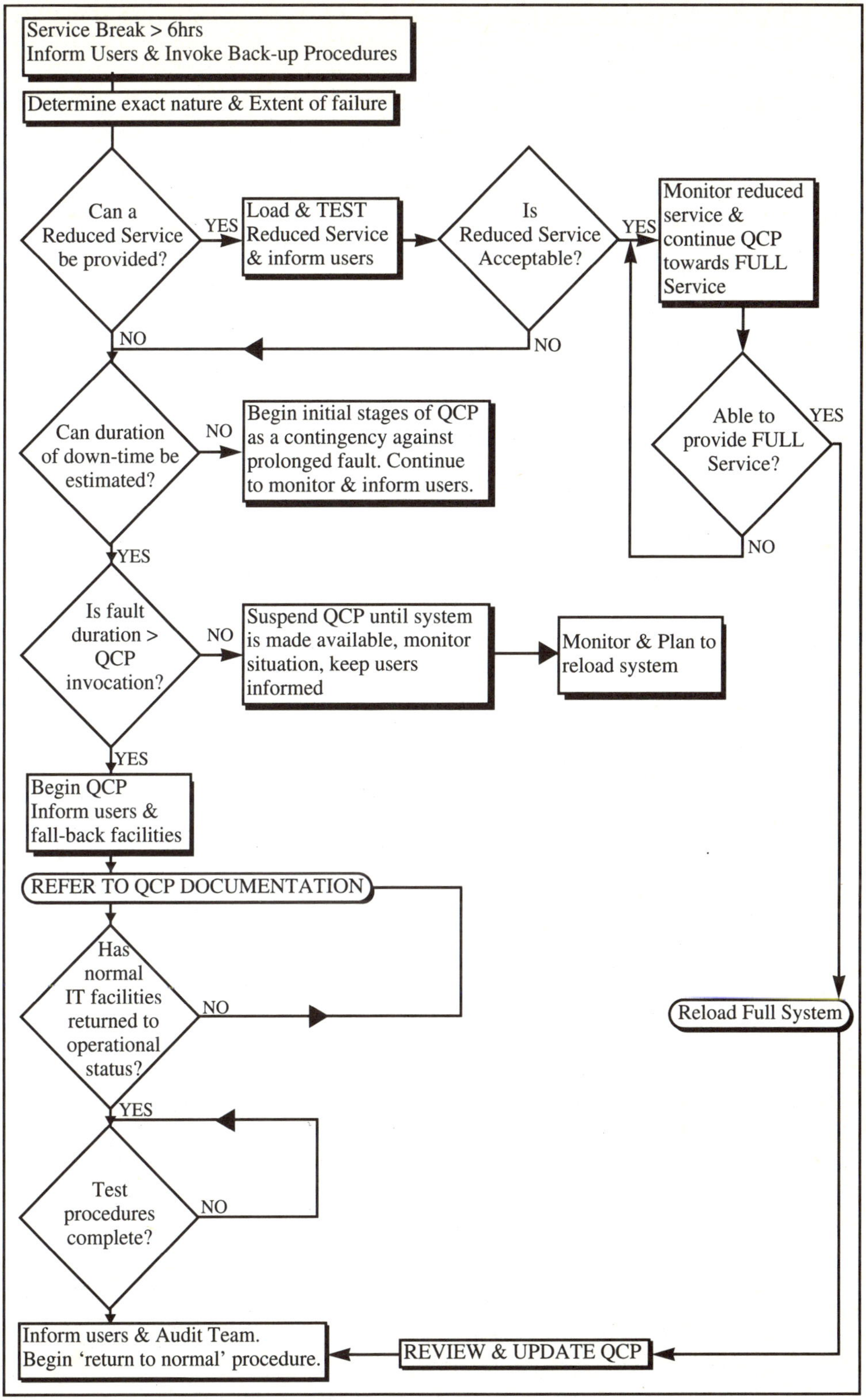

Figure 3.7 Contingency Planning (Testing and Decision Flow Chart)

stagnate and only address past situations. Like the business, any procedure needs to evolve and facilitate change. It is obvious, therefore, that if your Quality Contingency Plan does not evolve, future threats that either have not been thought of or as a cause in the change in the business will not have any contingency.

For instance, several years ago the use of international mailbox would probably have been too futuristic. Today reliance on this tool is fast becoming a vital element in business. What happens when this service crashes, like in January 15th 1990, when AT&T's long-distance telephone switching system came to an abrupt stop? Can your business survive without this service?

Your Quality Contingency Plan must be as flexible and complete as you can possibly make it and when the unforeseen occurs, your Quality Contingency Plan must learn from its omission and evolve.

Therefore in summary a Quality Contingency Plan must address the following:

- Think of the business, not just IT recovery;
- The plan is only a list of good ideas unless tested;
- Recovery plans should include crisis management;
- Recovery plans should address vital records and data must be stored off-site;
- Denial of service could be the end of your business.

Security and Systems Audits

'Auditors seldom find a loss — what they do is mainly (and with a lot of luck) confirm it after it happens ...'. This idea is at the forefront of many professionals who have relied upon audits to assist them in identifying acts of fraud, embezzlement and thievery where IT is used as the principal tool for the crime. The basic problem affecting the auditor's detection process within an IT environment is that in dealing with digital information the auditor is at least once removed from the contents of the original record. This problem is obviously going to impair the auditor's findings and make his evaluation at best suspect to mis-interpretations and at worst mislead a company into believing that they are functioning to a required criteria when they are actually doing the total opposite.

Therefore what exactly is auditing and how does the auditor do his job?

In general, auditing can be defined as the systematic process of verifying specific records (a task performed by an independent qualified individual) to ensure the accuracy of the information within those records and that the records truly represent the past and present state of affairs.

In so doing, it also includes the expression by the auditor of some degree of knowledgeable opinion on the matter in question. For instance, if the audit is being carried out on a specific activity, this opinion can reflect the quality of performance or final product, etc.

For too many people the term 'audit' conjures up a certain degree of bureaucratic establishment and consequently a fear that being audited would mean simply the identification of 'errors' (whether they be accidental or not) that will lead to an individual at best losing his job and at worst prosecution. This idea has been promoted through established accountancy firms who perform specific financial audits for their clients. These audits have formed the basis for a company's future existence, identifying the major strengths and weaknesses of a company and its financial standing. However, there is evidence to suggest that even reputable auditing firms make mistakes, declaring that a company accounts reflect a company's true financial position, when in reality hidden errors and frauds have not been identified. The reasons for these types of mistakes are normally attributed to the audit not been undertaken according to general accepted accounting procedures or that critical areas of audits are undertaken by inadequately trained people.

Whether these reasons are true or not or if there are other reasons, the fact is that a company's reputation and financial credibility relies solely on the auditing firm doing its job properly and to a certain extent being 'lucky' in their endeavour to do their job. It is a well known fact that many of the identification of security breaches are found due to some un-foreseen circumstance or Act of God, likewise with the auditing practice. Auditing, therefore, although of paramount importance, must not be the only tool used for identifying problems and consequently rectifying them.

The trust that is placed on financial audits has obvious consequences for the business. Similarly, computer systems audits should be treated in the same way. The need of IT systems for audits is just as critical as anywhere else, and in some respects even greater.

The function of a computer auditor is similar to that of the financial auditor but concentrated on IT systems. The computer auditor is concerned with ensuring that IT systems contain sufficient checks (e.g., audit trails by which auditors can trace transactions backwards and forwards throughout the system) to meet the requirements of the current environment and that they are checked periodically and any non-conformances investigated.

However, it is not the intention of this section within this publication to expound on IT auditing on which much has been written already. Chapter 6 elaborates on the techniques required within a Quality and Security environment and discusses the main issues that need to be understood when auditing. The reader is therefore referred to this chapter for further information on auditing.

Managing Security within a Quality Environment

IT Security, like TQM, is concerned with the protection and continued success of a business. It is therefore imperative that IT Security is strategically managed within strict management guidelines and maintained within the 'pure' Quality ethos. In essence, IT Security, like TQM, is a management problem. Within the management of IT Security, several key security areas must be controlled, namely:

- Risk Management;
- Safeguards Management;
- Vulnerability Management;
- Security Awareness Management;
- Contingency Planning;
- Security Audits Management.

Each of these areas must be managed with a strict goal of safeguarding the business and therefore must include an analysis of the 'Business Impact' with or without IT Security. However, IT Security, like TQM, is dependent on the available resource that management can effectively apply to it. Too little and the level of quality and security is so small that you are in danger of creating a catastrophe. Too much and you are probably pumping capital into a black hole without the required return on investment. Therefore, unless an organization has unlimited cash to finance an exceptionally complete security system, the first step has to be to understand and manage the whole environment. Basically this means understanding the risks, threats and possible actions that must be taken in order to minimize the impact on the organization. In order to understand security and how it is going to affect your organization, you will obviously need to review (either in a brief manner or through the use of elaborate mathematical calculations using formal risk analysis methodologies) the obvious exposures and countermeasures.

All this requires a realistic appraisal of exactly how much it is going to cost the organization to be secure. However, management must be made aware that this costing exercise is not the typical type where you invest and expect a quantifiable return within quantifiable limits. Most investment in IT Security is based on prevention, but without an illness to cost, you cannot fully appreciate exactly how much you have 'saved' the company and therefore the real cost of IT Security. This type of awareness is important in order for management to appreciate the validity of investing in IT Security. An approach of estimating how much a threat will cost a company if it were perpetrated is to collect the results of a large surveyed population (e.g., insurance companies use this method to predict if and when a house may be burgled) and extrapolating it towards predicting the occurrence of a threat.

These statistics in conjunction with an evaluation of your assets (or loss of them) can form the basis of justifying the investment.

You must therefore understand your company's needs and requirements before calculating the cost to the company of IT Security. For instance, some basic questions that you should answer before implementing any safeguards are:

(a) What do you need to protect?

(b) Why do you need to protect it?

(c) How do you protect it?

(d) When do you protect it?

(e) Where do you protect it?

This list of questions is not meant to be an exhaustive list covering every issue a manager needs to investigate and understand. It is meant as a guide to the reader into the types of questions that he/she need to be aware of and will hopefully result in the reader analysing his/her business IT requirements in the light of them.

Let's take each question in turn and evaluate what it could mean to an organization.

(a) *What do you need to protect?*

As already discussed earlier, information security is concerned with the protection of the business from breaches of information availability, integrity and confidentiality.

Here we need to decide what needs protecting, for example, a typical communications network contains many assets, the loss of any of which may incur an unacceptable cost to the company. Each asset will probably need a specific way of protecting it, for example, basic physical security will ensure that hardware is not stolen or damaged. This can be achieved by making a secure perimeter around your IT environment.

(b) *Why do you need to protect it?*

There are many threats in the form of business risks and attacks (for example, information services and equipment can be destroyed, stolen, disclosed, delayed, corrupted, defrauded, etc.). Many of these threats can arise from accidents or Acts of God (although some people believe Acts of God to be malicious) or of course deliberate attacks. As already stated earlier, the level of loss due to any of these attacks or breaches may mean the survival of the business.

For example, within a networking environment (which incidentally has now become the backbone of IT systems and consequently has also become of great value to the company as a whole) there are various types of network threats, e.g., Denial of Service, Repudiation[52], Masquerading[53], Modification, Replay and Eavesdropping. All these threats may cause a loss of business.

(c) *How do you protect it?*

We need to implement protective measures that will result in making a loss bearable and therefore address the three basic security principles of CIA. In terms of availability, we need to provide resilience, recovery and contingency services. While with integrity and confidentiality, this can be achieved by providing specific security services such as authentication, access control, data integrity, data confidentiality and non-repudiation.

Examples of these types of IT Security mechanisms could be:

- Cryptography;
- Identification and authentication tools;
- Multi-level security domains.

(d) *When do you protect it?*

Information is under threat twenty-four hours a day, every day of the week. It can occur everywhere — on transit, in storage or within a network. Within a day-to-day activity cycle of any company there are obviously certain times when the business activity would be highly vulnerable to an attack. For example, at 5.30pm every day a company backs up all its data, which takes for the sake of argument, 2 hours to complete. If while this is happening, a vital piece of equipment fails, what contingency do you require? Can you live with the failure which could mean that you have lost your back-up information?

Identifying when you require the service (e.g., a network) also identifies the areas that needs protecting, for example, remote access to the system should only be allowed at certain times and only if the user uses a dial-back intelligent modem.

(e) *Where do you protect it?*

Answering all the previous questions should help you identify what and where your network (or the complete system) needs to be protected. For example, network access points (dial-up, gateways, bridges, etc.); network nodes/switches (access, transit, concentration, etc.); network routes (resilience, tables, planning, sizing, etc.); network management systems (logical access, diagnostic tools); network back-up (routing, dial-back-up, network software and distribution).

Once you have evaluated the cost of safeguarding the organization you must then select the right mechanisms for your company. Each mechanism would either prevent the possibility of a threat, control the threat (e.g., limit the loss), transfer the loss or of course retain the threat.

The history of liberty has largely been the history of the observance of procedural safeguards.
.. Felix Frankfurther

4

Quality Standards and their Association with IT

Quality standards merely assist in ensuring that quality specifications meet certain accepted criteria of technical or service performance, safety, etc. These standards are normally established by a National body, for instance:

- American National Standards Institute;
- US Military;
- Deutsche Institüt Normennaussdiuss;
- British Standard Institute.

We have already discussed how some of these standards (set by a national organization) have in the last three to four decades evolved, with the culmination of a generic ISO/BSI skeletal description that we will discuss in this section. In terms of IT Security, to be effective it demands co-ordinated actions within the different areas of protection — administration, physical, logical and data. In terms of the physical, logical and data protection areas, measures can be specifically defined and their implementation checked. However, administrative measures can never be completely specified.

IT Security therefore needs both technical standards and Quality standards. With Quality it would mean conformance to a value judgement.

When reading this section it is important to note that standardization does not guarantee that the best IT design and production methods are selected and in some instances, it may be argued that the whole process of standardization can slow down the rate and direction of IT development and consequently affect what is produced.

It is therefore important to strike a business balance between the requirements for IT innovation and standardization. I am not advocating that standards should not be used (let's not return to the bad old days of non-standard IT hardware that would not work together) as it is always desirable for IT designers to adhere where possible to proven procedures and methods in the interest of reliability, maintainability and open systems philosophy. However, it is also very important not to hinder designers in the use of new-untested processes and techniques as this will inevitably lead to better products in the long-run.

The requirement for striking a business balance depends greatly upon the common sense of the producers of IT products and services and therefore will inevitably affect the subsequent security and reliance of the systems as a whole. As a rule, these quality standards need, at a minimum, to be understood by the industry, where every element of IT (whether that be the production of a piece of hardware or the supply of a service) adheres to the majority of the areas described within these standards.

By doing this it will initially solve one of the main security concerns that many users have, e.g., when safeguarding against a security breach, can you at least rely on the product or will it 'crash' repeatedly? To answer this question you need some method that when adhered to satisfies user requirements. This method should incorporate all the activities associated with quality and consequently should be implemented in an organization to ensure that all the specified user and performance requirements are fully met. All standards, whether British Standard, ISO or other have this pre-requisite in common, i.e., fit for purpose.

BS5750/ISO9000/EN29000

These standards have, since their creation, caused huge controversy. The problem may stem from whether the adherence to them justifies the expense and whether they are effective.

It is quickly becoming apparent that to continue in business, let alone succeed, adhering to an established standard is vital. However, to date, many firms find that the process of achieving it is far from simple and/or cheap.

In the UK more than 20,000 organizations (by November 1993), from dental surgeries to large multinationals, have acquired the coveted 'kite-mark' BS5750/ISO9000 and the number is continually rising. The reason why so many of these firms are using BS5750 is not always quality oriented and in many cases stems from simply surviving — as one director of a small recruitment agency put it '... we are continually being asked by our clients whether we are BS5750 accredited or not and there will come a day when they will insist on us being registered. We need the BSI kite mark to do business ... '. The objective of this firm is simple — to have a Quality Paper System, but not necessarily a Quality Product. Although this is a perfectly legitimate business reason for going for BS5750, a substantial amount is lost on the way, with many key Quality issues missed out and consequently few Quality benefits being attained. The reason for this is obvious — if internally personnel do not believe that they have a quality product/service in the first place how on earth are they going to actually produce a quality product/service? The basic principle of quality is omitted: culture change and training.

In fact most of these types of organizations 'fudged' their quality initiative by not implementing the right Quality Ethos and therefore both misleading their business partners and themselves into believing that they how have a quality product/service. The fact of the matter is that their Quality System, while it is being created, addresses all the pre-requisites of adhering to all the sections within the standard but once they attain the 'kite-mark' everything returns to 'normal'. Attaining BS5750 and/or its sister standards should not only mean this but it should set out how to establish, document and *maintain* an effective Quality System which continually demonstrates to your customers that you are truly committed to quality and ultimately are able to supply their quality needs, now and in the future.

We therefore come to the standards themselves. In general ISO9000/EN29000/BS5750 are all identical in scope and content. In fact the ISO9000 standards have been directly adopted without change, as national standards in at least 51 countries (1993), including all of the European Community, EFTA, Japan and USA. Consequently this section will deal in the main with BS5750 and where appropriate discuss ISO and any variation that may exist. In terms of the standard we have ISO9001, ISO9002, ISO9003 and ISO9004 (with BS5750 equivalent in parts 0 through to 4). Table 1 below describes briefly each standard and cross-references them between ISO and the British Standard. Table 2 describes some useful standards that are still in draft form (1993) but will become of paramount importance in the future. Figure 4.1 shows the flow of these standards and Figure 4.2 their inter-dependencies.

ISO	British	Description Standard	Commentary
8402 (1986)	4778 Part 1 (1987)	Quality Vocabulary	This standard defines the basic terms and definitions that are required when formulating a Quality Manual. It defines quality as '.. the totality of features and characteristics of a product or service that bear on its ability to satisfy stated or implied needs ...' Other terms defined include policy, management, assurance, control, system and audit.
9000 (1987)	5750 Part 0 Section 0.1 (1987)	Quality Management & Quality Assurance Standards-Guidelines for selection and use.	Will assist in drawing up your internal Quality Management System and in selecting the specific model from 9001, 9002, 9003 and 9004 part 2. Within it, it defines a quality policy as '... the overall Quality intention and direction of an organization as regards quality, as formally expressed by senior management.' Furthermore, it goes on to define quality management as ' .. that aspect of the overall management function that determines and implements the Quality Policy.'.
9001 (1987)	5750 Part 1 (1987)	Quality Systems – Model for Quality Assurance in Design/ Development, Production, Installation and Servicing.	This is for those organizations that need to assure their customers that conformity to specified requirements is met 'throughout' the whole cycle from design to service. This applies particularly where there is a contract specifically requiring design and where product requirements are stated in performance terms (e.g., speed, capacity or integrity).

Table 1. Cross-referenced Quality Standards

9002 (1987)	5750 Part 2 (1987)	Quality Systems — Model for Quality Assurance in Production & Installation	If one has an established design or specification, this one is more appropriate. In this standard all that needs to be demonstrated is an organization's capabilities in production and installation. It is also less stringent than 9001/5750 Part 1.
9003 (1987)	5750 Part 3 (1987)	Quality Systems — Model for Quality Assurance in Final Inspection and Test	This applies when we can only demonstrate capabilities for inspection and test, where the product is supplied from a manufacturer for those requirements.
9004 (1987)	5750 Part 0 Section 0.2 (1987)	Quality Management & Quality Systems Elements — Guidelines	This is an extension to 9001 and BS5750 Part 0 and its main purpose is to highlight 'services' quality criteria

Table 1. Cross-referenced Quality Standards (Cont,d)

ISO	**Description**
9000-1 (1996)	Draft revision of 9000
9000-2 (1992)	Draft standard for Quality Management and Quality Assurance standard Part 2 — Generic Guidelines for the Applications of ISO9001, 9002 & 9003.
9000-3 (1991)	Draft standard for Quality Management and Quality Assurance Part 3 — Guidelines for the Application of ISO9001 to the Development,Supply & Maintenance of SW
9000-4 (1992)	Draft Standard for Quality Management and Quality Assurance Part 4 — Application for Dependability Management.
10011-1 (1990)	Guideline for Auditing Quality Systems Part 1 : Auditing
10011-2 (1991)	Guideline for Auditing Quality Systems Part 2 : Qualification Criteria for Quality Systems Auditors.
10011-3 (1991)	Guideline for Auditing Quality Systems Part 3 : Management of Audit Programme.
10012-1 (1992)	Quality Assurance Requirements for Measuring Equipment Part 1 : Metrological Confirmation Systems for Measuring Equipment.
10012-2 (draft)	Quality Assurance Requirement for Measuring Equipment Part 2 : Measurement Process Control.
10013 (1992)	Draft Guideline for Development of Quality Manuals.

Table 2.

Standards to watch for.

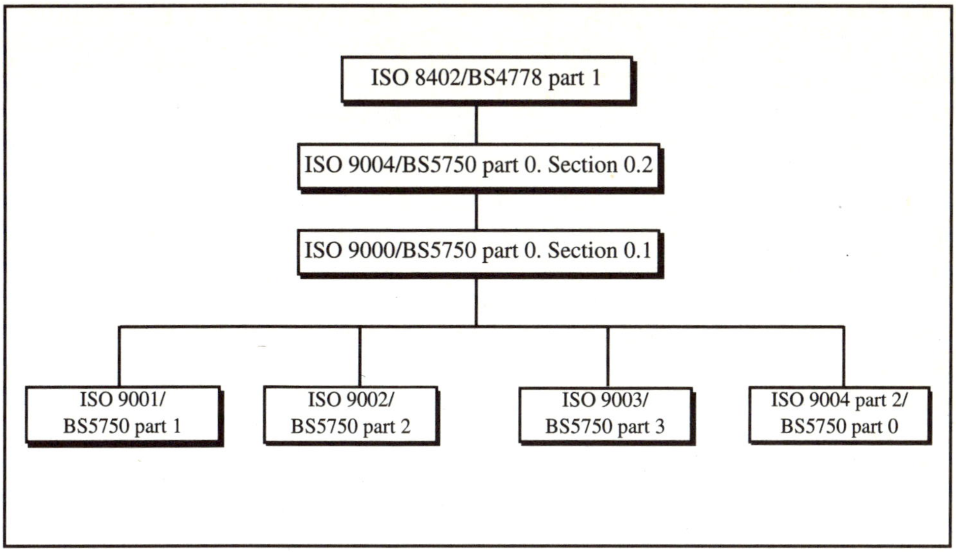

Figure 4.1 Quality Standards Flow

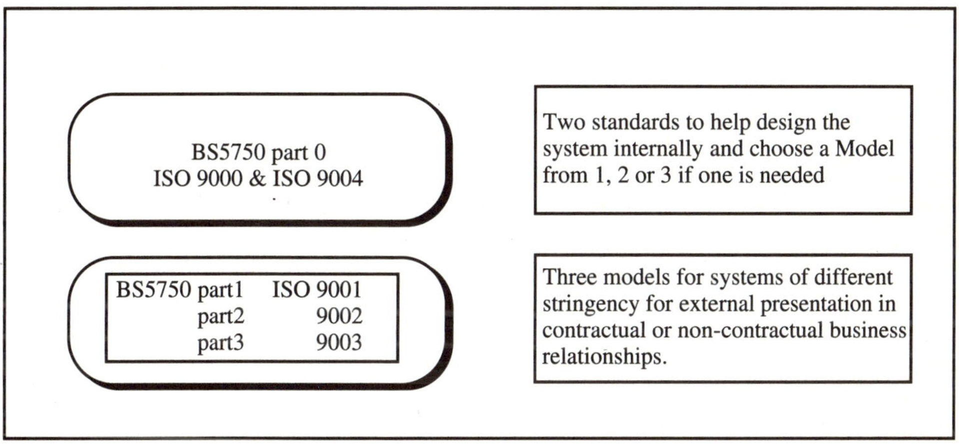

Figure 4.2 Dependencies

As we can see the standard is split into three models (with BS5750 having three parts). Each model consists of a number of clauses that need to be adhered to in order to meet the criteria set-out within the standard. Model 1 consists of 20 clauses, Model 2 consists of 18 clauses and is a subset of Model 1, Model 3 consists of 12 clauses and is a subset of Model 2. Therefore if we look at Model 1 in its entirety, we would understand the whole of the standard. Let's look at this standard (in terms of BS5750 Part 1) in detail and how it can be associated to IT & IT Security.

The following text will define the clauses (e.g., Clause 4.1), describe its use (e.g., USE: ..) and how IT & IT Security can utilize the clause (e.g., IT & IT SECURITY UTILITY of 4.1). Note, it will use the BS5750 numbering system — for a further information on the standard the reader is referred to the standard itself. Figure 4.3 below describes pictorially how BS5750 is defined within a complete organizational environment.

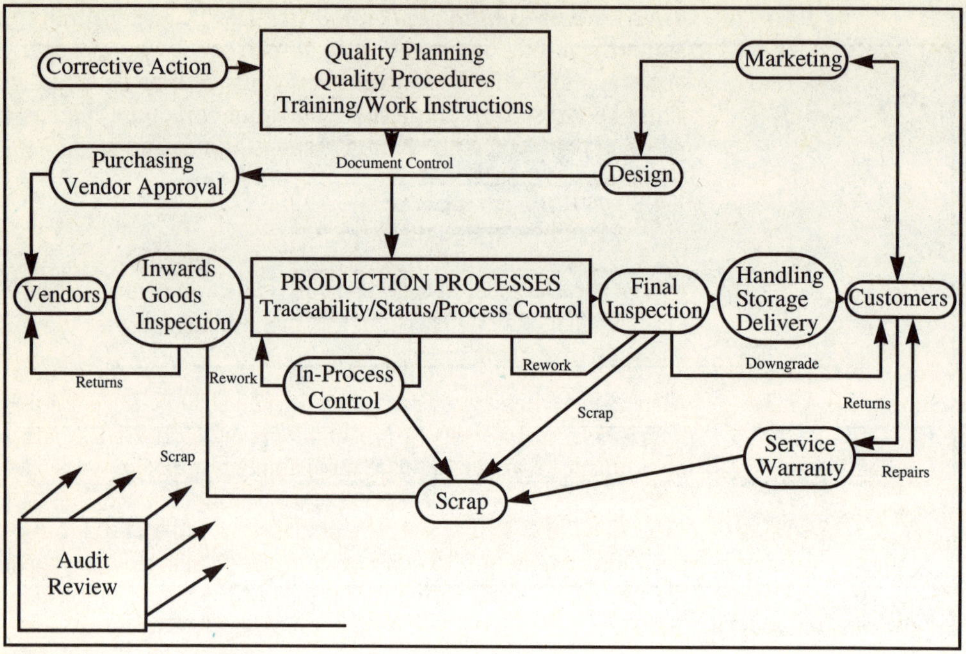

Figure 4.3 BS5750

BS5750 : Part 1 : 1987

Clause 4. Quality System Requirements

Clause 4.1 Management Responsibility

USE: As a prerequisite of adhering to this standard, this clause requires that the company management formally documents the objectives of the company and the policy for quality. Furthermore, it is management's responsibility that these objectives and policy are fully understood by all, put into action and kept that way. Management must also identify and assign responsibility to all personnel who manage and perform work affecting quality and assign trained personnel to verify that the work is performed correctly. This clause also requires management to review its objectives and policy at pre-determined scheduled intervals. These reviews should reveal any defects or irregularities and suggest corrective actions. All this is described within this clause as three sub-clauses that describe policy, responsibility, authority, verification, management and review.

Sub-clause 4.1.1 Quality Policy: Defines that the supplier will define and document its policy, objectives and commitment to quality. The supplier should ensure that its policy is understood, implemented and maintained.

Sub-clause 4.1.2 Organization: Management appoints a *management representative* with defined *authority* and *responsibility* for ensuring the *standard* is *implemented* and *managed*. This person will act as a focal point for quality, ensuring that the whole workforce understand their own specific responsibility towards the Quality System.

4.1.2.1 Responsibility and Authority: The ' ..responsibility, authority and the interrelation of all personnel who manage, perform and verify work affecting quality shall be defined..'. This means that a complete organization structure chart is required that depicts the duties, responsibilities and authority of all the staff.

4.1.2.2 Verification Resources and Personnel: This identifies in-house verification requirements, provide adequate resources and assigns trained personnel for verification activities. The verification includes inspection, test, monitoring, design reviews and audit of quality systems.

Sub-clause 4.1.3 Management Review: The quality System shall be *reviewed* at *appropriate intervals* to ensure *suitability* and *effectiveness* and conformance with the standard maintaining historical *records.*

IT & IT SECURITY UTILITY of 4.1: This management clause would be used in its entirety, no matter what industry, section or area within that industry. The main objective is the need for formality (since formality permits objectivity) within the documentation of the industry's objectives and policy. In terms of IT Security, one of the main areas of concern within this arena is management responsibility (or the lack of it). This clause highlights how important it is to have management commitment and to specifically define your quality needs and goals (i.e. policy) and consequently your security needs and goals (ie., IT Security policy). Although this clause does not explicitly define the contents of an IT Security Policy the reader is referred to Appendix B) it does define the scope of such a Policy, which goes in line with a Quality Policy.

Clause 4.2 Quality System

USE: This clause brings together all the areas, objectives and activities that contribute to the product's or service's quality. It does this by addressing all the requirements of the standard in terms of organizational structure, resources, responsibilities, procedures and processes and consequently writing these policies and procedures down in order to demonstrate how it will conform with the standard. The Quality System must as a result be planned and defined to be aware of all company functions, like customer liaison, training, manufacturing, etc. In a nutshell this clause defines the following flow diagram (see Figure 4.4 below)

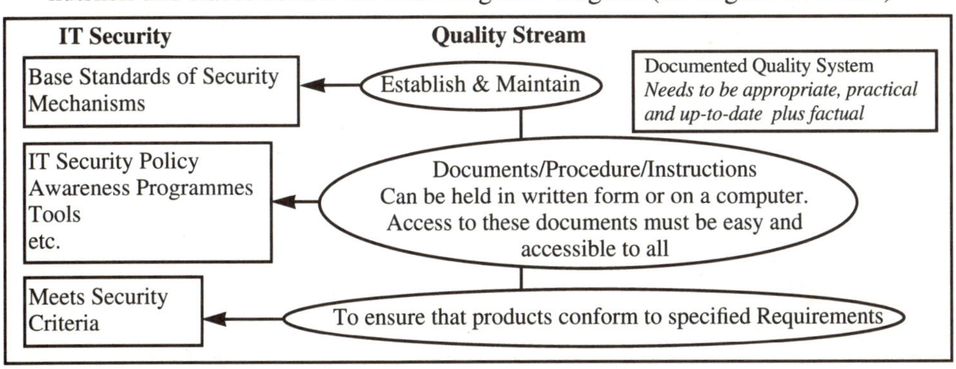

Figure 4.4 Clause 4.2 Relationship

IT & IT SECURITY UTILITY of 4.2: As with 4.1, this clause would be used in its entirety. All areas of a business produce a product or service — within IT, it is obviously the same, consequently these products or services must adhere to a minimum basic quality criteria defined within this clause. Within IT Security the Quality system can be defined as the overall Security Model for an organization. In Figure 4.4 above the IT Security/Quality System flow is depicted, with an overall view of the Security services defined.

Clause 4.3 Contract Review

USE: This is a recent addition to the standard and it requires that a company reviews all contracts before commencing work. This is achieved by ensuring that when a company takes in work from a customer they ensure that they can do it, to specification and without any alteration to the original tender, i.e., that you establish and maintain procedures for contract reviews, co-ordinating activities to ensure that:

- customer requirements are clearly defined and documented;
- differences resolved within the tender terms of reference;
- capability is met;
- contractual obligations are not broken.

IT & IT SECURITY UTILITY of 4.3: One of the criticisms of IT marketing and sales is the ease by which a sales person can offer the moon to a prospective client who finds out later that the company cannot supply what was originally agreed due to various business reasons but especially due to the technology not actually being available. This clause protects both the company from any future penalty for not delivering the goods as required and the client from receiving below-par products/services. It is too often the case that an IT product or service is supplied to a customer under 'false' pretences (whether directly written in the contract or implied within the literature/sales pitch — in either case criminal) and subjects the client to unwarranted risks to their business. For example, if a normal Personal Computer was sold for the control of a hospital electricity power-supply, that was not specifically built for this purpose (for instance has no fault-tolerant capability) and failed while in the process of supporting an open heart surgery session. The consequence of this could be catastrophic with the patient dying as a consequence, but who is at fault here? How secure should the system have been and would the adherence to this clause have avoided this disaster? Obviously it would have at least minimized the probability of it happening by at least supplying a product that was fit for its purpose.

A specific IT Security example within Contract Review can be seen within the establishment of a Contingency Plan and having to undertake a Contract for stand-by arrangements. All too often this type of contract is not properly defined and incomplete. For instance, ensuring that a 'cold' stand-by is not kept waiting too long for the supply of equipment, services, etc. In this situation the 'customer requirements' for a 'working' stand-by must be clearly defined (eg., an empty dedicated Computer Centre fully equipped) with the capability to fit within a specified time-frame the required hardware. Contractual obligations on both parties are then clearly defined.

Another example where contract review is of paramount importance is in the definition and specification of a contract between yourself and a developer (who may be developing some software for you). Specific importance should be given to defining which parts of the system are security-relevant and specifically describe what security features are required. Within this security software scenario additional protection can be attained by the use of a 'security ESCROW[54] Agreement'. This agreement defines the deposit of the 'security software source code' with a third party as an insurance against the owner of the software going bankrupt or liquidating and consequently unable to support/amend the software.

Clause 4.4 Design Control

USE: This clause is about design control and is probably one of the major functions within a business (the other being purchasing — clause 4.6 and manufacturing — clause 4.9). The aim here is to establish and control the functions of design and development planning, where qualified and trained personnel with adequate resources are able to perform their tasks effectively. This function would include the translation of customer requirements, often specified in terms of performance, into something from which other competent staff members can purchase, make, test, install, use and service, within specific cost and time limits. In other words identify problems, follow them through, document design input and output requirements in terms of specific customer needs and in so doing keeping strict, careful, planned document control at every stage (ie., the design stages include design and development planning, design input, design output, design verification and design changes) as per BS5750. Finally make sure they are 'closed' out showing evidence of the whole process.

Sub-clause 4.4.1 General

Sub-clause 4.4.2 Design and development planning: requires the design document(s) to state clearly each design and development activity, identifying who is responsible for what and keeping a log of the progress as the design evolves.

4.4.2.1 Activity Assignment: requires that those individuals assigned to do the work have both the knowledge and recourse to it.

4.4.2.2 Organizational and technical interfaces: requires that the staff and information needed from outside design be recognised and a controlled communications channel opened.

Sub-clause 4.4.3 Design input: this sub-clause defines the requirement and availability of all the information necessary for the design to be available before the design programme gets underway in a clear and unequivocal manner.

Sub-clause 4.4.4 Design output: this sub-clause defines the need for a company to demonstrate all the documentation, e.g., drawings, calculations, specifications, etc., pertaining to the design after completion (identifying the basis by which they are deemed complete and correct).

Sub-clause 4.4.5 Design verification: this sub-clause identifies the options available for proving design, e.g., design reviews, calculations, tests, comparison with similar designs, etc.

Sub-clause 4.4.6 Design changes: this sub-clause defines that any changes or modifications are fully and properly formally reviewed.

IT & IT SECURITY UTILITY of 4.4: Different areas of this clause can be applied to IT depending on whether you are producing hardware (to which the whole clause is applied), software (some areas are applicable) or supplying a service. For example, if we look at software development (which is described further within the TickIT section later) this clause can be applied within the following areas:

- software quality improvement function (referred to in sub-clauses 4.4.5 and 4.4.6);
- within the project plan stage (referred to in sub-clause 4.4.2);
- within product research and development (referred to in clause 4.4 et al);
- within the software specification stage (referred to in sub-clause 4.4.3);
- within the verification, validation and testing of software (referred to in sub-clause 4.4.5);
- within product acceptance (referred to in sub-clause 4.4.5);
- within the design and development stage (referred to in sub-clause 4.4.4 and 4.4.6).

It is obvious that this clause in its entirety has a paramount influence throughout the software development life cycle. Its correct implementation and utilization will maintain a balance between innovation and standardization, and therefore will encourage the use of new techniques while retaining reliable proven designs, materials and methods.

In terms of IT Security, this clause can be applied specifically to the evaluation of a particular security product or service. Its basic objective in terms of security is to establish the confidence that a security product or service is secure and fit for purpose. Such an assessment would require the examination of procedures, methods, tools and specific standards used in the development of the security product or service.

This assessment would consequently look at how the design process was set up, possibly adhering to a 'standard' design specification (note said standard would be defined by the organization as an internal process), such as:

- overall design;
- definition of constituent subsystems;
- interfaces between the subsystems;
- what type of subsystem was to be used;
- details of how each subsystem provides the required
- security functions.

In essence the design process would establish how the security relevant parts of the design specification corresponds to the security relevant parts required within the product.

Clause 4.5 Document Control

USE: Document control affects all areas of the business that have written procedures and processes, for example:

- quality manual;
- departmental work processes and manual;
- work procedures;
- health and safety guidelines;
- purchasing specification;
- lists of approved suppliers;
- specification of products and services;
- service level agreements;
- etc.

It is important within all these documents to ensure that there are procedures that dictate approval and issue of these documents in a controlled manner. This will obviously make available to all staff on demand only the most up-to-date issues (with obsolete documents being withdrawn). Obviously this means that it is of paramount importance to keep records of any changes to these 'controlled' documents (additionally a decision must be taken on the length of time that records will be kept for).

Sub-clause 4.5.1 Documentation approval and issue: this sub-clause defines the control of all documents relating to the standard. It is an all-encompassing clause, requiring review and approval of all 'controlled' documents by authorized personnel.

Sub-clause 4.5.2 Documentation changes/modifications: this requires any changes to be reviewed and approved on the same basis as that utilized for the original documents. Within it, it also requires indication on the document(s) which utilized the change and what the actual change is. It also requires a means of identifying the current and correct issue of a document via a master list so that wrong or irrelevant documents are not used. It also indicates that after a practical number of issues, a document should be re-issued from scratch.

IT & IT SECURITY UTILITY of 4.5: Documentation is the main way by which product and service information is presented, recorded and communicated. Consequently document control is of paramount importance within all areas of any production cycle, for example, in the creation and maintenance of documentation of systems and procedures. Consequently this clause *et al* is of paramount importance to IT and its various functions.

Documentation within IT comes in a variety of areas and forms, for instance, design documentation, user manuals, maintenance manuals, project plans, procedural documentation, etc.

Each element must come under the review of this clause and therefore will need to be audited accordingly. It is important to note that sometimes too many documents are placed under the watchful eye of Clause 4.5 and therefore make the administrative procedure of these documents endless. Care must be taken when choosing what documents to include within the rigorous control of this clause and this basically means only choosing those documents that 'directly' affect the final quality of the product or service. If a document is only used for guidance purposes or as an aide-memoir, it is unlikely that it requires strict document control.

This clause is also of great benefit to IT in terms of 'reducing' the number of trees destroyed as a result of utilizing IT. The so-called paperless office has never come to fruition, in fact, IT has increased the level of paper usage substantially — it is far too easy to get a personal print-out of a program, calculation, etc. By applying this clause, the number of documents used should be kept to a minimum since no Quality Manager wishes to have numerous manuals that he/she cannot control.

When it comes to IT Security products and the management of their production life cycle a method of development configuration management would fit well within this clause.

By configuration management I mean the managing of security products throughout their life-cycle from the original conception, through development, operational life until their eventual replacement or disposal (See Figure 4.5). Therefore for any IT Security product or service configuration identification information is required, e.g., Product/Service IT, Version, Date, Reason for issue, responsibility, etc.

Release C

Configuration Item	Version Number		
Requirement Spec	1.1	1.2	1.2
Functional Spec	1.1	1.1	1.1
Program Spec	1.0	1.1	1.4
Software Spec	1.2	1.2	1.2
User Documentation	1.0	1.2	1.4

Release B

Configuration Item	Version Number		
Requirement Spec	1.1	1.2	1.2
Functional Spec	1.1	1.1	1.1
Program Spec	1.0	1.1	1.4
Software Spec	1.2	1.2	1.2
User Documentation	1.0	1.2	1.4

Release A

Configuration Item	Version Number		
Requirement Spec	1.1	1.2	1.2
Functional Spec	1.1	1.1	1.1
Program Spec	1.0	1.1	1.4
Software Spec	1.2	1.2	1.2
User Documentation	1.0	1.2	1.4

Figure 4.5 Configuration Management

Consequently all deliverables within the life of the production of a security product needs to be under this control, including for example, any evidence that a particular security method has been utilized like a cryptographic algorithm.

Clause 4.6 Purchasing

USE: This is the second of what can be considered a major function, since all companies purchase. The objective of quality purchasing is very simple — to ensure that purchased products and services conform to pre-determined requirements. The way of achieving this may be concentrated on assessments of the suppliers' own quality systems, rather than by elaborate checking mechanisms on receipt.

Suppliers need to be chosen on the basis of their ability to meet the requirements and records should be kept showing whether the supplier:

- is able to supply the product or service;
- can supply the product or service in a reliable and consistent manner.

Note: the systems should allow for the imposition of quality requirements on supplier's suppliers, and so on, if specified in the contract. This may include independent third party certification, assessment of products, services and records.

Sub-clause 4.6.1 General: this requires that the purchased product conforms to specified requirements.

Sub-clause 4.6.2 Assessment of sub-contractors: this requires that suppliers be selected on the basis of specific quality requirements, and that the company should keep a record of acceptable ones. The criteria to judge whether the requirements are met can be made in terms of:

- purchasing specification;
- selection of suppliers by collaborators/competitors;
- assurance of quality of supplies;
- monitoring of suppliers performance;
- degree of standardization;
- inspectability and control;
- complexity and uniqueness of product or service;
- consequence of failure;
- special process control;
- records of past assessments and performance.

Sub-clause 4.6.3 Purchasing data: this requires that documents used for purchasing, e.g., purchase orders, clearly and unambiguously state requirements and all quality controlling information relevant to the purchase. Note, under Clause 4.5, all documents that are within the Quality Systems must also have review and approval logs before they are released.

Sub-clause 4.6.4 Verification of purchased product: this requires that where the customer requires the right to inspect and assess at source, then he shall be given access to do so. This sub-clause does not alter the responsibility of the supplier to supply quality products or to keep to contract and legal obligations. In basic terms, the purchaser must assure itself that their quality goals are being met. This process can be achieved by:

- the purchaser establishing the quality goals;
- the supplier specifying the measure or criteria which is to be used to meet the quality goals;
- the purchaser and supplier evaluate the product throughout its production life cycle.

IT & IT SECURITY UTILITY of 4.6: The quality of bought-in products and services is of prime importance to all business, but for IT security-conscious businesses, nothing would be more aggravating than purchasing a product or service, relying on its functionality and subsequently finding that it was not fit for its purpose. Even worse, causing a major security incident that could otherwise have been avoided. For instance, within the IT arena in the past twenty or so years, the use of temporary sub-contractors (normally hired via a third party agency) to produce programs that later need to be run and maintained by permanent staff has become a norm. These sub-contractors have been hired for fairly short periods and at a relatively high premium, but how does a company guarantee that what they produce adheres to their minimum quality requirements in terms of functionality, costs, time scales and maintainability? The selection of sub-contractors needs to be made on their ability to meet sub-contract requirements. This means that the only effective way of verifying the quality of the product is done in terms of periodic checks, inspections and monitoring throughout the development process.

IT Security purchasing (or procurement) is to date (1994) a relatively new discipline and most often buyers are unfamiliar with some of the security-related issues involved. Consequently it is important that before any purchase is undertaken buyers should seek advice from experts or Government Security Organizations like the UK Communications-Electronics Security Group (CESG).

The main objective is to ensure that the necessary documents defining the security requirements for a product or service are produced to a certain Quality Criteria. For example, the security product is accurate and structurally sound plus supplies all the security features needed by the buyer. (For example, this could mean the sum of a set of products that may deal with authentication, access control, accounting and auditing. Each individually can be defined requiring a certain level of security adherence but can also be defined together to form another product, eg., an operating system needs all four.) These documents consequently form the basis for a contractual agreement between the buyer and developer.

Clause 4.7 Purchaser supplied product

USE: Where a customer supplies materials or a product to which further work is going to be carried out, it is important to be able to assure its suitability for use and consequently execute a trace mechanism of the product through all its additional processes and ultimate storage. The company needs to check that the correct quantity has been received and that they are undamaged and must report to the customer any materials which are lost, damaged or unsuitable for any reason. Special consideration may be necessary when the customer supplies materials or products that may be owned by your customer but supplied to you for use whilst fulfilling your contract.

IT & IT SECURITY UTILITY of 4.7: In the era of outsourcing and the use of external agencies for the supply of specific specialist tasks, it is important that the company does not jeopardize its quality needs just because it has handed control of a specific task to a third party. Usually this third party supplier simply fills in a gap (normally due to lack of internal resources) which means that the ball is handed over temporarily and then taken back. An appropriate example in this situation is seen within the communications arena where the use of a local or international PTT is used to do business. The service provided by the PTT is the 'supplied product' that is going to be used within /outside the company. Any failure of this product would have some dramatic effect on the business and leave it vulnerable.

This example can be expanded upon within the Electronic Document Interchange arena. Various National and International companies provide this service via their networks. Within such an area there are various security concerns that need to be addressed, for example:

- loss of confidentiality of sensitive information due to an insecure network;
- increased exposure to fraud-blackmail due to lax security (not only are you vulnerable but also your trading partner);
- manipulation of payments (accidentally via an error or purposely by the introduction of rogue information);
- communications errors may result in the transmission of incorrect trading information;
- potential loss of trading audit trail since less trading paper is available for verifying and reconciling transactions.

Therefore it is obvious that the best means of protection against the above threats is to have the proper contractual agreement with your third party supplier and assurance that said third party is subject to regular independent audits. Such an agreement could include at least the following:

- nature of services to be maintained, such as the network and mailbox;
- service levels required and agreed with providers;
- backup and contingency arrangement and who is responsible for what;
- minimum security requirements of the network, mailbox, audit trails, software, data, etc.;
- rights and obligations of all parties;
- charges (network access, transmissions, etc.);
- independent auditing and reviews.

Clause 4.8 Product identification and traceability

USE: Identification and traceability throughout the production life cycle (e.g., delivery, production and installation — from raw materials to finished goods) are essential and provide important protection for effective process control and the identification of quality problems. An example where this strict clause could be applied is within 'bought-in' products that will be used in manufacturing prior to evidence of conformance being available — in this situation it is essential to track and identify the product.

Another area where it can be applied is in adherence to safety and statutory regulations, where product identification provides the capability to trace and recall non-conforming and dangerous products delivered to a customer.

IT & IT SECURITY UTILITY of 4.8: Although this clause can be clearly applied to any manufacturing environment in terms of tracking a product and safeguarding a customer, it can also be used to control the production of software. Within this environment, procedures are used to ensure that control of software is achieved within strict configuration management guidelines as described in Clause 4.5 and Figure 4.5. Configuration management addresses identification, fault reporting, modification (of the software itself and any associated products, like its documentation), product library and build status and tracking, version control and change request control.

Within this clause however, a major part is configuration audit where at regular intervals checks are made to ensure:

- products are consistent with the products from which they have been derived;
- information held within the configuration management system is consistent with the actual state of the physical products.

Clause 4.9 Process control

USE: This is the third (and the broadest in scope) major function, as all companies have some type of process control function. To a greater or lesser extent, everyone in a company performs processes of which most are carried out under some type of control. In order for this to occur, documented work instructions must be available to staff. These work instructions do not need to actually regurgitate the basic skills of the operator, but must, however, contain enough information to enable the process to be executed under the required quality conditions. For instance, a documented work instruction would be described as follows:

- a full description of the process;
- a full description of hardware needed to carry out task;
- any special process for 'start up', etc.;
- reference to any instrumentation/calibration standard;
- simplified operator instructions.

Sub-clause 4.9.1 General: This sub-clause is further divided into four basic control functions:

(a) requires documented work instructions to be available where needed, the use of suitable equipment, environment and compliance with specification and quality plans;

(b) requires that controls of products and the process producing it are operated, i.e., knowing the process capability;

(c) requires that approval and qualification if required be done of processes and other equipment;

(d) requires that there should be a method of knowing what is correct or not.

As a whole this sub-clause can be viewed in terms of what conditions exist to control the production life cycle of a product as described in Figure 4.6 below:

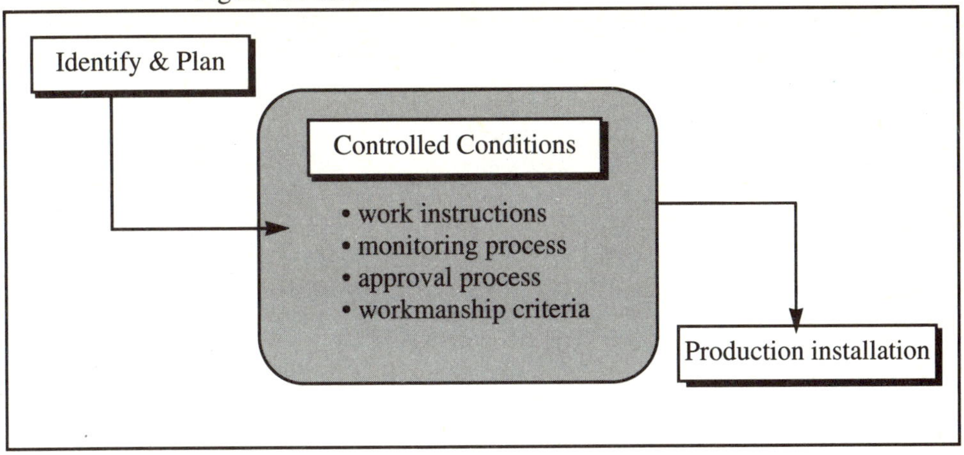

Figure 4.6 Process Control 4.9.1 General

Sub-clause 4.9.2 Special processes: This sub-clause caters for certain processes that cannot be checked fully and therefore the only way of ensuring a sound process is to closely control the process itself and provide minimum qualification on at least the known variables.

IT & IT SECURITY UTILITY of 4.9: In essence this clause is basically applied to production (whether that be within a manufacturing environment or not). It consequently follows that production needs to be identified, planned and carried out under controlled conditions. Therefore, in a similar way as clause 4.8 and 4.5 relate to IT & IT Security, clause 4.9 covers all areas of IT, for example, software production and replication, in process training, validation of results, configuration control, software tools, etc.

An IT Security example could be the design of some cryptographic software. Figure 4.7 below depicts the typical life-cycle of software development.

System Requirements ↓	• an overall statement is described, including overall security requirements. This can be based on the overall Security Policy.
Functional Specification ↓	• defines the highest level statement of what the system does, and should be as far as possible implementation free. It defines all the functions to be provided, secure inputs/outputs and any secure interfaces to other systems.
Design Specification ↓	• defines how the functions defined in the functional spec. are to be provided.
Programming ↓	• involves coding the requirements.
Developed System ↓	• this is the final product and could be the collection of smaller individual modules once they have been integrated. Within it you may also see security test material.
Operational System	• encompasses the software and any required data.

Figure 4.7 Software Development

Within this typical system development life-cycle, several security tests will also be carried out in order to establish confidence. Examples of such tests include control of access to data, control of state changes (eg., start-up, close-down, failure, recovery) and control of users, devices, etc.

Clause 4.10 Inspection and testing

USE: This clause caters for four aspects of inspection and testing of incoming goods. The amount of inspection depends on the situation (e.g., for process control or to ensure that quality criteria are being met) and consequently might simply be just checking a product label or delivery rate against a purchase order or visual examination for damage in transit or checking against a certificate of conformity. Whatever is done must operate according to your quality written work-procedures.

Sub-clause 4.10.1 Receiving inspection and testing : This sub-clause is further sub-divided into two areas — incoming product verification and un-inspected use of incoming products.

4.10.1.1 This requires a company not to use purchased materials until they have passed the incoming inspection and test procedures for conformance to specification — this could be source inspection or accepting it due to faith in supplier.

4.10.1.2 This requires that a company when releasing material for urgent production can positively identify it for recall if later found to be non-conforming to specification.

Sub-clause 4.10.2 In-process inspection and testing: This sub-clause requires that the inspection and testing required by procedure are done (which includes process and product monitoring, i.e., are we doing the job properly?). In reality, it is the actual process parameter, like temperature or speed, typing speed, flow rate, etc., that is monitored to ensure feed-forward control of the process. It also requires that if inspection and testing has not been carried out, the material should be 'held' unless released for urgent production where sub-clause 4.10.1.2 comes into effect. In a nutshell, this sub-clause can be viewed pictorially as shown in Figure 4.8 below.

Sub-clause 4.10.3 Final inspection and testing: This requires that finished product or service also needs to be inspected and tested to complete the evidence of its full conformance with the specified requirement (this also means that all other previous inspections and tests have been carried out and that the data is acceptable). Implicit within this sub-clause is that a product cannot be despatched without the completion of all activities within the quality plan. The sub-clause can be viewed pictorially as shown in Figure 4.9 below.

Sub-clause 4.10.4 Inspection and test records: This requires that records be kept of past inspection and/or tests against specified acceptance criteria.

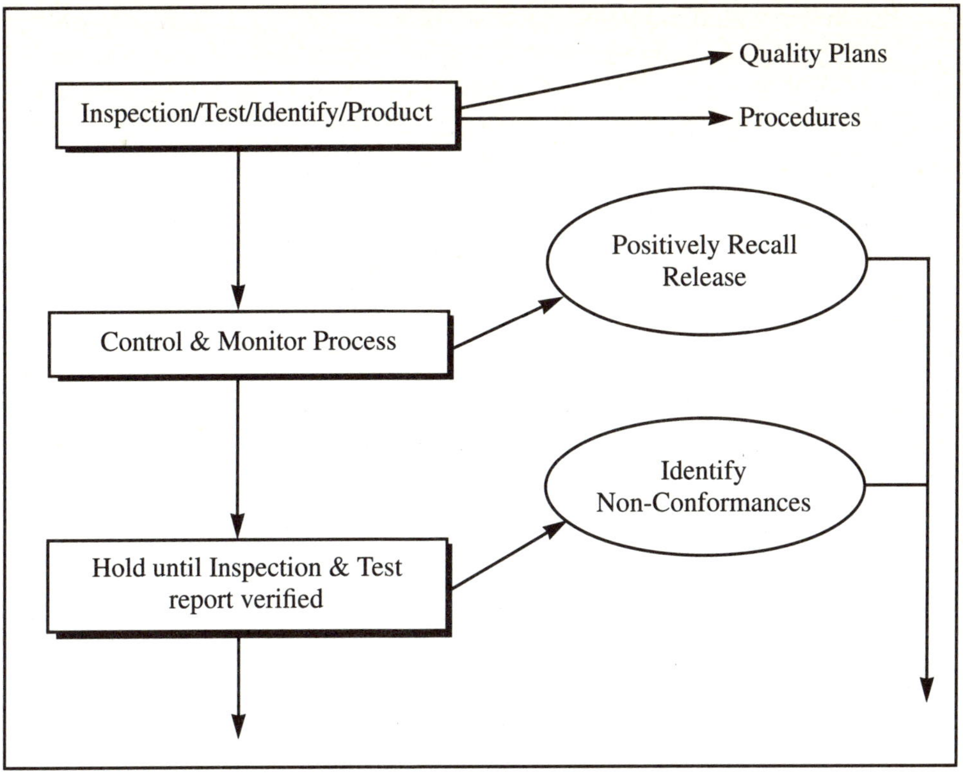

Figure 4.8 In-process Inspection and Test

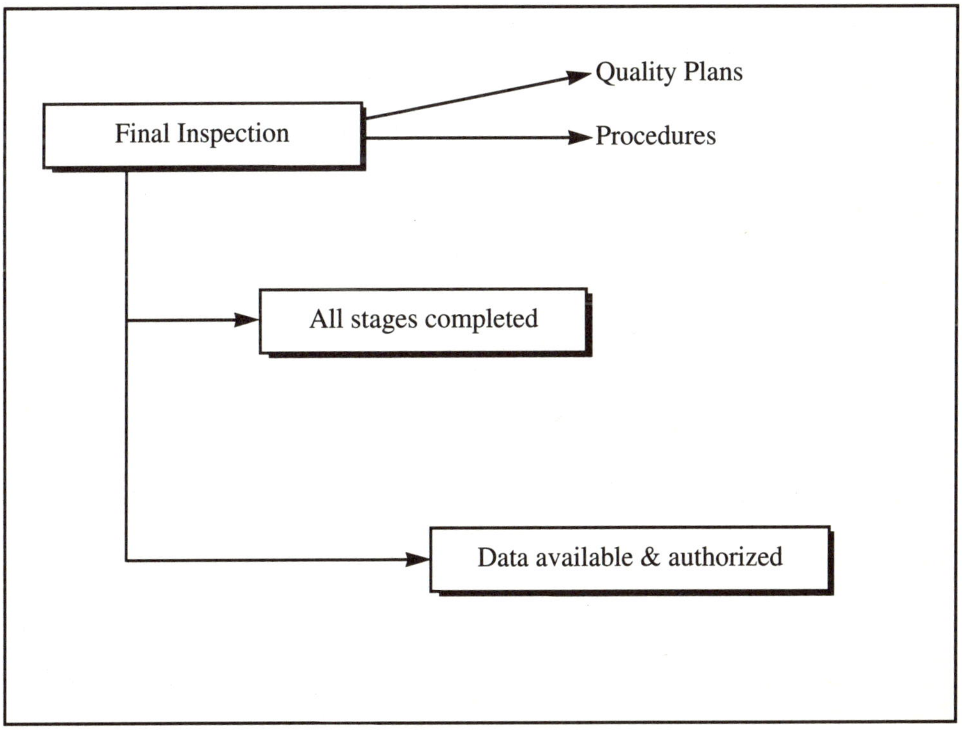

Figure 4.9 Final Inspection and Test

IT & IT SECURITY UTILITY of 4.10: The clause covers any product supplied in terms of demonstrating to a purchaser that the total requirement has been met. In terms of IT all areas are impacted by this clause. In terms of software, for instance, this testing may be done as part of a phased delivery of the total product, where a hierarchy of test modules and a structured approach of testing from coded modules upwards to system tests is implemented. This approach will reveal any hidden errors that were created during the specification, design or coding stages of the development. Traditionally within IT, software development, 'maintenance' (or fixing) debugging and error correction has formed a major part of software development.

Within IT Security, this clause can be interpreted as the evaluation process that can be carried out on IT Security tools throughout the life-cycle of the security product production. Said evaluation could take the following format:

- definition of the security evaluation baseline, which is needed in order to define the requirements against which the evaluation is to be conducted. It will describe the functional security requirements and the corresponding confidence level requirements;
- investigation into any system fault that could lead to possible breaches of the security of the system. This investigation will disclose potential vulnerabilities;
- once the product is at its final stage of production, you can perform 'penetration' tests to attempt to find possible security faults;
- report the findings.

Clause 4.11 Inspection, measuring and test equipment

USE: This is an extensive clause where a supplier is required to ensure consistency throughout their measurement and calibration procedures, This includes:

- Planning for measurement requirement accuracy;
- Traceability and evidence of calibration;
- Calibration procedures within a periodic schedule;
- Identification of calibration status;
- Historical record keeping for all inspection, measuring and test equipment.

The purpose of this clause is simple: to ensure that there is confidence in any measurements made.

IT & IT SECURITY UTILITY of 4.11: Within IT, this clause covers any area that is controlled under some type of configuration management process, e.g., the use of tools to measure system performance. It will also be concerned with the use of 'metrics' as a standard way of measuring the failure rate of software, or computer aided inspection/ computer aided testing tools for testing equipment. Within IT Security this would be defined by measuring a particular security product against an industry standard, eg, standard encryption algorithm (i.e., DES). You can calibrate your security tool accordingly.

Clause 4.12 Inspection and test status

USE: This requires that it be clear exactly what test status a product is in within its production life cycle. This could be:

- Not inspected, awaiting test, checks, etc.;
- Inspected and approved;
- Inspected and failed.

This process should provide records of the inspection process to ensure that only material and services that conform to requirements are passed onto the next stage or despatched.

IT & IT SECURITY UTILITY of 4.12: In a similar manner to 4.11 and 4.5, this clause identifies areas within IT & IT Security that require control procedures within a development environment. Within a large software projects (large or small), it will be composed of numerous modules that interact with each other and that require independent testing. As each passes its test stage, this should be highlighted and recorded. Configuration Management procedures discussed in clause 4.5 provide the level of traceability required under this clause.

Clause 4.13 Control of Non-Conforming Products

USE: This requires that items which do not conform are not used inadvertently with items that do. A control documented system is required here that clearly identifies and segregates each non-conforming item. This system should also identify how the non-conforming item will be dealt with (ie., re-worked, repaired, concession raised, regraded, rejected, scrapped, etc.).

Sub-clause 4.13.1 Non-conformity — review and disposition: This requires that review and disposition of non-conformity items be carried out to formal procedures and consideration given to re-working to meet quality criteria, used 'as is' by concessions, regraded for alternative use or scrapped. When this affects directly a customer's specification, then they must be advised formally and a record retained of the event.

IT & IT SECURITY UTILITY of 4.13: There are many sources of non-conformances (e.g., design, planning, suppliers, materials supplied, assembly, test and inspection, warehousing, transportation, etc.). With IT & IT Security this is also the case with literally every area being subject to some type of non-conformance due to products or services not adhering to Quality and Security standards. Examples where this clause could be used is when investigating the adherence of a security product or service to a particular security standard, e.g.,

- standard for techniques of risk analysis (CRAMM);
- standard for the scope and format of a Security Policy;
- standard for auditing;
- specific technical standards.

Clause 4.14 Corrective Action

USE: This is one of the most important areas of any Quality system. It requires a company to determine the cause of non-conforming products or services so that corrective lasting action can be taken to put it right. It also requires analysis of trouble areas or potential trouble areas to detect and eliminate potential problems. Once a corrective action has taken place, new controls and changes to procedures may be required to ensure that they last and are effective.

IT & IT SECURITY UTILITY of 4.14: This is similar to 4.13. In essence the fault and failure recording systems should be appropriate to the type of IT system used providing a means of ensuring that management corrective action is completed during all stages of the product development plan and in production, distribution and operational use. Corrective action applies to whatever product or service is being produced/delivered, for example, when developing the IT Security Policy, several iterative corrective processes occur, i.e.,

- Security Consultant produces skeletal Policy Document;
- Sends Draft 1. to a pre-defined group of reviewers (consisting of relevant people with knowledge and experience in the subject area and the business as a whole);
- reviewers review document for omissions, errors, suggestions, etc.;
- corrective process takes over to produce Draft 2 of the IT Security Policy;
- at this stage it can go back for review again or go straight for approval;
- approval process and release.

Clause 4.15 Handling, storage, packaging and delivery

USE: There should be written instructions and procedures that dictate how a product is handled and protected in process, ensuring that any 'special' product is not mixed with similar product, that there is no contamination, that delicate parts are protected and that product does not miss any operation and inspection, etc. It has five sub clauses covering each specification area of the clause.

Sub-clause 4.15.1 General

Sub-clause 4.15.2 Handling: Defines ways of handling which prevent damage or deterioration.

Sub-clause 4.15.3 Storage: Requires secure storage areas, including controlled receipt into and issue from such areas. It also requires stocks to be assessed periodically for any damage or deterioration.

Sub-clause 4.15.4 Packaging: Requires the recognition that responsibility ceases in despatching the product and to make sure that the packaging continues to identify and protect the product.

Sub-clause 4.15.5 Delivery: Requires that the product is protected properly after final inspection and test including delivery of contractually specified products or service.

IT & IT SECURITY UTILITY of 4.15: Similar in nature to clauses 4.13 and 4.14, there exist areas of IT that can directly be defined within this clause. For instance in terms of 4.15.2, the handling of media and electrostatic sensitive devices or 4.15.3, storage of media, must adhere to certain prescribed standards. In terms of IT Security, it is obvious that total control is required of any security product. For instance, the delivery of a secure fax with 'secure card keys' that will be used in a secure area must be protected from any theft of cards or physical damage.

Clause 4.16 Quality Records

USE: Within any Quality System you need objective evidence that you are meeting your customer's quality requirements and this is normally done via records which can include audit reports, results of inspection and tests, calibration tests, approvals, concessions, corrective action reports, etc. In order for this to be effectively managed, this clause stipulates that there must be a method of identifying, collecting, indexing, filing, storage, maintenance and disposition of these records. Easy access to these records is vital.

IT & IT SECURITY UTILITY of 4.16: In IT & IT Security documentation is part and parcel of any System, this clause simply formalizes the procedure. In terms of being able to 'trace' the product it is important that this documentation is maintained and is accessible. For instance, evidence of test results, standards adhered to etc.

Clause 4.17 Internal Quality Audits

USE: These audits set out to determine whether the Quality Management System is being operated according to the written procedures. This should be done on a planned and systematic basis. The audit plan, procedures for audit and records of audit results shall be formally prepared and retained. Any non-conformances identified should be reported to management and subsequently corrected and a follow-up review conducted to ensure that the corrective action is effective and remains so.

IT & IT SECURITY UTILITY of 4.17: The impact on IT & IT Security within this clause can be viewed in a similar way to the other clauses. Auditing is simply used to ascertain whether the operation of a system is functioning according to a previously agreed criteria. In IT this process should already be in place, covered by electronic audit trails and procedures. Principally, the auditor here is acting like a 'watchdog', studying and evaluating the operation of the internal controls for development and adherence to standards. The reader is referred to Chapter 6 for further information on auditing.

Clause 4.18 Training

USE: This should be defined and implemented for all staff, where written procedures need to be established and maintained for identifying training needs, carrying out the training and keeping records of the training.

IT & IT SECURITY UTILITY of 4.18: One of the main elements in any Quality System is the need for training. This clause simply re-enforces and formalizes this need. This has been described both in Chapter 2 in terms of Quality and in Chapter 3 in terms of Security.

Clause 4.19 Servicing

USE: This requires that companies involved contractually in this activity do carry out this activity and can verify in some way that it is done correctly.

IT & IT SECURITY UTILITY of 4.19: Within IT & IT Security this can be one of the most important clauses, as it defines the need for a Quality criteria in servicing. This can include the servicing of IT equipment, contractual staff, Facilities Management or as described in Clause 4.7, the purchase of a secure EDI service from a third party.

Clause 4.20 Statistical Techniques

USE: This requires that the company considers all the processes within it and the products processed and identifies appropriate statistical techniques (e.g., Statistical Process Control).

IT & IT SECURITY UTILITY of 4.20: IT can assist in imposing this clause as it can supply the means by which data can be easily collected and allow the implementation of statistical process control. The essence here is to continually measure the process over time by the collection of metrics (as described in Chapter 2).

The reader is referred to Appendix A — ISO9001 — An Example Quality Manual, for further information on clauses 4.1 through 4.20. In this appendix a Quality Manual for a fictitious company Ibertalia SA is described.

Software Quality

Software quality has always been an area that has not commanded a great deal of attention, since quality assurance and quality control were mainly the prime concern for preventing hardware failures. However, this situation has in recent years changed, since hardware reliability has increased dramatically, highlighted by the increased need to create quality software. Owing to the growth in the number of software applications available and the level of awareness within the user community for quality software, there has been a phenomenal growth in standards and guidelines. It is impossible to exhaustively list here all these standards and guidelines; however, the most important are:

- The safe use of programmable electronic systems *(Health and Safety Executive, 1987)*
- Guidelines for the documentation of software in industrial computer systems *(The Institute of Electrical Engineers, 1985)*
- Guides of software quality *(Electronic Engineering Association)*
- Software Engineering Standards *(Institute of Electrical and Electronic Engineers (USA Branch))*
- The STARTS Guide *(Department of Trade and Industry)*
- TickIT — Guide to Software Quality Management System Construction and Certification using EN29001 *(Department of Trade and Industry)*

Software Inspection

One of the fundamental criteria for a secure business environment is reliability and availability. IT is now, and will be for a long time, the nucleus of many businesses. Any failure within the IT system will at best cost a substantial amount of money and at worst put you out of business. Consequently, software development must rigorously impose strict Quality Criteria in order to reduce the likelihood of software error to zero.

Software inspection started back in the 1970s with the now famous 'Fagan Inspection' paper. Michael E. Fagan at IBM developed 'statistical quality control methods' to control a software project he was managing in 1972/74. The project was to translate Assembler Language to PLS. His achievements in this project led to the publication of his process. Later AT&T Bell Labs. started to use the method reporting improvements in their development process of 14% increase in productivity, better tracking and phasing plus early defect detection.

By 1990, the culmination of work from Carole L. Jones and Robert Mays (1985), all from IBM, enhanced Fagan's inspection technique, developing their defect prevention process as additions to Fagan's defect correction process.

Throughout this period an ANSI/IEEE standard was released — 729(1983) IEEE Standard Glossary of Software Engineering Terminology defining inspection as '... a formal evaluation technique in which software requirements, design, or code are examined in detail by a person or group other than the author to detect faults, violations of development standards and other problems'.

It also defines the objective of software inspection as

' .. to detect and identify software elements defects. This is a rigorous, formal peer examination that does the following:

(a) verifies that the software element(s) satisfy its specification;

(b) verifies that the software element(s) conform to applicable standards;

(c) identifies deviation from standards and specification;

(d) collects software engineering data;

(e) does not examine alternatives or stylistic issues'

It is obvious that in order to safeguard against the security implications of bad/ineffective software, that you must preferably catch and correct the problems at an early stage. Prevention is better than the cure.

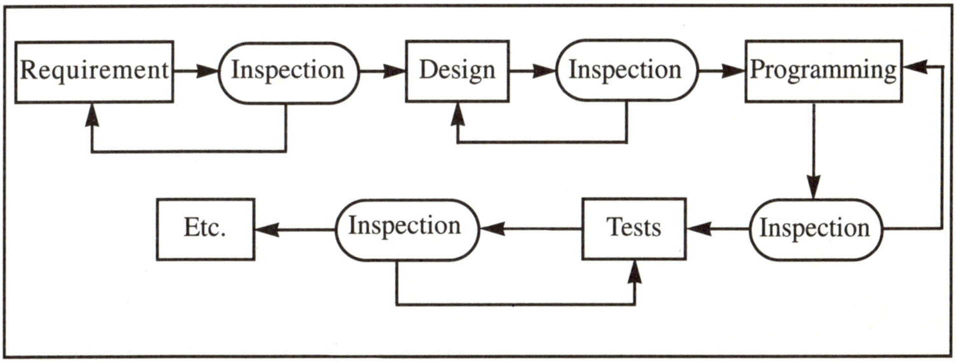

Figure 4.10

Figure 4.10 depicts product software inspection taking place within the development life cycle, with each inspection feeding results back to each development stage. Each stage will produce a 'product' (document or code) that has by default various defects. The purpose of inspection is to look at it through a microscope so that each defect can be discovered and any corrective action executed.

This process can be described at each development stage as follows:

Requirements stage:

– Initiate inspection:

- define inspection objectives;
- define who is going to do the inspection;
- check the product;
- log issues-errors found.

– Improve product (Edit);

– Go back to Inspection if appropriate

This inspection process fits neatly into BS5750 within clauses 4.4, 4.5, 4.9 and 4.10, as the whole process would go through each clause.

TickIT described below formalizes and documents this process by using BS5750 part 1 (ISO9001) towards the production and management of software development.

TickIT — Software Standard

TickIT is mainly a certification scheme that assists developers in the definition of quality within software (any software including security software) and how it can be achieved. It is devised by IT professionals and supported by the Department of Trade and Industry and the British Computer Society.

The TickIT manual is composed of five sections, namely:

- Part 1, Introduction;
- Part 2, ISO 9000-3 Guidelines for the application of ISO9001 to the development, supply and maintenance of software;
- Part 3, Purchasers' Guide;
- Part 4, Suppliers' Guide;
- Part 5, Auditor's Guide.

Since TickIT is based around ISO9001 (BS5750) the reader is referred back to the previous section for specific IT Security example within each clause associated with BS5750 and consequently TickIT.

Part 1 — Introduction

This provides information on costs of certification, benefits and quality, highlighting the following areas:

- cost of assessment and certification and the benefits of being certified;

- TickIT quality themes giving information on the setting up of a Quality Management System;
- types of assessments available, first, second or third party assessments and how to get accredited with the TickIT certificate. The reader is referred to Chapter 6 in this publication for further information on these types of assessments and audits.

It also describes four models for certification purposes, e.g.,

Model 1. — Complete Information System Supply (e.g., System House)

System Development —> Manufacture, software replication —> Supply and Maintenance

Examples of this could be a complete Access Control System encompassing Hardware and Software. In the above model the organization has the responsibility for the systems development, manufacturing, software replication, supply and maintenance.

Model 2. — Information System Supply (Software) (e.g. Software House)

System Development —> Software replication —> Supply and Maintenance

In this model the organization does not supply the hardware, although the developer still has the responsibility of verifying performance on the client's system,. Example of this could be software encryption for an EDI service.

Model 3. — Information System Supply (Package based)(e.g., Software product vendor)

Software package development —> Software replication —> Supply and Maintenance

In this model the system may be developed using multiple packages or only one package. Example of this could be the use of a PC tool as part of a Backup Facility.

Model 4. — Customer support and maintenance (e.g., a third party)

Software modification and enhancement —> Software replication —> Supply and Maintenance

In this model the development activity consists of software modifications and enhancement to a supplier system, eg., EDI service modifications.

All these models include:

- software forming the fundamental control facilities of computer hardware (e.g., Operating Systems);
- software providing development facilities, such as compilers, linkers and testing tools;
- software supporting applications, such as transaction processing, Database Management Systems, etc.;
- software providing applications, such as stock control, Management Information Systems, etc.;

- software embedded within a device, providing control of facilities for that device;
- analytical software used in engineering.

Part 2 — ISO9000-3, Quality Management and Quality Assurance Standards, Part 3, Guidelines for the application of ISO 9001 to the development, supply and maintenance of software.

This section provides a detailed description of the standard, using its own numbering system. Its contents include:

1 Scope — description of ISO9000 and the use of ISO9001 to organizations developing, supplying and maintaining software.

2 Normative references — terms of reference based on:

- ISO 2382-1:1984, Data Processing — Vocabulary — Part 01: Fundamental Terms;
- ISO 8402:1986, Quality — Vocabulary;
- ISO 9001:1987, Quality Systems — Model for quality assurance in design/development, production, installation and servicing;
- ISO 10011-1:1990, Guidelines for auditing quality systems — Part 1: Auditing.

3 Definitions

- Software (intellectual creation comprising of the programs, procedures, rules and any associated documentation);
- Software product (complete set of computer programs, procedures and associated documentation and data);
- Software item (any identifiable part of a software product);
- Development (all activities to be carried out to create a software product);
- Phase (defined segment of work);
- Verification (the process of evaluating the products of a given phase to ensure correctness and consistency);
- Validation (the process of evaluating software to ensure compliance with specified requirements).

4 Quality system — Framework — this defines the supplier/purchaser management role within a Quality Management System and in terms of software development.

4.1	Management Responsibility	[ISO9001:1987, 4.1]
4.2	Quality System	[ISO9001:1987, 4.2]

4.3	Internal Quality System Audit	[ISO9001:1987, 4.17]
4.4	Corrective Action	[ISO9001:1987, 4.14]

5 Quality system — Life-cycle Activities — software development life-cycle model is discussed here, giving particular attention to planned quality related activities.

5.1	General	
5.2	Contract Review	[ISO9001:1987, 4.3]
5.3	Purchaser's requirements spec.	[ISO9001:1987, 4.3 and 4.4]
5.4	Development Planning	[ISO9001:1987, 4.4]
5.5	Quality Planning	[ISO9001:1987, 4.2 and 4.4]
5.6	Design and Implementation	[ISO9001:1987, 4.4,4.9, 4.13]
5.7	Testing and Validation	[ISO9001:1987,4.4,4.10,4.11,4.13]
5.8	Acceptance	[ISO9001:1987, 4.10 and 4.15]
5.9	Replication, Delivery and Installation	[ISO9001:1987, 4.10,4.13,4.15]
5.10	Maintenance	[ISO9001:1987,4.13, 4.19]

6 Quality System — Supporting Activities — this section covers areas that assist in the control, monitoring, tracking, identification and use of the final software product.

6.1	Configuration Management	[ISO9001:1987,4.4,4.5,4.8,4.12,4.13]
6.2	Document Control	[ISO9001:1987, 4.5]
6.3	Quality Records	[ISO9001:1987, 4.16]
6.4	Measurement	[ISO9001:1987, 4.20]
6.5	Rules, practices and conventions	[ISO9001:1987, 4.9 and 4.11]
6.6	Tools and Techniques	[ISO9001:1987, 4.9 and 4.11]
6.7	Purchasing	[ISO9001:1987, 4.6]
6.8	Included software product	[ISO9001:1987, 4.7]
6.9	Training	[ISO9001:1987, 4.18]

Part 3 — Purchasers' Guide

This section addresses the need to reduce the level of failure of projects involving software due to the lack of well defined quality criteria. This problem stems from the very nature of software (e.g., ease of change, volatility, etc.) and its development process plus the lack of supplier commitment on design.

This section describes how a purchaser's quality needs should be defined within a purchaser — supplier agreement and in relation to ISO9001, highlighting the importance of:

- Management Responsibility (ISO 9001:1987 4.1.1, 4.1.2 and 4.6.4);
- Standards (ISO 9001:1987 4.4.2);
- Methods and Tools (ISO 9001:1987 4.8 and 4.11);
- Assessment and Accreditation (ISO 9001:1987 4.6.3);
- Contractual Requirements (ISO 9001:1987 4.3);
- Verification, validation and testing (ISO 9001:1987 4.4.5).

Part 4 — Suppliers' Guide

In a similar way to the previous section, this section addresses the requirements on a supplier. In particular it describes the main Quality System and Control Elements of supplying software. Within the Quality System Elements it describes in detail:

- Implementing and Maintaining a Quality System
  [ISO9001:1987, 4.1.2 and 4.2 — this defines scope and objectives of the Quality System];
- Managing the Organization and its interfaces
  [ISO9001:1987, 4.1.2.1, 4.1.2.2 and 4.4.2.2 — this establishes clear communications lines and responsibilities];
- Reviewing
  [ISO9001:1987, 4.4.5 — provides the assurance that specific requirements are being met];
- Documenting Projects and Products
  [ISO9001:1987, 4.5.1 and 4.5.2 — conveys relevant information when needed and in the appropriate manner];
- Recruitment, Training and Staff Development
  [ISO9001:1987, 4.18 — maintains staff morale];
- Configuration Management
  [ISO9001:1987, 4.4.6, 4.8, 4.12, 4.13 and 4.14 — controls and administers each 'product' of the development life cycle];
- Backup, Security and Archiving
  [ISO9001:1987, 4.5 and 4.15.3 — provides protection against loss];
- Quality System Reviews and Audits
  [ISO9001:1987, 4.1.3 and 4.17 — reviews the Quality System according to standards];
- Procurement
  [ISO9001:1987, 4.6, 4.7 and 4.10.1 — assures products against a quality criteria];
- Progress Monitoring and Reporting
  [ISO9001:1987, 4.3 and 4.4.2 — project monitors against plan and solves potential problem before they arise];

- Non-conforming Material

  [ISO9001:1987, 4.13 — makes sure that bad products are identified and dealt with accordingly];
- Corrective Action

  [ISO9001:1987, 4.13.1, 4.14 and 4.20 — ensures that procedures are in place to identify and correct non-conforming products];
- Quality Information

  [ISO9001:1987, 4.1.3, 4.2, 4.14, 4.16 and 4.20 — metric collection process].

Within the Quality Control Elements it describes in detail:

- Identify Task [ISO9001:1987, 4.3];
- Prepare Proposal [ISO9001:1987, 4.3];
- Initiate Project [ISO9001:1987, 4.3 and 4.4.2];
- Analyse Requirements and Specify System [ISO9001:1987, 4.4.3];
- Produce High Level Software Design [ISO9001:1987, 4.4];
- Produce Detailed Software Design [ISO9001:1987, 4.4];
- Code and Unit Test [ISO9001:1987, 4.4 and 4.10]
- Integrate and System Test [ISO9001:1987, 4.10 and 4.11]
- Perform Acceptance Test [ISO9001:1987, 4.10 and 4.16]
- Handover/Release [ISO9001:1987, 4.4.4, 4.12 and 4.18]
- User Training [ISO9001:1987, 4.4.4 and 4.18];
- Storage and Shipment [ISO9001:1987, 4.15];
- Replication [ISO9001:1987, 4.10, 4.11 and 4.15];
- Deliver and Install [ISO9001:1987, 4.15];
- Maintain and Enhance [ISO9001:1987, 4.19];
- Support [ISO9001:1987, 4.19];
- Phase-out Product [ISO9001:1987, 4.19].

Part 5 — Auditors' Guide

This provides general information on auditing and Quality Management System assessments. Within this section it includes a full description of the European IT Quality System Auditor Guide which is utilized by the Information Technology Quality Sector (ITQS).

ITQS is a European Recognition Arrangement which has been provisionally accepted by the European Committee for IT Testing and Certification (ECITC).

Since this section simply describes the requirements for an auditor and how to carry out the audit, it is not deemed applicable to describe its contents in this publication. However, readers are referred to Chapter 6 if they require further information on Auditing.

TickIT takes BS5750 part 1 and applies it specifically to software development in a structured and rigorous manner. It is the basis for confirming a developer's ability to produce Quality Software. Accreditation on this scheme goes some way in reducing the threat of bad bug-ridden software and therefore reducing the security risk this brings. However, it is important to note that Murphy's Law does not take into account any Quality Standard or Accreditation and will still impact when least expected. What TickIT and similar standards does is to impose a documented management and administration process that is auditable and traceable. Although software may still fail, we can now evaluate and pinpoint exactly where it has failed and correct the problem and even avoid it occurring in the future.

No amount of inspection and the use of standards will solve poor design, organizational, cultural or production problems. The keys to successful Quality Control within Software Development (as is to the production of any other product) are:

- good communications throughout the company;
- publicity of the results (Quality achievements);
- dedication by *all*;
- commitment by *all*;
- understanding;
- not being too ambitious at the beginning;
- have a champion to market Quality;
- enrol Management;
- training.

It is not in the nature of reason to regard things as contingent, but as necessary
... Baruch Spinoza

5

IT Security Standards and their Relation to Quality

As with quality, the need for IT Security Standards stems from the need to maintain an overall effective quality business environment. This need has further been highlighted by the ever increasing threats to information from hackers, viruses, etc. The main aim of these security standards is to facilitate a guide for business users to help them implement a secure cost-effective IT environment. Such a guide will assist business users to answer their main basic criteria — do security standards, like quality standards, supply them with a product or service that is fit for its purpose?

IT Security Standards definitions have been evolving since the late 1960s. Most maintain the simple nucleus that addresses the confidentiality, integrity and availability of information. Therefore, it is inevitable that a certain amount of re-inventing the wheel goes on when a new security standard is defined. The main offering comes from the USA, namely the 'Trusted Computer System Evaluation Criteria (TCSEC)', more commonly known as the 'Orange Book', published by the US Department of Defense's National Computer Security Center (NCSC) in 1983, significantly revised in 1985. In the UK, the DTI in collaboration with the Communications, Electronics Security Group (CESG) of the Government Communications Head Quarters (GCHQ) have produced a series of 'Green Books' of a similar nature to their US counterpart. Similarly Germany produced in 1989 their 'Criteria for the Evaluation of the Trustworthiness of Information Systems' (ZSIEC) and in France, they produced their 'Red-White-and-Blue Book' — 'Catalogue de Critères Destines à Évaluer le Degrée de Confiance de Systèmes d'Information' (SCSSI).

With the colours of the rainbow defining various national IT Security Standards and since all are based on a harmonized nucleus of IT Security needs, it is inevitable within such an environment of European harmony that a European definition should evolve. This evolution comes from four of the leading European nations in the field of IT Security Standards — Germany, France, UK and Netherlands. Between them in 1990 they came up with a new set of harmonised IT Security Evaluation Criteria (ITSEC). This immediately became known as the White Book.

This chapter therefore attempts to describe two of the most important IT Security Standards (e.g., the Orange Book and the White Book) in relation to the business need for them and consequently the need for quality throughout the organization (i.e., not only of a physical product but also within internal and external services).

Orange Book

Security within various environments has been addressed within the US Department of Defense (DOD) in their manual 'Trusted Computer System Evaluation Criteria', or 'Orange Book'. This section attempts to describe the more pertinent issues within this Orange Book which apply to IT Security and Quality.

Background

The 'Trusted Computer Systems Evaluation Criteria' manual, alias 'Orange Book' or 'TCSEC' was first published in August 1983 by the US DOD Computer Security Centre. It defines criteria to be used in terms of sensitivity levels in the evaluation and selection of Automatic Data Processing (ADP) systems being considered for the processing and/or storage and retrieval of sensitive or classified information by the Department of Defense.

This manual is written in a very academic manner, defining three basic security 'control objectives':

The Security Policy: this section identifies that before it is possible to protect a computer system it is necessary to define exactly what is to be protected. This definition spells out how an IT product or service will be protected, giving it a minimum Quality criteria to adhere to. The security policy therefore defines the protection requirements in terms of the perceived threats, risks and objectives of the organization. Obviously this means that a system is only deemed to be secure with respect to the enforcement of the security policy.

Note that a well defined security policy within any organization is of paramount importance, since without it, it would be impossible to measure the effectiveness of the security measures being taken to secure the environment. In essence what we have here is the clear understanding of how an organization will handle security. This therefore forms our terms of reference when reviewing the security of an organization (just like the Quality Manual defined by ISO9001) and can be used for auditing purposes.

Accountability: this defines a fundamental issue of security, namely that of individual accountability, i.e. it would be of no use to have a 'secure' system in which the designated administrator does not know who or what has done what. This reinforces the Quality ethos of making everyone responsible for their actions and how that action will impact on their environment.

Assurance: this deals with providing the guarantees that the security policy has been correctly and accurately interpreted and cannot be distorted. In a similar way to stamping a Quality kite mark on a product or service to show that the product adheres to a 'minimum' quality standard, we also need to 'assure' ourselves that an IT system adheres to a minimum Security Standard.

Certification Levels

There are four sensitivity divisions defined in the Orange Book, with Division D being the lowest, offering no security protection, through to A which offers substantial protection. Within each division there have also been defined various intermediate classes of trusted system definitions. These intermediate classes have been defined in order to identify those systems that:

- are viewed to offer significantly better protection and assurance than would systems that satisfy the basic requirements for their evaluation division.

- would eventually be developed in order that they would satisfy the requirements for the next higher evaluation grade.

It is important to note that upwards movement from division to division (i.e. from grade C to B) generally takes a substantial amount of investment and effort on the part of the developers, implementors and the users of the systems. However, it is worth pointing out that each 'higher' class or sub-class is defined in the Orange Book as a superset of the one below it, therefore, class C2 is a superset of class C1.

Division D — Minimal Protection

This division contains only one class, with all systems by default belonging to this division. In essence this is the minimal set of quality standard required of a system encompassing **integrity** and **reliability** as its fundamental features, two Quality elements required of any system but most of all a secure system. Would you have any confidence in a system or product without these two features?

Division C — Discretionary Protection

This division is divided into two sub-classes called 'C1- Discretionary Security Protection' and 'C2 - Controlled Access Protection', with C1 being lower than C2. Here is where we start to define countermeasures to protect against malicious or accidental security breaches. Again in a Quality environment we need to ask ourselves whether the system is fit for its purpose and consequently does it adheres to C1 or C2? We could take as our baseline for evaluation (both in terms of Security and Quality) that adhering to C1 is our minimum Security/Quality Criteria. However, such an adherence implies that you may be omitting vital security measures (see end of section).

Class C1 is based on the concept of a trusted computing base (TCB), which identifies and authenticates users on the system. This is normally achieved by the [55]TCB requesting and verifying a user name and password prior to granting access to the system or allowing the user (or process) the privilege of performing some action.

Note that once access has been granted, protection from reading and writing to a file, and/or executing a program, is normally at the discretion of the file/program owner. For example, if Michelle creates a document, i.e. a spreadsheet called *Accounts*, she is the *owner* of said document, which means that she can *read, write* or *alter* it at will. Michelle is also a member of the 'Office System Group (OSG)'. As the owner of *Accounts* she can grant or deny access to this document to other members of the OSG, for example, she can grant them access to read *Accounts* but *not* write to it. Michelle could also give different types of access (e.g. execute) to this file to other users and groups at her discretion.

In Class C2 users are individually accountable for their actions, through the use of login procedures, resource [56]isolation/control and audit trails[57]. This means that as well as the authentication and access control rules applicable to C1, within this class, systems must also enforce a more stringent discretionary access control policy than required in C1.

Division B — Mandatory Protection

This division is divided into three sub-classes called 'B1- Labelled Security Protection', 'B2-Structured Protection' and 'B3-Security Domain', with B1 being lower than B2 and subsequently B2 being lower than B3.

Any system that meets any of the sub-classes defined within Division B must first meet Division C totally, with Division B adding a mandatory access control[58] (MAC) policy.

In this Division, who has access to what is no longer exclusively at the discretion of the owner (or creator) of the file, although the discretionary access control rules must still be obeyed before access is granted. Here, the system itself must maintain and control a security policy that has been defined in advance by the system administrator within certain guide-lines required by this Division. In Class B1, we must first have a statement of the security policy (whether formal or informal) to be followed.

With this, sensitivity labels[59] can subsequently be associated to each subject[60] or object[61] that is under the mandatory access control system of the TCB. Any data that is to be imported/exported into or from the trusted system must also be labelled by an authorised user, with all such action being auditable. Hence the main aim in this environment is to have a multi level security approach to the system.

This means that different levels of protection for varying types of information are held on the same host system.

Class B2 includes structured protection with a clear formal security policy with access control mechanisms enforced for all subjects and objects in the system.

A further requirement at this level is the use of a trusted communications[62] path between the user and the TCB for initial login and authentication.

Covert channels are also addressed at this level, where a covert channel is defined as any communications channel than can be used by a process to transfer information in a manner that violates the system's security policy.

Class B3 defines security domains (in terms of various access control lists) with the system being tamper-proof and small enough for analysis and testing. This includes a security administrator role, more audit mechanisms and system recovery procedures.

In much the same way as with Class C, fitness for purpose is the fundamental issue here. It becomes a major issue when applying this Division (especially Class B3 and possibly even Class B2) to identify to what level within a business you require such a level of security. Obviously, within Defence and similar organizations, the application of this level is fundamental to its requirements for security and consequently applying B2/B3 would satisfy their fitness for purpose issue of security (see end of section for further details).

Division A — Verified Protection

This division verifies the design and implementation of the operating system using formal methods. There is no fundamental difference between systems at class B3 and those in this division. The basic difference is mainly in terms of the use of a formal security verification mechanisms used to assure that the controls employed in the system can effectively protect the information.

Summary

The above brief description of the Orange Book should give the reader a feel for the different levels of functionality required for a secure system. Note that this book is over 130 pages in length. However, for commercial and normal government security, the Orange Book Standard (i.e. Military Standard) is generally considered to be 'over the top'. It is again like wanting the quality of a Rolls Royce for the production of a Mini — what exactly is required and will satisfy the business need? This is the question that needs to be answered, not whether we are trying to satisfy some esoteric security criteria.

In order to attempt to evaluate whether adherence to the Orange Book supplies you with a product or service that is fit for purpose, you must define your 'statement of requirements' for a secure system. In general, secure systems will control access to data. In order to meet this basic criterion (i.e., define a system as 'trustable') you must define the three basic 'control objectives' discussed in the Orange Book:

- Security Policy;
- Accountability;
- Assurance.

Therefore by applying these three key security objectives, specifically to a security product or service, you can move onto defining what certification level is appropriate for your business. Consequently adhering to this certification level could prove your 'fitness for purpose'.

Typically, most organizations would only be interested in maximum assurance up to B1 and even this may be too high. Experience of various systems shows that given the auditing and authentication requirements within class C2, along with certain basic additions (e.g. password ageing, password formal control, action on failed login and shadow passwording) to the Orange Book, would be sufficient for many.

It must be remembered that the Orange Book was written to deal with the requirements of the US DOD and hence reflects this. Therefore many of the features identified within it are seldom required within normal business practices.

This is not to say that the Orange Book supplies business with every conceivable security aspect possible. There are various areas not considered. For example:

- *Automatic Log Out* — This is the most often requested requirement in business and omitted from the Orange Book. Much unauthorised access has been perpetrated via an 'inactive' terminal. Since the Orange Book is directed at MoD sites, it assumes that all terminals are within a secure perimeter. However, within business this is seldom the case, e.g., a reception area. Reception areas are ideal places for 'visitors' to get access to the system, when the reception area is unmanned;
- *Password Ageing* — This is of paramount importance in any environment. It is surprising that this has been omitted from the Orange Book — again possibly it assumes that people do not leave the military. However, in business this is not the case. How many times have 'contractors' in business been given a password which stays active after their departure?;
- *Password Format Control* — Although the Orange Book discussed passwords in its broadest sense — access control and authentication (C2 and B) it does

not give any guidelines on how these should be used and managed. Surprisingly, again, trust is placed on the users to be knowledgeable enough to use proper passwords (i.e., not trivial and/or guessable);

- *Terminal Dependent Login* — A very useful way of protecting the use of remote terminals is to make sure who is utilizing the links by restricting access via them, i.e., only a previously defined user can use a receptionist terminal. Anyone else, even if they are an authorised user to the system, will not be able to use the receptionist terminal. Care, however, should be taken with this restrictive practice as it may go against company policy of working outside your normal working environment;
- *Time of Day/Day of Week Access Control* — Another purely business requirement is to define the hours and day of work of an individual, e.g., a reception area may be manned Mon-Fri 9-12, 13-17. In the military, it is assumed that a terminal is always required, therefore the Orange Book does not cater for this requirement.

Going back to the start of this chapter, I defined the aim of any security standard as providing business with an easy cost-effective secure IT environment. By doing this it then supplies business with an IT secure product or service that is 'fit for purpose'. Looking at the Orange Book specifically applied to business, it does not supply this. It does set the scene for a secure environment but assumes that you had a secure area to work with in the first place.

As a guide for better security it is 'fit for purpose'. However, business applicability, to date, is limited, unless you are a military style establishment, e.g., a Police Force. This is reflected in the development of the UNIX Operating System in recent times, although several manufacturers are producing their UNIX version with adherence to C2 or even up to B2 as a standard to meet. They are also adding general security features normally seen in mainframe operating systems environments but not mentioned in the Orange Book.

As has been mentioned at the start of this chapter, in order to give business and IT manufacturers some clear guidelines, in 1989 the Department of Trade and Industry (*dti*) in the UK developed the Green Book for commercial security products, with other European countries developing a similar document. These documents were later harmonised to form the Information Technology Security Evaluation Criteria (ITSEC), the 'White Book', Europe's answer to the kaleidoscope of colours, in May 1990 which is described in the next section.

European Security Standard (ITSEC)

Information Technology Security Evaluation Criteria (ITSEC) requires that information security products and systems must have appropriate security functions such as access control and auditing. It defines ten classes, five of which have the same functional requirement as the Orange Book in the previous Section. It also takes some of its functionality from ZSIEC, published by the German Information Security Agency in 1984.

Background

Its main objectives are:

- to have an agreed set of terminology throughout European participating countries;
- the security fundamentals would be applicable to all sectors, from defence to commercial organizations;
- coverage of the complete IT system;
- coverage for all classes of security policies;
- confidentiality, integrity and availability is its nucleus;
- compatibility with other *de facto* security standards, particularly TCSEC.

These objectives go some way towards establishing flexible IT Security criteria with differentiation between functionality and assurance. In terms of functionality it addresses the 'Target of Evaluation (TOE)' or product in terms of its security functions as a whole, i.e., the why, what and how of security, in a similar way to defining the quality criteria of a product or service. In terms of assurance, it defines the correctness as seven hierarchical evaluation levels and effectiveness of the TOE or product.

These two areas (functionality and assurance) covered by ITSEC form the basis for the possible evaluation of a security product or service. But, like any other standard, before one can judge whether a product meets a certain level within this standard and consequently its fitness for purpose one must first decide what operational requirements are needed of the security product or service. One must also identify the threats which the Target of Evaluation is expected to deal with.

Once this is established one can proceed and define the security objectives needed for the product or service. From the security objectives can be derived the security functions required to achieve the intended effect and an indication of the appropriate evaluation level to which to aim for. This then becomes the Target of Evaluation with pre-defined functional elements.

Let's first look at the TOE and its Functionality Classes.

Functionality Class F1 — (Corresponds to C1 in Orange Book)

This class is divided into two areas: Identification and Authentication[63] (i.e., the system should identify and authenticate users prior to all other interactions between the system and the user) and Access Control[64] (i.e., the system shall distinguish and administer access rights between users, groups and objects). In terms of how this function applies to meeting any quality criteria, it defines the need for technical standards within two basic elements of security administration (Authentication and Access Control). This requirement is at the heart of any secure system of any worth and consequently forms the basic quality criteria to achieve.

Functionality Class F2 — (Corresponds to C2 in Orange Book)

This class has five areas of concern: **identification and authentication** (i.e., it shall be unique and for every interaction the system shall be able to establish the identity of the user); **access control** (i.e., it shall be possible to restrict a user's access privileges in terms of Read, Write and Delete as appropriate); **Accountability**[65] (i.e., a log should be maintained that lists the use of Identification and Authentication mechanisms, attempted access to objects, creation and/or deletion of objects and actions by authorised users); **Audit**[66] (i.e., tools should be available to examine the accountability files) and **Object Reuse**[67] (i.e., all storage objects returned to the system shall be treated before reuse by other subjects, in such a way that no conclusions can be drawn regarding the preceding content).

Building upon F1, it enhances the security requirements needed for a 'complete' secure system, making it fit for a 'secure' purpose. Its main addition is in the audit facilities required to manage and control the system. This audit can become not only a way of supplying confidence in the system but also a way of assuring that the security of the system adheres to standard. This ties in nicely with BS5750, Clause 4.7, where an internal audit is carried out to verify whether quality activities comply with planned requirements.

Functionality Class F3 — (Corresponds to B1 in Orange Book)

This is split into two major areas: access control and accountability. Within access control it defines the need to provide all subjects and storage objects with attributes in terms of mandatory access rights. Said access rights are defined in two parts. Part One has hierarchically ordered values, Part Two represents a set — i.e., an attribute A is said to dominate an attribute B if Part One of A is hierarchically >= Part One of B and Part Two of B is a proper subset of, or equal to, Part Two of A.

Accountability is defined within four events:

- use of the identification and authentication mechanism, including the authorisation of the user;
- attempted access to an object which is subject to the administration of rights including the attribute of the object;
- creation or deletion of an object which is subject to the administration of rights including the attribute of the object;
- actions by authorised users or roles affecting the security of the system including the attribute of the object to which the action related.

This clause enhances Class F2 in terms of access control mechanisms, elaborating on how to manage and administer access control in terms of hierarchical subsets. This is defined in terms of the attribute of a subject (agent, user, etc.), e.g., a user can only access an object (data, information, etc.) if and only if his or her attributes (i.e., their access rights) are higher than that assigned to the object.

This links straight into the accountability of an action. This, as is seen above, is defined in terms of four events. As already described earlier in this book, accountability is one of the fundamental concepts of Quality Management. Within BS5750, Clause 4.1.2.1 (Responsibility and Authority) defines the need for '.. the responsibility authority and the interrelation of all personnel ...' in order to manage the whole Quality Process.

To manage the whole process within access control you need very specific technical mechanisms to control 'access' to something. Failure of the said mechanism implies that you have a 'non-conforming' situation. Again BS5750, Clause 4.13 (Control of non-conforming product) defines the requirement to establish and maintain procedures 'to ensure that a product that does not conform to specified requirements is prevented from inadvertent use'. Non-conforming here is defined in the four events described above.

Each class (F4-F10) elaborates and enhances specific security elements within:

- access control;
- audit;
- identification and authentication;
- accountability;
- reliability.

The applicability of quality procedures to each is defined in terms of specific fitness for purpose of each class. So if you were to audit against F7, the main areas of concern would be reliability of service — if your requirement is to have a service 100% of the time. F7 conformance would imply fitness for purpose of a system required for 100% of the time.

Functionality Class F4 — (Corresponds to B2 in Orange Book)

This class elaborates on three areas of concern: identification and authentication where identification and authentication shall be handled via a trusted path; access control in terms of group access, roles and attributes and audit (this includes all of 'F' plus where the system should be able to audit known events).

Functionality Class F5 — (Corresponds to B3/A1 in Orange Book)

This class elaborates on three areas of concern: identification and authentication (as in F4); access control (as in F4 plus with specific roles being separated within its own unique domain) and audit (as in F4 plus a mechanism for monitoring the occurrence of any event).

Functionality Class F6 — (Systems with High Integrity needs)

This class has four areas of concern: identification and authentication (as in F5 plus the identification of users prior to any interaction between the system and the user takes place); access control (as in F5 plus the administration of access rights of users, roles and processes); accountability (as in F2 plus the system shall contain accountability components that logs the definition or deletion of types, the assignation of a type to an object and the granting or revocation of access rights) and audit (as in F2 in its entirety).

Functionality Class F7 — (No Orange Book equivalent)

Its main area of concern is the 'Reliability of Service[68]', where the system should be able to recover from any failure without loss of service at any time.

Functionality Class F8 — (No Orange Book equivalent)

This class identifies four areas of concern: identification and authentication (as in F6 plus prior to the establishment of a connection, the peer entity shall be identified and authenticated); data exchange[69] (i.e., methods of error detection and correction shall be applied); accountability (as with F2 part 1 plus the monitoring of data exchange) and audit (as in F2).

Functionality Class F9 — (No Orange Book equivalent)

This class is intended for systems with high demand on the confidentiality of data during data exchange. Therefore its main area of concern is confidentiality and the use of encryption.

Functionality Class F10 — (No Orange Book equivalent)

This class is intended for networks with high demands on CIA of data exchange. It contains three elements, Identification and Authentication (as in F8); Accountability (as in F8 plus connection establishment and special data exchange transactions) and Audit (as in F2).

As has been seen, these classes can be viewed in terms of Quality as were the divisions within the Orange Book. Each class defines a specific requirement to be met by the system that covers specific security needs. If a product or TOE meets a certain level and that is the required level for the business then we have met both the security and quality requirements for the system and it can be said that it is 'fit for purpose'.

In terms of assurance, ITSEC defines seven levels applicable to the development process, development environment and operations. The following tables summarise these levels (Note level E0 is omitted since this represents inadequate assurance).

	E1	E2	E3	E4	E5	E6
Security Target	X	As for E1 ——>				
Formal Security Policy Model				X	As for E4	
Informal Architectural Design Spec.	X	As for E1 ——>				
Semiformal Architectural Design Spec.				X	As for E4	
Formal Architectural Design Specification						X
Informal Detailed Design Specification		X	As for E2 ——>			
Semiformal Detailed Design Specification				X	As for E4	
Informal External Interface Spec.	X	As for E1 ——>				
Informal Interface Specification Security Component		X	As for E2 ——>			
Informal Mapping Security Object to Low Level		X	As for E2 ——>			
Design Vulnerability Analysis				X	As for E4	
Identification of Covert Channels				X	As for E4	
Implementation Vulnerability Analysis					X	X
Source Code			X	As for E3 —>		
Mnemonic of the Object Code						X
Test Documentation		X	As for E2 ——>			
Independent Objectives testing	X	As for E1 ——>				
Separation Security Relevant to Non Security Relevant		X	As for E2 ——>			

Table 5.1 Level Requirement — Development Process

	E1	E2	E3	E4	E5	E6
Complete List of Provided Documents	X	As for E1 ——>				
Configuration List		X	As for E2 ——>			
Configuration Control		X	As for E2 ——>			
Authorised Changes Only		X	As for E2 ——>			
Tool Support				X	As for E4	
Version Control and Audit Facility				X	As for E4	
Audit Information on Changes				X	As for E4	
All objects subjects to configuration control					X	X
Relationships between objects					X	X
All tools subject to configuration control						X
Completely Defined Roles						X
Acceptance Procedure			X	As for E3 —>		
Integration Procedure					X	X
Standardized Implementation Languages			X	As for E3 —>		
Evaluated or Tested Compilers				X		
Validated Compilers					X	
Approved Compilers						X

Table 5.2 Level Requirement — Development Environment

	E1	E2	E3	E4	E5	E6
User Documentation	X	As with E1 ——>				
Administration Doc.	X	As with E1 ——>				
Identification of Control and Information	X	As with E1 ——>				
Description of Admin. Procedures	X	As with E1 ——>				
Description of Security Relevant Aspects	X	As with E1 ——>				
Impact of Different Configurations	X	As with E1 ——>				
Delivery of Generation Procs.	X	As with E1 ——>				
Approved Distribution Procedure		X	As with E2 —>			
Audit of System Generation		X	As with E2 —>			
Secure Start up and Ops.	X	As with E1 ——>				
Insecure Maintenance Description		X	As with E2 —>			
Administrator Informed before HW/SW Maintenance			X	As for E3 —>		
Administrator Acceptance before HW/SW Maintenance					X	X
Secure Restart procs after HW/SW Error				X	As with E4	
Self-Testing Procedures in HW		X	As with E2 —>			

Table 5.3 Level Requirement — Operations

Summary

As both the Orange Book and ITSEC stand at the moment (1994) they go some way in defining specific security procedures that need to be taken to assure a system. However, both may be viewed by many to be of little use, since they may be considered to lack commercial awareness and tangible procedures. Both standards provide a fundamental nucleus of security issues and define how systems can be evaluated against a set of basic security criteria. They do not, however, explain how the security of a system should be evaluated. But you can say this of most standards, including the Quality Standards.

As with any standard initiative, failure to keep pace with technology will be seen as a fundamental flaw. However, most standards, although seemingly developed in a vacuum, must evolve in order to meet future expectations. This evolution does not necessarily mean the rewriting of the standard itself but how one uses it and applies it to your own particular need. This application will define the utility of the standard in days to come.

I submit that security standards can be applied to any business (whether public or private) organization in terms of the basic philosophy it proposes but requires creativity or lateral thinking in terms of applying quality based standards for:

- techniques in risk analysis;
- methodologies;
- format of security policies;
- techniques in auditing security;
- codes of conduct / practice.

This creative link between Quality and Security will bring with it substantial benefits within a secure environment that is fit for purpose.

He has a right to criticize who has
a heart to help
... Abraham Lincoln

6

Auditing IT Security in Terms of Quality

The aim of audits within the IT environment is to ensure that what is being audited adheres to formal procedures and more importantly whether what is being audited is effective. This encompasses the inspection of systems and procedures by an 'autonomous' individual not intimately involved in the system or procedure's development or day-to-day use.

Many would argue that the auditor consequently can be too divorced from what is being audited, with many auditors criticising the failures after they have occurred but not recommending any preventative measures beforehand. What tends to occur in this situation would be more destructive than anything else — both in the relationship between the auditor and the audittee and in future audit exercises. This is, to say the least, bad auditing practice.

The function of an auditor is to examine the accuracy of the system and records kept by a business function. He is also responsible for reporting any discrepancy identified. This definition applies to all types of audits, including IT Security.

However, although the auditor may in theory do the same job, there are some minor differences in the audit process. Table 6.1 below describes the main differences between financial and product specific audits.

	Financial Audits	Product Specific Audits
Status	Confirms status of business in relation to accepted standards	Must create basis for and form status of each product
Predictions	Company's state economic well-being	Future status of product
Measurement	Mostly in financial terms.	Financial terms plus adherence to standards
Record Keeping System	Format dictated by legal regulations and professional standards	Standard system based on ISO 9001
Existence of IT	Minimal records needed to start audit.	Database of 'controls' used to start audit.
Recommendations	Usually few or none, often restricted to management of accounting system	Often required and may cover any aspect of the product or its management.
Qualifications	Customary to qualify statements if conditions dictate.	Qualifications focused on shortcomings of audit process, e.g., lack of funds, time, etc.

Table 6.1

However, a spanner in the works will be to what depth you can (or want to) apply an audit. There are several practical constraints that may limit this. Time and money are two of the main problems, as lack of either of them will limit the depth of investigation and consequently what is presented in the audit report.

Assuming that you have the prerequisite resource to effectively conduct a quality/ security audit you can quickly see that the actions taken by the audit will impact on the 'quality' of the whole system. As discussed in Chapter 2, the main cost of quality is the 'cost of prevention' — auditing within these two environments (Quality and Security) act as preventative measures.

All this leads to providing a 'Quality and Secure' environment, where the audit process will assist in maintaining said environment. In order to do this we have to redefine how we look at IT Security and the IT systems it uses. So how do we audit IT Security in terms of Quality?

In terms of IT Security an auditor will wish to identify the areas where fraud, misuse and error are most likely and institute controls before they occur. These controls could be, for example, (list not exhaustive):

- Access Control (e.g., restriction matrix of staff versus access type);
- Validity Checks (e.g., an exceptionally large sum in a payment field);
- Control Totals (e.g., total value of a group of product fields);
- Batch Totals (e.g., total of a group of tasks);
- End User Prints (e.g., when any change occurs to a file own by a user, the user receives a print of when, who, etc. to action the event);
- Exception Reports (e.g., a report highlighting all payments over a certain limit);
- Audit Trails (e.g., a secure log of all transactions).

Evaluating the information collected from these controls will provide the auditor with the data he/she requires on how a 'system' is functioning and whether there are any errors or discrepancies, plus, more importantly, how future 'attacks' could develop.

Consequently, auditing becomes much more of a preventative measure instead of prescriptive measure, since the audit task will not simply be to check the controls but to advise on how best to safeguard the 'system'.

Auditing IT Security in terms of Quality can only really be viewed if we define IT security and its constituent IT parts as products, in a similar way to how PRINCE defines the project planning environment. In other words, every deliverable is a product, providing product based planning via the use of product breakdown structures, flow diagrams, descriptions and transformations. Therefore, we can define IT Security in the same way, i.e., Security Products are defined as any individually produced entity that has a purpose, composition and quality criteria. These products could therefore be defined to be entities like contingency plans documents, risk analysis reports, encryption algorithms, standards, training, access control mechanisms, etc. etc.

By doing this we can go forward and implement an IT Security Quality Plan that encompasses all the elements of quality monitoring, assurance, control and rectification. This definition ensures that the IT Security products conform to a pre-defined set of criteria and have been produced according to agreed methods and standards. With this in mind we can progress and define how the IT Security products will be audited, whether formally or informally. The choice of these would depend on the type of IT Security product that is being 'audited'. Certain IT Security products are obviously going to be more critical than others and consequently will require more rigorous audits, which could be based on adhering to the Quality Standard ISO9001 or a Technical Standard like POSIX.

This chapter is therefore divided into two major sections, Formal Quality Audits and Informal Quality Audits.

Formal Quality Audits

What is a Quality Audit?

Before I describe how a formal quality audit is conducted what exactly is a Quality audit? Clearly any company that decides to carry out audits as part of their quality management system must have a clearly defined method that describes the procedures for planning, doing, reporting and following-up an audit.

The British Standard Institute have a Guide (BS7229, 1989) that defines the Quality Auditing Process. It covers audit objectives and responsibilities, corrective actions and follow-up, giving guidance on:

- Initiation (includes scope and frequency);
- Preparation (includes review of documentation);
- Execution (includes opening meeting, examination, evaluation, collecting evidence, observations and closing the audit);
- Report (includes report submission and retention)

In addition to this, ISO have ISO-9000-3 'Guidelines for the application of ISO 9001 to the development, supply and maintenance of software' that alludes to the auditor's tasks as:

- Confirm that the documented Quality Management System has the capability to be effectively used in the management of the organization and the products of the organization;
- Confirm by way of sample auditing the use of the documented Quality Management System in the management of current work;
- Confirm that the practices employed meet the methods and principles contained in ISO9001.

In order to adhere to these guidelines it is very important that a clear statement of fact is defined at an early stage that describes the company's objectives for auditing, for example:

> *IT Security Quality Audits Definition*: A systematic investigation of the intent, the implementation and the effectiveness of selected IT Security Products that are part of the IT Security quality systems of an organization or department.

As can be seen, part and parcel of this definition is that the audit itself must be systematic in the way it is organized and conducted, carrying the full support of management. The intent of the system must be established within the Quality documentation, e.g., manuals, procedures, work practices, etc. Consequently, the audit must first examine what system is intended (i.e., the intention against the requirements of the standard being utilized, for instance, the use of security access control mechanism within a specific software environment). Secondly, the audit needs to establish the extent to which that intent has been implemented.

Thirdly, the audit must demonstrate whether the practice is effective in achieving what the procedure or mechanism being examined is designed to achieve.

It must be noted that within any audit it would be virtually impossible to examine every conceivable activity, document, decision, etc. that an organization generates during a normal working day. It is therefore important to understand that the audit will only examine selected random aspects of the quality system and this must be understood by all concerned in the audit — the auditor and the auditee.

This means that audits cannot by their very nature establish that there are any errors or problem areas within the quality system. Within the audit many areas will be found to be working very effectively; but it is the factual evidence of failures that is utilized by the auditor and the reporting of this which forms the audit report. This particular ethos means that the auditor must always assume that the auditee is innocent until proven guilty; even in the absence of information to the contrary, the benefit of the doubt must go to the auditee.

Therefore in general a Quality audit can be defined as:

> A formal exercise, undertaken by an independent competent individual(s) that checks against aides-memoires, procedures, checklists, policy, to independently examine objective evidence and verify or otherwise compliance with specified requirements.

This means that as part of the quality system, audits are carried out against written formal procedures and checklists with formal reports and records. Compliance with specified requirements could mean meeting contract requirements, quality manuals/procedures/instructions, Quality Assurance standards (e.g., BS5750) and Technical Standards (e.g., POSIX, DES). By its very nature, independence is a major requirement and therefore implies that self-audits are not encouraged.

Within most audits a large amount of information is collected. It is the auditor's responsibility to use that information which is directly relevant to the audit process and is therefore based on fact. Opinions, feelings, rumour, etc. cannot form a base for objective conclusions and, if acted upon normally, creates little progress and much confusion. Therefore, only objective evidence must be used, i.e.:

- evidence which exists (it is important that when conducting the audit that meticulous notes are kept of every item);
- uninfluenced by emotion or prejudice;
- can be stated;
- can be documented;
- is about quality;
- can be quantitative;
- can be qualitative;
- can be verified.

Audit Stages

Once these issues are understood, we can progress with the audit. Normally this will encompass two distinct stages. The first one is to collect information about and establish the intention of the quality system. This evidence may be produced in the form of a Quality Manual, which can be reviewed by the auditor to ascertain whether the system outlined in the manual complies with the standard being checked against.

The second stage involves the auditor 'visiting' the evaluation area and identifying specific areas within the manual that need to be checked in a physical manner. In the case of actually 'visiting' the evaluation area, this could simply mean attaining the 'product' which within IT Security could be the Security Documents, mechanism or procedure. Depending on the rigour required you may feel that simply attaining the security documentation is not enough. In such a situation physical evidence may be required in the form of independent security tests, e.g., an evaluation of the breakability of an encryption algorithm, smart card, etc.

Types of Audits

This leads onto defining the 'type' of audit we are conducting. If you refer to the numerous number of accounting and financial publications, you will come to realize that there are numerous types of audits; however, for our purposes, there are really only two types — external and internal audits. Within the external arena they can be split up into two, Second and Third party audits. Internal audits are normally classified as First party audits.

First party audits are audits that an organization conducts on itself in order to confirm to their management that the system or product being audited is working effectively and according to standards. The reasons for conducting this type of audit are therefore obvious and include:

- Quality Assurance standards requires it;
- Control mechanism utilized by management;
- To correct noncompliances before external bodies find them;
- As a powerful tool for auditing improvements.

In terms of IT Security, this is the normal type of audit carried out by most organizations. However, as mentioned earlier, time and money may be lacking (or the foresight in management to see the benefits) and consequently this type of audit is seldom effective.

Second party audits are audits carried out by one organization on another and are those which originally promoted the idea of quality assurance since major purchasers would audit its suppliers in order to assure themselves that the service or product that they were going to receive met their requirements. Within IT Security there are numerous examples of this type of audit, for instance, the auditing of a supplier of a Wide Area Network, an EDI service, a security mechanism, smart cards, etc. Each audit will depend greatly on the final application of the service or product and subsequently the breadth of the audit will change accordingly.

Therefore, the reasons for conducting this type of audit are therefore also obvious and include:

- Quality Assurance standards require it;
- Provides input to selecting, grading and improving suppliers;
- Provides help to improve quality systems of suppliers;
- Increases mutual understanding of quality requirements;
- Leads to 'supply chain tuning' towards JIT, TQM, etc., by improving the interface with suppliers.

This type of audit has recently had a major impetus in the EDI market-place. Security within this environment is of paramount importance, with a major concern being the avoidance of 'repudiation' — i.e., the user may deny sending or receiving a transaction or message. When this situation involves vast amounts of money (movement of), it is, of course, not allowed.

Finally, Third party audits are audits that are conducted by a company on another company on behalf of a third organization. The basis of this type of audit is that upon payment of a fee to a certification body, they will assess an organization's quality management system to an agreed standard (normally ISO9001). Depending upon the result of the assessment the organization would become a registered company on their list. All this indicates is that at the time of the assessment, the company had the systems potentially capable of supplying the product to their customer's requirements.

Within the IT Security arena, an example of this type of audit could be classed as the assessment of a security mechanism by an authorized body (e.g., a national DOD) within a 'black box' which 'stamps' an adherence label on it. This could be adherence to the US Orange Book, ITSEC or similar standard.

Preparing for the Audit

It is obvious that the reason for the audit and type of audit may vary but the processes of preparation and performing them do not by any great degree — what may differ is the scale of effort needed.

Once we have established that an audit needs to be carried out (normally a management decision) we then need to define/investigate the objective of the audit (e.g., is it to assess an organization for its degree of compliance to a standard or to determine where the major problems lie or the company's ability to produce a product?). These objectives could be numerous and diverse, but it is very important that whatever they are, they are understood by everyone concerned with the audit and are applicable.

Consequently, we will need to establish the scope of the audit. If an organization produces various types of IT Security Products and parts of products but the client conducting the audit is only interested in one in particular, then that will limit the effort.

Once this is established it is normal practice to nominate the 'lead auditor' or managing auditor, whose responsibility it is to plan, perform and report the audit. This lead auditor will need to be briefed on the objectives and scope of the audit and is required then to specify the resources required (e.g., man-days to carry out the audit, personnel, etc.). In general, a group of auditors is formed of two or three people.

When the audit team is ready to proceed, an opening meeting with management is always recommended. At this meeting the basic audit terms of reference are discussed plus how the audit will be conducted. At this stage the documents within the auditee's company that define the quality system (or product(s)) will be passed onto the auditing team. This could include a Quality Manual, procedures, product specification, etc.

Once this has been carried out the team will normally split up into separate teams of one, two or three. Each team will require an escort and consequently will take up auditee time. Although the teams may be working separately, they share a common goal and will meet regularly to review progress. These review get-togethers will form the basis for checking across different team responsibilities.

The Audit Programme

Although the previous section briefly described the process of conducting an audit as simply getting together with the management team and then proceeding with the audit, in practice this task is much more complicated.

A detailed Audit Programme is required to defined exactly what will occur before, during and after an audit. Normally the programme will take a 'top-down' approach, with the auditor and his/her team following the quality process from inception to its conclusion. For instance, if the auditor is conducting a Quality review of the whole Quality System, then it would be obvious to start with the Quality Manual and follow the manual's structure compared to whatever Quality Standard is being adhered to. This may mean following a specific order through the system and examining how it is being handled along the way. This has a basic advantage that the auditing team will attain an overall view of the company.

Within this programme it would be very beneficial for the audit team to have ready a checklist of tasks to do. The purpose of this checklist would be to collect objective evidence to permit an informed judgement, about the status of the quality system or product. In order to come to that informed judgement, the auditors must take samples from selected areas and check for implementation and effectiveness in the areas chosen. The checklist defines that sample. The benefits of the checklist include formality (as it defines the audit procedure), imposes research, helps maintain the pace of the audit, keeps the audit objectives clear, can act as a historical reference, reduces workload on auditor during the audit and assures auditee of auditor's professionalism.

This checklist must therefore be as representative as the auditors are able to make it, bearing in mind the objective of that audit. Within it, broad and specific questions must be raised to ascertain the reality of the quality system or product.

An example checklist that an auditor may have could be the following:

Auditor's Checklist

Area audited:	IT System Development Department
To Examine:	* IT Security Manual (Copies No. A21 and A22) * Quality Manual (Copy No. 5) * Previous Audit Reports
To Assess:	* Are they there? * Are they assessable?

To Examine:	* Development Controls
To Assess:	* Are Cost of rework figures collected? * What is done with this information? * Do new systems incorporate appropriate controls? * Are systems tested independently before they are accepted for line use? * Are amended systems subject to testing? * Is the first live output scrutinised from new or amended systems by an independent auditor?
To Examine:	* Operational Controls
To Assess:	* Are controls checked regularly? * Are reported incidents investigated? * Are controls amended if they are found to be ineffectual? * Are audit records available? How secure are they? * Check non-conformance against IT Security Manual * Are controls functional? Are any missing? * Is test data collected? What happens to the test data once it is collected? * Are recovery procedures adequate? * Are any mandatory security requirements bypassed/ ignored/etc.?
To Examine:	* The system as a whole
To Assess:	* How are specific areas to be protected (e.g., physical access evaluation ca be achieved through the use of locked doors, etc.)? * Are the facilities to be protected distributed geographically? If so, how are they controlled? * Is the system as a whole covering CIA in its entirety?
To Recommend:	* Specific alterations or amendments to controls (if needed)` * Additional controls (if required) * Short terms plan of action * Long term strategic plan * Awareness training requirements.

In summary, preparation for an audit is the most important task an auditor should undertake in order to conduct an effective audit and consequently not miss any pertinent issue. He or she should therefore make sure that they have covered the following points:

- Have they established the purpose of the audit?
- Has the scope been defined?
- Do you know all the Quality Assurance requirements?
- Has the Lead Auditor/Manager been appointed?
- Has the scale and resource requirements for the audit been identified?
- Have you considered past audit results?

- Have you considered current problems?
- Have you considered management concerns and priorities?
- Has an agenda and programme for the audit been established and agreed?
- Have the required checklists been defined?

Performance of the Audit

Within this section an audit has a number of distinct events, namely:

(a) *Opening Meeting*; also called the Pre-Audit or Start-up meeting and its main aim is to act as a preamble to the audit where the objectives and terms of reference of the audit are discussed. Normally this is the first time that the auditor and auditee may have met and therefore the way it is carried out will set the style and tone of the consequent audit. A typical agenda for such a meeting could be:

- introduction of personnel;
- audit purpose and scope;
- review of audit programme;
- guide(s) for the team(s) (this is an important part of the audit as these individuals will show the auditors where departments, files, etc. are situated);
- logistics (e.g., transport, protective clothing, lunch, etc.);
- clarification (i.e., there may be points that the auditor wish to raise);
- reporting methods (e.g., the way non-conformances are to be presented to auditee);
- confidentiality and restrictions;
- sampling scheme.

(b) *The Audit Itself*; at any time within the audit process, the number of people can be quite high and can include the audit team, the guides, a management representative and staff of the area, observers, etc. etc. It is obvious that this number must be kept to the minimum, it is up to the Team Leader to maintain control of his/her audit.

Once the auditor gets to their objective audit area it would be wise to run over their audit plan for that area with his/her guide. The amount of time the auditor spends talking to management and staff in each area about the audit will vary according to how much information was originally supplied to the auditors. If the auditor finds no evidence of discrepancies he or she should go to their next task quickly. A witch hunt in one area will probably not produce the desired non-conformances and will detrimentally affect the audit schedule as a whole (apart from the obvious consequence of adding bias to the sample). Therefore the auditor must simply satisfy his/her sampling objective, looking for objective evidence in all its forms. Deficiencies should be investigated to the depth judged to be necessary.

The most important aspect of this audit is to remember to take meticulous notes of all that is observed. These notes should include reference to documents, items identification, batch numbers, statements and who said them, etc. A most apt quotation which truly depicts the basis for all research and should be every auditor's motto is:

'.. I keep six honest serving men,
They taught me all I know,
Their names are What and Why and When
and How and Where and Who...'
— *R. Kipling,* The Elephant Child.

(c) *Recording Discrepancies*; Although an audit should not be viewed as a witch-hunt, it must always be remembered that one of the main objectives of an auditor is to identify non-conformances and to honestly and completely record the facts. The reason for such non-conformances could be because:

- the written procedure does not comply with the requirement of the standard;
- the written procedure has not been put into practice in the way the procedure describes;
- the practice is not effective.

If any of the above situations arises, then a statement (normally written) of non-conformance must be drawn up in a format understandable both to the auditee and the audit team.

- The corrective action necessary will often be carried out by people not present at the audit. A common format for writing non-conformances could be the following:
- Exact observation of the facts;
- Where was it found?
- What was found?
- Why is it a non-conformance?
- Who was there?

An example of such a non-conformance report could be as follows:

IBERTALIA S.A. IT SECURITY AND AUDIT DEPARTMENT NON-CONFORMANCE REPORT			
Observation: Use of Un-Encrypted modem for transatlantic communications. Where: IT System Development Department, User Support Section.			
AUDITOR	GUIDE	Technical Standard Ref.	IT Security Manual Ref.
MD	FG	DES	1.7.11[70]

Table 6.2

Note, the use of local terminology is advisable.

(d) *Closing Meeting*

This is the final meeting of the audit and normally is the formal presentation of the findings and conclusions of the audit. The following issues are normally covered within it:

- objectives and scope, as terms of reference for the audit;
- outline of the way the audit will be formally reported;
- limitations since the audit is only a sampling exercise the possibility may still exist after an audit that deficiencies are present in areas not covered by the audit;
- presentation of non-conformances;
- summary, conclusions and recommendations;
- clarification;
- agreement.

Informal Quality Reviews

Within National Quality Standards like BS5750, formality and strict procedural auditing is a requirement. However another type of audit is the informal quality audit otherwise known as the Quality Review. The main difference between them is the informality of the proceedings (e.g., within the Quality Review it could simply consists of a desk check of a product by one or more people) but the objective and output of both is identical.

Therefore the main aim is to obviously improve product quality by identifying any errors or non-conformances as early as possible.

Remember that at the beginning of this chapter we mentioned that the best way to treat IT Security was to defined it within the confines of a product based environment. Within Quality Reviews you will be reviewing the product in terms of pre-defined quality criteria. This is depicted graphically in Figure 6.1 below

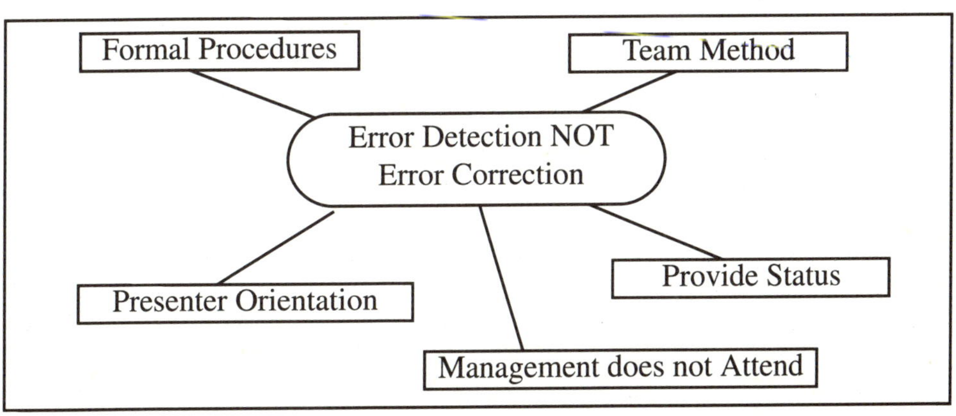

Figure 6.1 Quality Reviews

The Roles within such a Quality Reviews include:

- Chairperson, whose main responsibilities include:
  - selection of reviewers to represent all parties interested in the product;
  - control agenda of allocation of time;
  - ensure each reviewer makes a reasonable contribution;
  - avoid repeated identification of the same error by several reviewers;
  - log errors/non-conformances by each reviewer;
  - involve reviewers in deciding overall acceptability of the product;
  - involve the presenter in estimating completion if follow-up action is required.
- Presenter, whose main responsibilities include:
  - present the product for review in its intended final form;
  - state any special objectives/quality criteria for the product;
  - keep the overview short and concise;
  - record the reviewers' comments by highlighting on the presenter's copy of the product;
  - walk-through the product in page order and respond to the reviewers' recorded comments.
- Reviewers, whose main responsibilities include:
  - prepare thoroughly;
  - look for strength as well as weaknesses in the product;
  - contain comments within the product Quality criteria;
  - make your comments and identify errors, do not try to correct the product in the meeting;
  - use checklist/experience to help identify missing items in the product;
  - on completion of the review, all reviewers become jointly responsible for the quality of the product.

Within such Quality Reviews there are three distinct steps (see Figure 6.2) to follow.

Step 1 The aim of this step is to examine the product under review and to create a list of questions (or errors) for the review. Each reviewer will study the product and supporting documents, annotate the product and complete their Quality Review Question List.

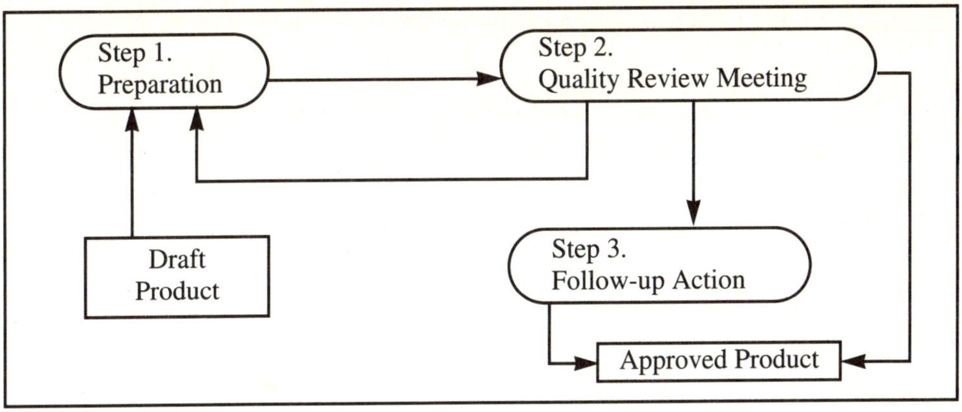

Figure 6.2 Quality Review Steps

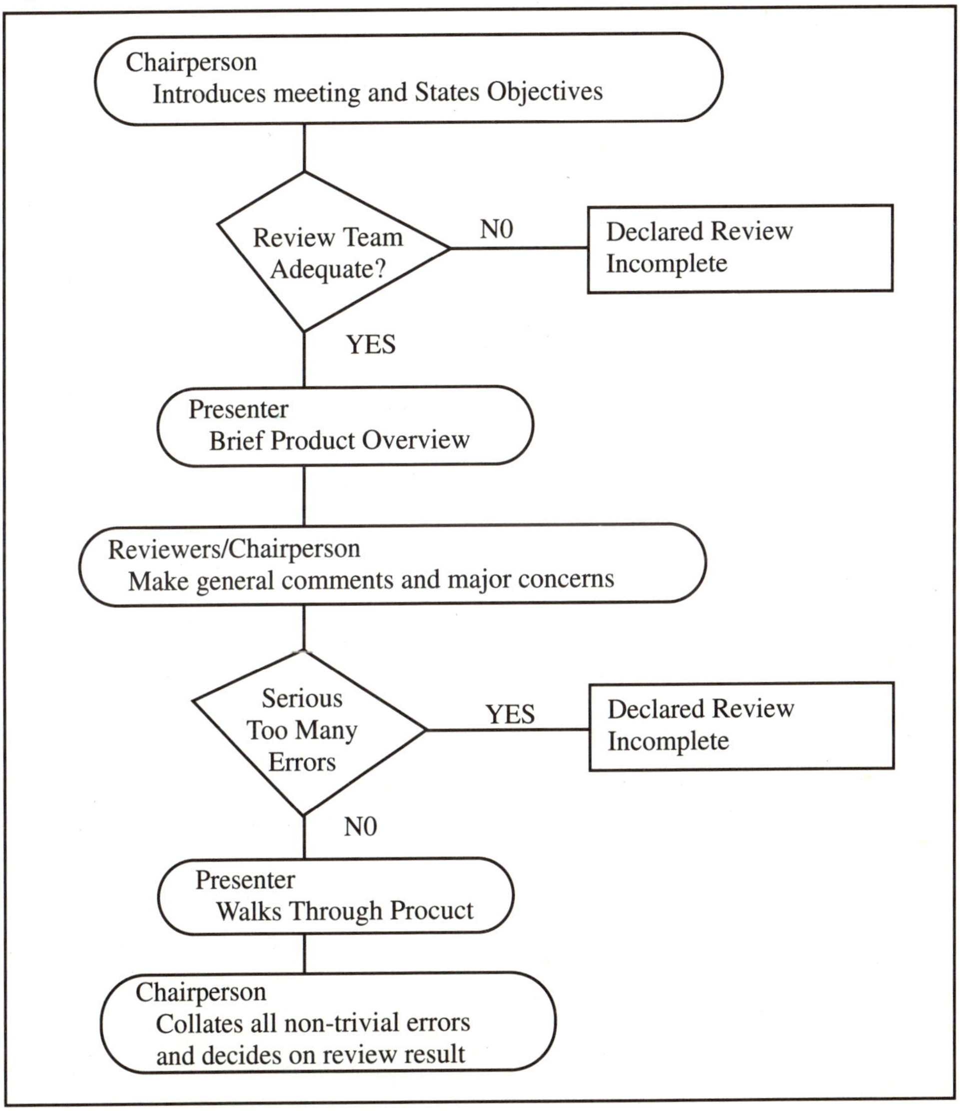

Figure 6.3 Quality Review Meeting

Step 2 The aim of this step is to agree a list of actions required to complete or correct the product if any non-conformances exists. This is depicted graphically in Figure 6.3 .

Step 3 The aim of this step is to ensure that all actions identified on the Quality Review Follow-up Action List are dealt with. This is depicted graphically in Figure 6.4 below.

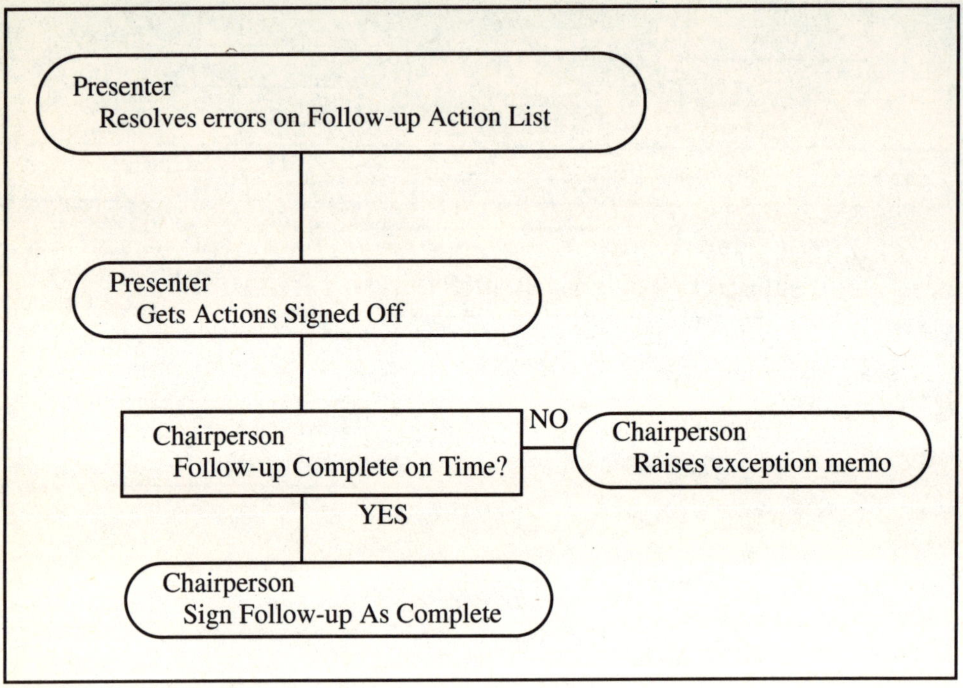

Figure 6.4 Quality Review Follow-up

In essence, therefore, even though this may be classed as an informal quality audit procedure it is still a structured way of reviewing all aspects of a product properly. The degree of formality in the Quality Review process will vary from product to product, with key products being 'formally' Quality reviewed and audited.

Now this is not the end. It is not even the beginning of the end.
But it is, perhaps, the end of the beginning.

... Sir Winston Spencer Churchill

Appendix A

ISO9001 - Example Quality Manual

Quality Manual

IBERTALIA S.A.

Ctra. Valencia Klm. 124.5
Polígono Industrial Los Olivos
Alicante
España

		Page No. 01
Standard Title:	*ISO 9001 – 1987 (Quality Manual)*	
Std Ref. No.	*QM.93/94*	
Issue No.	*010*	Change No. 02
Issue Date:	*26th August 1993*	Change Date: 8th June 1994

Foreword

Ibertalia's mission is to increase constantly its determination to serve its customers better and improve its operating efficiency. It will do this by consistently providing quality of products and services that meets our customer's needs and our contractual obligation. Our main goals are:

- To respect and understand our customer.
- To maintain well-trained dedicated personnel to serving our customers.
- To become the Number One travel company servicing Europe, USA and the Far East.

The company has some years of experience in the Travel Industry with its headquarters based in Alicante, Spain and offices in France, Italy, UK, USA, Hong Kong and Russia. The level of success achieved so far can only be maintained and improved upon by our continuing commitment and support to Quality. However, while Quality procedures can be defined and supported by senior management, their effectivenes can only be assured if staff at all levels within the organization work towards it. The aim therefore is to promote quality awareness by all the means available.

This Quality Manual is devoted to describing the activities within Ibertalia SA, the aim of which is to provide products and services to satisfy the standards and requirements of our customers.

The objective of the company's Quality Assurance System is to deliver the agreed product through a policy of set procedures operated throughout the whole organization.

Declaration

The provisions of this Quality Manual have been reviewed by me and I certify that it will be used as a working document, enforced by the Quality Assurance Manager, who has the required authority for ensuring that the requirements are implemented and maintained.

Signed ______________________

Chairman and Managing Director.

		Page No. 02
Standard Title:	*ISO 9001 – 1987 (Quality Manual)*	
Std Ref. No.	*QM.93/94*	
Issue No.	*010*	Change No. 02
Issue Date:	*26th August 1993*	Change Date: 8th June 1994

0 Introduction

1 Scope

2 Applicable References

3 Definitions

4 Quality System Requirements

- 4.1 Management Responsibility
- 4.2 Quality System
- 4.3 Contract Review
- 4.4 Design Control
- 4.5 Document Control
- 4.6 Purchasing
- 4.7 Purchaser Supplied Product
- 4.8 Product Identification and Traceability
- 4.9 Process Control
- 4.10 Inspection and Testing
- 4.11 Inspection, Measuring and Test Equipment
- 4.12 Inspection and Test Status
- 4.13 Control of Non-Conforming Product
- 4.14 Correction Action
- 4.15 Handling, Storage, Packing and Delivery
- 4.16 Quality Records
- 4.17 Internal Quality Audits
- 4.18 Training
- 4.19 Servicing
- 4.20 Statistical Techniques

5 List of Quality Procedures

6 List of Work Instructions

7 Company Organizational Chart

		Page No. 03
Standard Title:	*ISO 9001 – 1987 (Quality Manual)*	
Std Ref. No.	*QM.93/94*	
Issue No.	*010*	Change No. 02
Issue Date:	*26th August 1993*	Change Date: 8th June 1994

0. Introduction

The Ibertalia quality assurance procedures and work instructions have been compiled to ensure that products are designed and produced to the requirements of ISO9001, 1987 (BS5759: Part 1: 1987 equivalent).

The responsibility for ensuring compliance with contract requirements and standards has been delegated to the Quality Manager by the Chairman, although quality is the responsibility of every member of staff.

Section 4 of this manual is numbered using the identical paragraph numbers to the requirements of the Standard.

0.1 Distribution and updating of the manual

The Quality Manager or his appointed deputy is responsible for distributing and updating the manual. The Quality Manager alone is responsible for the administration of all amendments. Each holder of the Quality Manual is responsible for maintaining and keeping his/her copy up to date when revisions are issued by the Quality Manager.

All copies of the Quality Manual shall be returned to the Quality Manager when a registered holder resigns, or for any other reason has no further need of it.

The Quality Manager may distribute 'uncontrolled copies' of the Quality Manual to external companies. These copies will not be updated. He will periodically review and revise the quality system.

1. Scope

This Quality Manual describes and designates the management responsibilities and procedures in design, planning, procurement, manufacture, inspection, test and quality that will be applied by Ibertalia SA to meet the requirements of ISO9001, 1987. The contents of this manual are mandatory and must not be altered or omitted without the written authority of the Quality Manager.

		Page No. 04
Standard Title:	*ISO 9001 – 1987 (Quality Manual)*	
Std Ref. No.	*QM.93/94*	
Issue No.	*010*	Change No. 02
Issue Date:	*26th August 1993*	Change Date: 8th June 1994

2. Applicable References

(i) ISO9001, 1987 — Quality Systems, Model for Quality Assurance in Design/Development, Production, Installation and Servicing.

(ii) ISO9000, 1987 — Quality Management and Quality Assurance Standards (Guidelines for selection and use).

(iii) ISO9004, 1987 — Quality Management and Quality Systems Elements Guidelines.

(iv) ISO8402, 1986 — Quality Vocabulary.

(v) Ibertalia SA quality procedures and work instructions referred to in several sections in this document and listed in Sections 5 and 6 respectively.

3. Definitions

For the purpose of this document, the definitions given in ISO8402, 1986 - Quality Vocabulary shall apply.

4. Quality System Requirements

4.1 Management responsibility

4.1.1 Company Quality Policy

The objective of management policy is to ensure that products and services supplied by the company to our customers are fit for their intended purpose. This policy is implemented and understood at all levels within the company and is described in company procedures and work instructions. These company procedures and work instructions adhere to ISO9001, 1987.

		Page No. 05
Standard Title:	*ISO 9001 – 1987 (Quality Manual)*	
Std Ref. No.	*QM.93/94*	
Issue No.	*010*	Change No. 02
Issue Date:	*26th August 1993*	Change Date: 8th June 1994

4.1.2 Organization

4.1.2.1 Responsibility and Authority

Ibertalia SA Headquarters are based at the address shown on the front sheet of this Quality Manual. It is an independent company owned by Mancera Incorporated, Madrid, under the direction of Miss Isabel Mancera.

Ibertalia SA is a medium sized company, staffed by a mixture of professional staff and semi-skilled staff in the design and servicing of travel related products (e.g., propaganda items like T-Shirts, cups, maps, ethnic memorabilia, etc.) and travel servicing (e.g., air, sea, train and car tickets/vouchers). The Chairman and the Managing Director of Ibertalia SA is Mr. Juan Mancera who is the main authority over all matters pertaining to quality. Through the Quality Manager he has the responsibility of ensuring that procedures, work-instructions and documentation used by any member of staff are coordinated so that the products and services supplied to our customers are in full compliance with contract requirements. Note, Ibertalia supplies products both direct to the public and to smaller travel organizations.

The organization of the company is shown in Chart 1. Job Descriptions are held with the Personnel Department.

4.1.2.2 Verification Resources and Personnel

The need for in-house verification of design, procurement, manufacture, testing, installation and servicing of all Ibertalia SA products are identified in the company procedures and work-instructions. See Section 5 and 6 for details.

Inspection, internal audits and design reviews are carried out by staff independent of those responsible for the work being performed.

		Page No. 06
Standard Title:	*ISO 9001 – 1987 (Quality Manual)*	
Std Ref. No.	*QM.93/94*	
Issue No.	*010*	Change No. 02
Issue Date:	*26th August 1993*	Change Date: 8th June 1994

4.1.2.3 Management Representative

The Chairman and Managing Director reviews the quality system by assessing the results of internal audits and by arranging third party audits (ie., this is normally carried out by an independent consultant or the company accounts managers - Peters, Peters and Peters Associates, London). A file of planned and past reviews will be maintained by management with the details of results and corrective action.

4.2 Quality System

The elements of the Quality System include:

- (i) Applicable international standards;
- (ii) Formalized company procedures;
- (iii) Company work-instructions.

The effectiveness of the quality system is the responsibility of the Quality Manager will full support of the whole work-force and on behalf of the Chairman and Managing Director for the:

- (i) Coordination and monitoring of the quality system;
- (ii) Resolution of any non-conformances in the system;
- (iii) Implementation of effective actions to be taken by appropriate personnel to ensure compliance with specific requirements;
- (iv) Updating of quality control procedures, work-instructions, procedures and testing techniques as required;
- (v) Identification and preparation of Quality Records;
- (vi) Internal Quality Audits.

		Page No. 07
Standard Title:	*ISO 9001 – 1987 (Quality Manual)*	
Std Ref. No.	*QM.93/94*	
Issue No.	*010*	Change No. 02
Issue Date:	*26th August 1993*	Change Date: 8th June 1994

4.3 Contract Review

A contract is defined as an agreement, verbal or written, to perform a service (e.g., organize all travel arrangements for a client) or provide a product (e.g., produce a quality 'cup'), at some future time, for a price. It is the responsibility of the Branch Manager to conduct reviews of any activity that reflect on the ability of the company to meet the requirements of each order. He/she will involve the Quality Manager in the review of each contact involving non-standard items.

Sales and Contract procedure is defined in *IBQP.01 - Sales And Contract Procedure*

4.4 Design Control

4.4.1 General

Compliance to this clause is attained by verifying that the design criteria complies with the requirements and that completed designs satisfy user and design requirements. The implementation of company procedures is the mechanism by which control of design is achieved. Design within our company applies to all areas that supply our customers with a 'product', whether that be holiday memorabilia, a video or a brochure.

4.4.2 Design and Development Planning

For each product or service item, design and development is subject to a prior design description form agreed prior to the contract commencing. Said description must be in a written form (verbal descriptions are not accepted).

4.4.2.1 Activity Assignments

Design and verification activities are the responsibility of the Quality Department to ensure that adequate resources are provided so as to permit effective execution of the development. Individual design alterations are not permitted.

		Page No. 08
Standard Title:	*ISO 9001 – 1987 (Quality Manual)*	
Std Ref. No.	*QM.93/94*	
Issue No.	*010*	Change No. 02
Issue Date:	*26th August 1993*	Change Date: 8th June 1994

4.4.2.2 Organizational and Technical Interfaces

Technical interfaces will be at the Branch Management Level.

4.4.3 Design Input

Design requirements for holiday products are clearly identified by discussion with the customer. These are documented and agreed by means of the design description form. Incomplete or conflicting requirements of the contract are to be resolved prior to proceeding with the work.

4.4.4 Design Output

The design of holiday products must adhere to customer specification and performance needs, this is covered within *IBQP.02 - Performance Service Level.*

4.4.5 Design Verification

Original design data is independently verified for compliance with specific criteria and any project work is documented and maintained in a project file, adhering to the PRINCE standard.

Design is controlled by:

IBQP.03 — Holiday Service Design and Review

IBQP.04 — Contract and Sales Control

IBQP.05 — Request for Change

IBQP.06 — Configuration and Change Control

IBQP.13 — Project File Configuration Items

IBQP.14 — Project Management Standard — PRINCE

IBWI.01 — Marketing and Sales Design Drawing

		Page No. 09
Standard Title:	*ISO 9001 – 1987 (Quality Manual)*	
Std Ref. No.	*QM.93/94*	
Issue No.	*010*	Change No. 02
Issue Date:	*26th August 1993*	Change Date: 8th June 1994

4.5 Document Control

4.5.1 Document Approval and Issue

The procedures established cover all documents relating to the performance and quality of work in progress such as procedures, work-instructions and general office administration. The control of such documents is a task which is the responsibility of all, in order to authenticate the work undertaken.

The preparation, issue and change of documents is controlled to ensure that correct documents are being employed. Such documents, including changes, are reviewed for adequacy and approval for release by authorized personnel.

The approval of documents that form part of the final documentation will be a continuous process throughout any given contract. Proposed changes within the content of particular contracts initiated by either the company or its clients are agreed by the Branch and Quality Managers. A formal written transmittal, between both parties, on the nature of the change proposal and the action to be taken, is then sent.

A pertinent number of issues of appropriate documents are then brought under internal change control. The internal control of drawing issues is through a document register.

Document control is controlled by:

IBQP.06 — Configuration and Change Control

IBWI.02 — Archiving

Page No. 10

Standard Title:	*ISO 9001 – 1987 (Quality Manual)*	
Std Ref. No.	*QM.93/94*	
Issue No.	*010*	Change No. 02
Issue Date:	*26th August 1993*	Change Date: 8th June 1994

4.6 Purchasing

4.6.1 General

The purchase of material, components and services is the responsibility of the Administration Manager who shall endorse purchase orders raised by the branch. Where necessary a quotation will first be requested.

4.6.2 Assessment of Sub-Contractors

All sources of supply must be evaluated and approved by the Quality Manager prior to the placement of the order. The type and extent of the evaluation shall depend on the nature of the goods or services to be provided and the degree of previous experience with the supplier.

Where possible suppliers shall be ISO9001 accredited.

To enable the Quality Manager to carry out an onsite supplier evaluation, a checklist is available. Suitable suppliers will be placed on an approved suppliers list. The Quality Manager shall be responsible for ensuring that the records of suppliers' performance are kept and that regular assessments are made. A history of all rejected goods will be maintained in respect of individual suppliers and this will be used to monitor their performance. Suppliers regularly appearing on the rejected section of component preparation and conformity sheets are first advised that they must improve their quality. If no improvement is noted their names will be removed from the Approved Supplier List.

4.6.3 Purchasing data

All purchase orders will contain adequate data to enable the supplier to provide the correct quantity and quality of material or services requested. All purchase orders of a value of more that 500,000 ptas (or its equivalent in any other currency) will be reviewed and signed by the Managing Director.

		Page No. 11
Standard Title:	*ISO 9001 – 1987 (Quality Manual)*	
Std Ref. No.	*QM.93/94*	
Issue No.	*010*	Change No. 02
Issue Date:	*26th August 1993*	Change Date: 8th June 1994

4.6.4 Verification of Purchased Product

Facilities are provided at Ibertalia SA for customers to witness the production of holiday memorabilia at any stage of manufacture.

Purchase goods are controlled by:

IBQP.07 — Purchasing and Supplier Assessment

IBQP.08 — Goods Inwards and Inspection

IBWI.03 — Statistical Analysis

4.7 Purchaser Supplied Product

In some instances the customer may supply free issue material which will be treated as a purchased item and will follow the appropriate procedures, including inspection, storage and maintenance. If any such material is lost, damaged or otherwise unsuitable it shall be recorded and reported to the purchaser.

This is controlled by:

IBQP.07 — Purchasing and Supplier Assessment

IBQP.08 — Goods Inwards and Inspection

IBWI.03 — Statistical Analysis

4.8 Product Identification and Traceability

All material which has passed the goods inwards inspection is transferred to the appropriate store, segregated and individually identified where possible.

All packages containing products are marked with appropriate product identification labels, when in the manufacturing areas. Cartons or boxes are marked with similar labels for identification. Large items of equipment also have labels attached for identification.

		Page No. 12
Standard Title:	*ISO 9001 – 1987 (Quality Manual)*	
Std Ref. No.	*QM.93/94*	
Issue No.	*010*	Change No. 02
Issue Date:	*26th August 1993*	Change Date: 8th June 1994

This is controlled by:

IBQP.10 — Job Control

IBQP.11 — Control of Production

IBQP.12 — Stores

IBWI.04 — Product Identification and Traceability

4.9 Process Control

4.9.1 General

Manufacturing, assembly and testing operations are performed under controlled conditions. These conditions include work instructions and test procedures. Testing and inspection procedures, which define the method and sequence of all manufacturing operations and quality criteria, are provided.

4.9.2 Special Processes

From the final inspection sheets, data is collected for reporting the long term performance of products installed as operations systems. Appropriate records are maintained for analysis by design and manufacturing.

4.10 Inspection and Testing

4.10.1 Receiving Inspection and Testing

All goods that arrive at Ibertalia SA are received at goods inwards. The goods will be placed on the appropriate shelf in the goods inwards area to await inspection.

All finished items, sub-assemblies and assemblies are inspected and tested in accordance with appropriate specifications, and are identified as follows:

Green Label — Goods which have passed inspection

Yellow Label — Goods offered for concession since they do not meet requirements. These goods are kept in a secure storage area.

Red Label — Non-conforming goods — these are normally returned to the supplier

4.10.2 In-process Inspection and Testing

During the course of product assembly, inspection and tests are carried out in accordance with applicable documented procedures and specifications. The results of inspection and tests are recorded on jobsheets attached to each batch of manufactures items to cover various stages in their assembly. Non-conforming items are identified, noted and reported to the Quality Manager for segregation and appropriate action.

4.10.3 Final Inspection and Testing

All assemblies are tested functionally prior to despatch. Such tests can be witnessed by the client. Test processes and acceptance criteria are agreed with the client prior to testing. Note that no test certificates are produced unless the client specifically asks for one.

4.10.4 Inspection and Test Records

Material certificates, test results, etc. are all collated as a contract progresses and are maintained in the specific client control file. At the end of the contract the file is archived according to *IBQP.15 - Security Procedures (Information Storage).*

Inspection and test are controlled by:

IBQP.16 — Calibration of Measuring Equipment

IBQP.10 — Job Control

IBQP.08 — Goods Inwards and Inspection

IBQP.17 — Non-conformance, Corrective Action and Records

IBQP.18 — Final Inspection and Test

IBWI.03 — Statistical Analysis

		Page No. 14
Standard Title:	*ISO 9001 – 1987 (Quality Manual)*	
Std Ref. No.	*QM.93/94*	
Issue No.	*010*	Change No. 02
Issue Date:	*26th August 1993*	Change Date: 8th June 1994

4.11 Inspection, Measuring and Test Equipment

All inspection and test equipment used to verify compliances is subjected to regular in-house calibration checks where applicable.

Each instrument is allocated a unique reference number and is checked against master references which are traceable to International Standards. A label is fixed to each instrument stating the date on which it was last calibrated; a record of this is kept with the Quality Manager and adheres to *IBQP.16 — Calibration of Measuring Equipment.*

4.12 Inspection and Test status

Goods inwards status is referenced in Section 4.10. The inspection status of items (i.e., with each item within a batch being uniquely identified) during assembly is recorded in the client control file. A copy is attached to each batch for information.

Completed items are not released until final inspection and testing has been carried out. Note this can be done in the presence of the client if the client wishes, however if this occurs the client will be asked to sign-off the acceptable items as they are produced.

This Section is covered by *IBQP.10 — Job Control.*

4.13 Control of Non-conforming Product

The control of non-conforming products is executed at the goods inwards inspection area where they are segregated and stored in a locked area. Items that fail during assembly and test are also segregated and stored in a locked area and actioned by the Quality Manager.

A record is always kept of any non-conforming items and sent to the Quality Manager. This section is covered by *IBQP.17 — Non-conformance, Corrective Action and Records.*

		Page No. 15
Standard Title:	*ISO 9001 – 1987 (Quality Manual)*	
Std Ref. No.	*QM.93/94*	
Issue No.	*010*	Change No. 02
Issue Date:	*26th August 1993*	Change Date: 8th June 1994

4.14 Corrective Action

At various stages of a contract, it is sometimes necessary to initiate corrective actions to ensure compliance with the standards and more importantly customer requirements. The corrective actions carried out depend on the circumstance of the items. This is covered by *IBQP.17 - Non-conformance, Corrective Action and Records.*

4.15 Handling, Storage, Packaging and Delivery

4.15.1 General

Items and completed assemblies are moved around the workshop by OSCAR, the Ibertalia robot systems.

4.15.2 Handling

Items are stored by OSCAR in the correct area. No human intervention is required.

4.15.3 Storage

Items are stored within a secure storage area.

4.15.4 Packaging

Items in stores are boxed and kept on shelves marked with appropriate labels.

4.15.5 Delivery

Packing and crating of completed items is done in accordance with contract specification. No external carriers are used to deliver items and the Distribution Departments handles all deliveries. This is covered by *IBWI.05 - Packaging and Despatch.*

		Page No. 16
Standard Title:	*ISO 9001 – 1987 (Quality Manual)*	
Std Ref. No.	*QM.93/94*	
Issue No.	*010*	Change No. 02
Issue Date:	*26th August 1993*	Change Date: 8th June 1994

4.16 Quality Records

Records are maintained which verify the effective operation of the quality system. These records include, specification, procedures, work instructions, reports, corrective action forms, inspection results, calibration results and internal audit reports. All records are kept for a minimum of 5 years or longer if the contract stipulates it in a secure off-site location. A client requiring access to these records will need to obtain permission from the Managing Director of Ibertalia.

4.17 Internal Quality Audits

Internal quality audits are carried out to verify that quality activities comply with ISO9001. These audits are carried out on a scheduled basis, with the results and corrective actions documented. A re-audit may be appropriate if the corrective action is considered to be highly important as it may affect the business detrimentally.

4.18 Training

Training is the responsibility of the training department who carry out any training needs identified during appraisals of staff. Records of training are kept with the Personnel Department in each member of staff's record.

New personnel will receive on joining the company, a 5 day Induction Training programme. This is covered by *IBWI.06 - Induction Training.*

4.19 Servicing

Servicing of holiday items is not included within the normal day-to-day activities of Ibertalia. However, an after-service agreement (described in *IBQP.19 — Customer Servicing* and *IBQP.03 — Holiday Service Design and Review*) is part of the service provided to customers who purchase our 'travel' product.

		Page No. 17
Standard Title:	*ISO 9001 – 1987 (Quality Manual)*	
Std Ref. No.	*QM.93/94*	
Issue No.	*010*	Change No. 02
Issue Date:	*26th August 1993*	Change Date: 8th June 1994

4.20 Statistical Techniques

Procedures are established that verify the acceptability of the products and any processes. This is covered by *IBWI.03 - Statistical Analysis*.

5. List of Quality Procedures

IBQP.01 — Sales And Contract Procedure

IBQP.02 — Performance Service Level

IBQP.03 — Holiday Service Design and Review

IBQP.04 — Contract and Sales Control

IBQP.05 — Request for Change

IBQP.06 — Configuration and Change Control

IBQP.07 — Purchasing and Supplier Assessment

IBQP.08 — Goods Inwards and Inspection

IBQP.10 — Job Control

IBQP.11 — Control of Production

IBQP.12 — Stores

IBQP.13 — Project File Configuration Items

IBQP.14 — Project Management Standard — PRINCE

IBQP.15 — Security Procedures (Information Storage)

IBQP.16 — Calibration of Measuring Equipment

IBQP.17 — Non-conformance, Corrective Action and Records

IBQP.18 — Final Inspection and Test

IBQP.19 — Customer Servicing

6. List of Work Instructions

IBWI.01 — Marketing and Sales Design Drawing

IBWI.02 — Archiving

IBWI.03 — Statistical Analysis

IBWI.04 — Product Identification and Traceability

IBWI.05 — Packaging and Despatch.

IBWI.06 — Induction Training

Page No. 20

Standard Title: *ISO 9001 – 1987 (Quality Manual)*
Std Ref. No. *QM.93/94*
Issue No. *010* Change No. 02
Issue Date: *26th August 1993* Change Date: 8th June 1994

7. Company Organization Chart

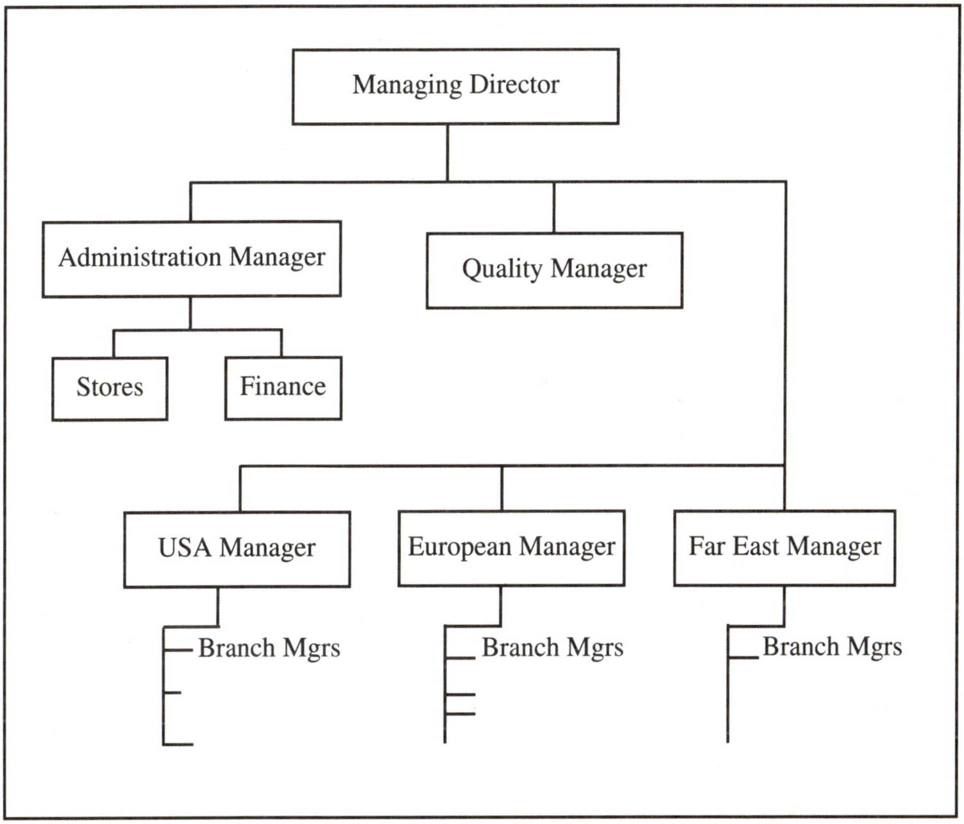

Appendix B

IT Security Policy and Strategic Standards Manual

UK Version

		Page No. 01
Standard Title:	*IT Security Policy and Strategic Standards Manual*	
Std Ref. No.	*SP.94*	
Issue No.	*3.1*	Change No. 3
Issue Date:	*June 1994*	Change Date: June 1994

IBERTALIA S.A.

Information Technology Department

IT Security Policy & Strategic Standards Manual

UK VERSION

Contents:

Amendment History

Circulation

1. Security
   - 1.1 Objectives
   - 1.2 General IT Security Guidelines
   - 1.3 Responsibilities
   - 1.4 Physical Security
   - 1.5 Personnel Security
   - 1.6 Procedural Security
   - 1.7 Technical Security
   - 1.8 Other
2. Legislation
3. Audit Procedures

Signed ______________________________

Managing Director

		Page No. 02
Standard Title:	*IT Security Policy and Strategic Standards Manual*	
Std Ref. No.	*SP.94*	
Issue No.	*3.1*	Change No. 3
Issue Date:	*June 1994*	Change Date: June 1994

Amendment History

Issue 0.0 January 1989	Draft Issue
Issue 1.0 June 1990	First Issue
Issue 2.0 January 1992	Second Issue
Issue 3.0 January 1993	Draft Third Issue
Issue 3.1 June 1994	Third Issue

Circulation

1. Managing Director
2. Computer Manager
3. Network and Communications Manager
4. IT Development Manager
5. Finance Director
6. Marketing Director
7. Quality Manager
8. Personnel Manager
9. Special Projects Manager

		Page No. 03
Standard Title:	*IT Security Policy and Strategic Standards Manual*	
Std Ref. No.	*SP.94*	
Issue No.	*3.1*	Change No. 3
Issue Date:	*June 1994*	Change Date: June 1994

1. Security

1.1 Objectives

1.1.1 This Security Policy and Standards manual is a set of guidelines for the implementation of 11 Security throughout the organization.

1.1.2 The basic and prime objective of this manual is to maintain adequate Business Continuity. Inadvertent or deliberate corruption of our systems can affect every business transaction. The longer errors or threats remain undetected, the greater the impact with cash flow, adverse publicity and loss of business confidence.

1.1.3 This manual is intended to outline the controls that are required to secure the IT environment and subsequently the business plus manage adequately and effectively those security controls.

1.1.4 This manual applies to ALL members, employees and agents of the organization whenever they are using or changing any part of the system(s) or the information stored or processed within them for any purpose.

		Page No. 04
Standard Title:	*IT Security Policy and Strategic Standards Manual*	
Std Ref. No.	*SP.94*	
Issue No.	*3.1*	Change No. 3
Issue Date:	*June 1994*	Change Date: June 1994

1.2 General IT Security Guidelines

1.2.1 Security measures shall be taken against unauthorized access to, or alteration, disclosure or destruction of information and IT systems, and against accidental loss or destruction of information and IT systems.

1.2.2 Subsections 1.4 -1.7 inclusively address the basic IT Security criteria of:

(a) Maintenance of the confidentiality of all software and information held within the organization's systems whose disclosure could harm the organization.

(b) Maintenance of the integrity of all software and information held within the organization's systems whose unauthorized amendment or deletion could harm the organization.

(c) Maintenance of the availability of all hardware, software and information whose temporary or permanent loss could harm the organization.

1.2.3 In this respect regard should be:

(a) To the nature of data and the harm resulting from unlawful access, alteration, disclosure, loss or distinction; and

(b) To the storage place, the security measures programmed into the relevant equipment and to the security measures taken for ensuring the reliability staff having access; and

(c) To the observance of relevant legislation, including that covered in Section 2; and

		Page No. 05
Standard Title:	*IT Security Policy and Strategic Standards Manual*	
Std Ref. No.	*SP.94*	
Issue No.	*3.1*	Change No. 3
Issue Date:	*June 1994*	Change Date: June 1994

(d) To the measures taken enabling effective implementation and administration of security procedures.

1.2.4 Company IT equipment will only be operated by authorized personnel.

1.2.5 Access to company data is permitted ONLY for purposes necessary for the official discharge of official company duties and personal plus private use of company systems is *strictly forbidden.*

1.2.6 Nominated personnel will maintain a list of all authorized users of IT equipment within their sphere of responsibility.

		Page No. 06
Standard Title:	*IT Security Policy and Strategic Standards Manual*	
Std Ref. No.	*SP.94*	
Issue No.	*3.1*	Change No. 3
Issue Date:	*June 1994*	Change Date: June 1994

1.3 Responsibilities

1.3.1 All personnel must be constantly alert to IT Security Principles described in this Policy. There are no circumstances that can relieve any employee of this responsibility.

1.3.2 IT Security overall responsibility is defined as:

(a) IT Security Committee; this is a top level management forum representing technical and user departments. Its main responsibilities include:

- advice to the Executive on matters of IT Security and Planning;
- update and maintain the IT Security Policy;
- translates the policy into an IT Security Programme;
- monitors the implementation;
- reviews the effectiveness of the policy;
- promotes awareness of IT security issues;
- overall accountability to the Executive Board.

(b) IT Security Manager; this is a senior manager with the following responsibilities:

- assists the IT Security Committee in the formulation and maintenance of the IT Security Policy;
- advice on the implementation of the IT Security Programme;
- monitors security daily;
- advice on specific IT Security issues;
- delivers Security awareness.

	Page No. 07	
Standard Title:	*IT Security Policy and Strategic Standards Manual*	
Std Ref. No.	*SP.94*	
Issue No.	*3.1*	Change No. 3
Issue Date:	*June 1994*	Change Date: June 1994

(c) Departmental Security Liaison Officer, this is a senior manager with the following responsibilities:

- liaison with IT Security Manager;
- assist the IT Security Manager in threat/risk assessment;
- has a wide appreciation of security within his/her business context;
- assist in the creation of IT contingency plans;
- creates departmental recovery plans.

		Page No. 08
Standard Title:	*IT Security Policy and Strategic Standards Manual*	
Std Ref. No.	*SP.94*	
Issue No.	*3.1*	Change No. 3
Issue Date:	*June 1994*	Change Date: June 1994

1.4 Physical Security

1.4.1 Access to the site, buildings and IT computer room(s) is restricted to those authorized to the extent necessary for the execution of their duties, or the purpose for which they are authorized. Visitors must always be accompanied by a member of staff. Photographic cameras are strictly prohibited and should be left with the House Manager at reception.

1.4.2 All staff have a responsibility to ensure that reasonable precautions are taken to protect the installation, staff, equipment and data from natural and other hazards. This should adhere (in the UK) to the 'Health and Safety Act Work Act (1974)'.

1.4.3 In this respect regard should be had for:

(a) The maintenance of an effective IT contingency plan (IT Security Manager responsible);

(b) The interface/integration to the Business Recovery Plan (refer to Ibertalia's Recovery Plan);

(c) The measures taken enabling the proper and effective use of physical security tools;

(d) Strict adherence to Ibertalia's Recovery Plan (appendix C in this publication).

1.4.4 Strict control must be kept of the movement of all IT equipment. IT equipmnet will NOT be moved without the written authorization of a senior manager (form IBEQUIP must be filled in and filed with the Administration Department for audit purposes).

1.4.5 Strict control must be kept over the storage availability and use of all computer storage media and logs will be kept of the existence and movement of storage media, showing the content and disposal of such material.

1.4.6 The level of security for the location of IT equipment will be that which applies to the type of data that is accessible. However, screen displays must not be located in public view under any circumstances.

1.4.7 Eating, drinking and smoking is prohibited whilst using any IT equipment.

1.4.8 Care should be taken when:

(a) Placing diskettes next to certain electrical appliances as it can cause information corruption or loss;

(b) Obstructing air vents;

(c) Cable layout - care should be taken with power and communications lines;

(d) Storage media (e.g, PC diskettes) must be stored away when not in use. Any company confidential media should be stored in lockable cabinets.

1.4.9 Where the location of Personal Computers are defined as 'open to the public' (e.g., Reception), all such equipment must be 'bolted' to the table they sit on.

1.4.10 Access to IT equipment within the 'open to the public' environment must be kept to a minimum. Regard should be had for:

(a) No system is to be linked in any way to the corporate communications network;

(b) No Corporate information should be held on these systems;

(c) Visitors found using this equipment must be challenged;

(d) All systems function solely as 'stand-alone';

(e) All equipment shall be kept in a clean and tidy environment (e.g., no papers, manuals should be in view).

		Page No. 10
Standard Title:	*IT Security Policy and Strategic Standards Manual*	
Std Ref. No.	*SP.94*	
Issue No.	*3.1*	Change No. 3
Issue Date:	*June 1994*	Change Date: June 1994

1.5 Personnel Security

1.5.1 The roles of all personnel involved in or associated with IT systems are defined in the IT Standards Manual (a copy can be attained from the Computer Manager) and all tasks falling outside those specified must be authorized by a senior manager.

1.5.2 All staff must undergo the basic IT Security awareness 1 day training session.

1.5.3 On accepting an offer of employment, new members of staff must be given:

(a) The conditions of employment;

(b) The security policies guidelines;

(c) The Health and Safety procedures (inc. emergency procedures);

(d) Personal IT Security responsibility guideline – note each new member of staff must acknowledge receipt of these details.

1.5.4 As far as possible contract staff (e.g., maintenance, manufacturers, programmers, etc.) will not have access to live data, and where access is permitted, it must be strictly controlled and documented. Access to the Corporate Network is restricted to local applications.

	Page No. 11	
Standard Title:	*IT Security Policy and Strategic Standards Manual*	
Std Ref. No.	*SP.94*	
Issue No.	*3.1*	Change No. 3
Issue Date:	*June 1994*	Change Date: June 1994

1.5.5 Where practical, logs (computer based or manual) will be kept of all transactions carried out on terminals/PCs/ etc.

1.5.6 Regular checks will be made of IT logs and/or system management reports to detect attempts at unauthorized access.

1.5.7 The following legal consideration will apply to all areas of IT systems within the organization (Note: These are only applicable in the UK, please refer to your local IT Department for the equivalent legislation pertaining to your country.):

(a) Data Protection Act 1984 – this applies to all users dealing with personal data (see Section 2 in this Policy and the Data Protection Guideline for further details);

(b) Companies Act 1985 – this applies to the protection of company registers and records (see Companies Act Guidelines for further details);

(c) Copyright, Design and Patents Law 1988 – this makes specific provision for the protection of computer software (see the Copyright Guidelines for further details);

(d) Computer Misuse Act 1990 - the abuse of computers, of unauthorized access, use of stolen software is a criminal offence and will be dealt with according to subsection 1.5.8 below (see Section 2 of this Policy and the Computer Misuse Guidelines for further details).

		Page No. 12
Standard Title:	*IT Security Policy and Strategic Standards Manual*	
Std Ref. No.	*SP.94*	
Issue No.	*3.1*	Change No. 3
Issue Date:	*June 1994*	Change Date: June 1994

1.5.8 Any person found guilty of a criminal offence may be dealt with:

- (a) An indictment (unlimited fine);
- (b) An indictment and imprisonment;
- (c) Summarily – fine not exceeding the current maximum ($5,000)

1.5.9 All employees are personally responsible for their actions which may result in damages being awarded against them.

1.6 Procedural Security

1.6.1 Passwords will be issued by or on behalf of the system manager.

1.6.2 When notifying the users of their initial password, the following guidelines apply:

- (a) The password must not be disclosed to another person;
- (b) Responsibility lies with the user to exercise care that his/her password is not disclosed to other persons;
- (c) On initial use, the system will require the user to change it;
- (d) The password must not be written down;
- (e) Names, nicknames, obscene or obvious words should not be used as passwords;
- (f) Where possible passwords should be at least seven alphanumeric characters.

1.6.3 It is a disciplinary offence to write down your password. Furthermore any employee who attempts to discover, or is found using, another employee's password will be dismissed.

1.6.4 The use of home computers for company purposes or the use of company computers for unauthorized purposes is prohibited.

1.6.5 An asset register shall be administered by the IT Administration Office. Part of its function will be to monitor and advise on:

(a) Requisition of new assets;

(b) Disposal of existing assets;

(c) Transfer of assets between users.

1.6.6 To avoid viruses regard should be had for

(a) Software developed in-house should be subject to thorough testing and inspection. All changes to existing software should be justified and subject to a formal approval procedure.

(b) Authenticated copies of all software should be kept available for restoring the system if the current software is corrupted.

(c) Software from outside the organization should only be accepted from known, reputable suppliers and be delivered to the central IT Administration Department. The central IT Administration Department will virus-proof each copy of PC software on their 'dirty' PC.

Users are not allowed to introduce their software, however acquired, and any packages received free of charge should be viewed with great suspicion.

		Page No. 14
Standard Title:	*IT Security Policy and Strategic Standards Manual*	
Std Ref. No.	*SP.94*	
Issue No.	*3.1*	Change No. 3
Issue Date:	*June 1994*	Change Date: June 1994

1.6.7 To remove an identified virus regard should be had for:

(a) If the users suspect a virus they should contact the IT Help Desk; they should not switch off their machine and, in particular, they should not try using different data or different machines as they will only help the virus propagate.

(b) If a virus is detected straight away, it can be circumvented by switching off the system concerned and then re-booting from a write-protected non-infected system disk. The unaffected files may then be copied from the infected disk to another.

(c) All infected media should be removed.

(d) Software should be restored from the copies taken before the virus was loaded.

(e) When these steps are taken, checks should be made to ensure that the virus is not sill present.

1.6.8 Incident reporting can be exercised by any member of staff and regard should be had for:

(a) The reporting of IT Security incidents is for the common good – the major concern is not to attach blame to an individual but to rectify the fault and prevent future incidents occurring.

(b) Failure to report incidents is a serious matter.

(c) All IT Security incidents should be reported to the IT Security Manager immediately.

(d) An IT Security incident is deemed to occur whenever the confidentiality, integrity or availability of a system is breached, intentionally or otherwise.

(e) All breaches (except trivial ones – see (f) and (g)) of CIA must be reported.

(f) The IT Security Manager does not need to be informed about one-off minor incidents, e.g., where a user has trouble keying in a password. Note, the definition of a minor incident cannot be 'strictly' defined, e.g., switching off the power to a mainframe or server is obviously not a minor incident – but switching off the power to your laptop personal computer could be.

(g) The definition of trivial is best left as a matter for judgement by those operating the system.

1.6.9 When an incident has been identified regards should be given to:

(a) All reports of IT security incidents should be made using the proper IT Security forms (available from the IT Security Manager);

(b) The forms should be completed by the individual best placed to provide maximum information re the incident. The reports should be forwarded to the IT Security Manager.

(c) Once a form has been completed it must be handled with the same security as that of the highest level of the data, processed on the system, e.g., if the data is 'classified' then the form is also 'classified'.

Page No. 16

Standard Title:	*IT Security Policy and Strategic Standards Manual*	
Std Ref. No.	*SP.94*	
Issue No.	*3.1*	Change No. 3
Issue Date:	*June 1994*	Change Date: June 1994

	Page No. 17	
Standard Title:	*IT Security Policy and Strategic Standards Manual*	
Std Ref. No.	*SP.94*	
Issue No.	*3.1*	Change No. 3
Issue Date:	*June 1994*	Change Date: June 1994

1.7 Technical Security

1.7.1 All reasonable steps must be taken to prevent and detect corruption of data and software.

1.7.2 System access is controlled within the first level by the use of personal smart cards which generates an authenticated ticket to the server. Second level access is defined by a personal password.

1.7.3 All data storage must be capable of recovery. Each storage medium must be strictly monitored (i.e.., movement and disposal). The level of protection for data which are temporarily inaccessible through fault or breakdown should be that which applies when the data are accessible.

1.7.4 Where possible a computer log should be kept of all transactions. Terminal logs and operators' manuals should be kept near the relative terminal/PC. They should not be left exposed or in view of visitors to the office.

1.7.5 Software and software testing must be monitored for compliance with specifications, technical and security standards. Under no circumstance can live data be used for testing or development.

1.7.6 All data entered into the 'live' system will, as far as possible, be validated automatically to ensure accuracy and integrity.

1.7.7 All IT equipment (whether computers, WPs, communications equipment, etc.) must be subject to strict control.

1.7.8 Faulty equipment must be treated with the same level of security as that applicable when the equipment is fully operational.

1.7.9 Strict security must be exercised over printouts and access to printout is denied to unauthorized persons. Careless handling of restricted printouts is a disciplinary offence.

		Page No. 18
Standard Title:	*IT Security Policy and Strategic Standards Manual*	
Std Ref. No.	*SP.94*	
Issue No.	*3.1*	Change No. 3
Issue Date:	*June 1994*	Change Date: June 1994

1.7.10 All printouts (printed materials) containing personal data or company confidential data must be disposed of as 'confidential waste' as soon as the information is no longer required for company purposes.

1.7.11 In terms of our networks, regard should be given to:

(a) All Local Area Network users outside the IT Department will only be given normal access;

(b) Data cannot be passed between computers without the written authority of a senior manager,

(c) Dial-up is strictly prohibited (under all circumstances);

(d) All terminals/PCs connected to a host/server will be automatically disconnected after a set time without activity. Time allowed to be set by the Systems Administrator and depends on system accessed.

(e) Transmission of all company information (irrespective of its security classification) outside the company secure boundary (e.g., via the public domain) must be encrypted. Encryption mechanism used to be defined by the IT Security Manager.

(f) Responsibility for overall control of network access rests with the Network Administrators.

1.7.12 Use of facsimile machines, regard should be given to:

(a) All facsimile machines must not be located within a public area.

(b) Secure facsimile machines must be located in the Executive Room, 10th Floor. Access to these will be strictly controlled via the use of personal Smart Cards.

Page No. 19

Standard Title:	*IT Security Policy and Strategic Standards Manual*	
Std Ref. No.	*SP.94*	
Issue No.	*3.1*	Change No. 3
Issue Date:	*June 1994*	Change Date: June 1994

1.8 Other

1.8.1 All manuals, books, letter, etc. relating to company computers are confidential and must not be viewed by unauthorized persons, neither must the contents be disclosed to such persons. They will not be removed from company premises other than for official purposes.

1.8.2 Risk analysis is performed by the IT Security Department using the company standard procedures based upon CRAMM.

1.8.3 An IT Contingency Plan exists (filed with the IT Security Manager) which covers emergencies and disasters.

1.8.4 All Contingency Plans (including Business Recovery) must be tested at least every six months.

2. Legislation

2.1 Data Protection Act 1984 (UK)

2.1.1 This act applies to all users dealing with personal data. Appropriate security measures shall be taken against unauthorized access to, alteration, disclosure or destruction of personal data and against accidental loss or destruction of the same.

2.1.2 The rules defined within the Act define the procedures to be followed by all staff of our organization concerning the obtaining, using, disclosing, security and general handling of personal data.

2.1.3 Copies of the Act will be readily available at each office and department having a computer/terminal/WP.

2.1.4 It is for each individual employee to make sure that the requirements of the Act are complied with.

2.1.5 Every system will be monitored to ensure that the Act, Principles, Codes of Practice and Rules are complied with.

		Page No. 20
Standard Title:	*IT Security Policy and Strategic Standards Manual*	
Std Ref. No.	*SP.94*	
Issue No.	*3.1*	Change No. 3
Issue Date:	*June 1994*	Change Date: June 1994

2.2 The Computer Misuse Act 1990 (UK)

2.2.1 This Act deals with the abuse of computers and in particular the use of unauthorized or stolen software.

2.2.2 It is a criminal offence for an unauthorized employee or any other unauthorized person to:

(a) access our IT Systems or data;

(b) access our IT Systems or data with intent to commit a further crime;

(c) modify any program or data held in our IT systems.

2.2.3 The full weight of the Law (British Justice System) will be utilized to convict any unauthorized usage of our IT systems.

2.2.4 In order to fulfil 2.2.3 above the IT department is responsible for collecting the required proof of unauthorized use of our IT systems. Secure audit procedures will be utilized.

2.2.5 When an investigation is authorized the Local Police Authority must be fully informed and collaboration sought.

	Page No. 21	
Standard Title:	*IT Security Policy and Strategic Standards Manual*	
Std Ref. No.	*SP.94*	
Issue No.	*3.1*	Change No. 3
Issue Date:	*June 1994*	Change Date: June 1994

3. Audit Procedures

3.1 Objectives

3.1.1 This Security Policy and Strategic Standard will be reviewed on a regular basis (at least once a year) by the Corporate Audit and Security Committee. The basic aim is to review the security measures as a whole and their effectiveness.

3.1.2 The Corporate Audit and Security Committee is responsible for frequent and irregular audits of all company IT systems with the following objective:

(a) To detect errors in data and to cause these to be rectified;

(b) To identify the causes of error found and to recommend improvements to existing administrative procedures;

(c) To report to the IT Steering Group Management Team any anomalies found and confidence level of the accuracy of the data held within our systems;

(d) To examine the security and use of data.

3.1.3 The Corporate Audit and Security Committee will evaluate on a regular basis the effectiveness of contingency arrangements for alternative support in the event of breakdown.

3.1.4 The Corporate Audit and Security Committee will use on a frequent but irregular basis the following IT controls as a mode of evaluating security: Access control, Validity checks, Control totals, End-user prints, Exception reports, manual totals, audit trails, authentication data.

Appendix C

IT Disaster Recovery Plan

UK VERSION

Page No. 02

Standard Title:	*IT Disaster Recovery Plan*	
Std Ref. No.	*DR.94*	
Issue No.	*4.1*	Change No. 1
Issue Date:	*June 1994*	Change Date: June 1994

IBERTALIA S.A.

Information Technology Department

IT Disaster Recovery Plan

UK VERSION

Contents:

Amendment History

Circulation

1. Introduction
   - 1.1 Objectives
   - 1.2 Scope
   - 1.3 Strategy
   - 1.4 Recovery Team - Organizational Diagram

2. Recovery Phased Approach
   - 2.1 Disaster Team Leader Responsibilities
   - 2.2 Temporary Recovery Centre
   - 2.3 Organization and Staff Support
   - 2.4 Plan Maintenance and Testing

3. Short Term Recovery

4. Long Term Recovery

Signed: ______________________

Managing Director

		Page No. 03
Standard Title:	*IT Disaster Recovery Plan*	
Std Ref. No.	*DR.94*	
Issue No.	*4.1*	Change No. 1
Issue Date:	*June 1994*	Change Date: June 1994

Page No. 04

Standard Title:	*IT Disaster Recovery Plan*	
Std Ref. No.	*DR.94*	
Issue No.	*4.1*	Change No. 1
Issue Date:	*June 1994*	Change Date: June 1994

Amendment History

Issue 0.0 January 1989	Draft Issue
Issue 1.0 June 1990	First Issue
Issue 2.0 January 1992	Second Issue
Issue 3.0 January 1993	Third Issue
Issue 4.0 January 1994	Draft Fourth Issue
Issue 4.1 June 1994	Third Issue

Circulation

1. Managing Director
2. Computer Manager
3. Network and Communications Manager
4. IT Development Manager
5. Finance Director
6. Marketing Director
7. Quality Manager
8. Personnel Manager
9. Special Projects Manager
10. Administration Manager
11. I.T. Project Office Manager

		Page No. 05
Standard Title:	*IT Disaster Recovery Plan*	
Std Ref. No.	*DR.94*	
Issue No.	*4.1*	Change No. 1
Issue Date:	*June 1994*	Change Date: June 1994

1. Introduction

1.1 Objectives

1.1.1 The aim of this IT Disaster Recovery Plan is to provide a set of effective and practical procedures to ensure recovery of the IT systems following a major disaster and enable normal working to be resumed in the shortest possible time.

1.1.2 This plan deals with the Long Term recovery of the IT Service (including Hardware, Software, People, Power, Communications) in temporary accommodation or the organization's Headquarters' site in Alicante, Spain.

1.1.3 This plan also includes preventative measures and operational practice with the objective of reducing the risk of a disaster and therefore limiting its impact.

Page No. 06

Standard Title:	*IT Disaster Recovery Plan*	
Std Ref. No.	*DR.94*	
Issue No.	*4.1*	Change No. 1
Issue Date:	*June 1994*	Change Date: June 1994

1.2 Scope

1.2.1 This Disaster Recovery Plan only defines the loss of or inability to use the computer centre at our Headquarters. Recovery in other areas is not included.

1.2.2 This plan does NOT include a general contingency for the Business as a whole as this is covered by the Strategic Business Recovery Plan. However, it forms a subset of the Strategic Business Recovery Plan and consequently must interface with it in its entirety.

1.3 Strategy

1.3.1 It is estimated that complete recovery from a major disaster can take in excess of one year while rebuilding takes place. To provide this degree of recovery capability a Contingency contract has been signed with Teleinformatica S.A. who undertake to erect, within a seven day period (continuous) following a disaster, a portable air-conditioned computer room of 1500 square metres, complete with its own electricity supply and communications lines. This portable building would be erected on the HQ South car park.

1.3.2 In addition to the period needed to construct the recovery building, our Hardware supplier will require time in which to deliver, install and test the replacement equipment. It is estimated that this will not be greater than two weeks.

		Page No. 07
Standard Title:	*IT Disaster Recovery Plan*	
Std Ref. No.	*DR.94*	
Issue No.	*4.1*	Change No. 1
Issue Date:	*June 1994*	Change Date: June 1994

1.4 Recovery Team - Organizational Diagram

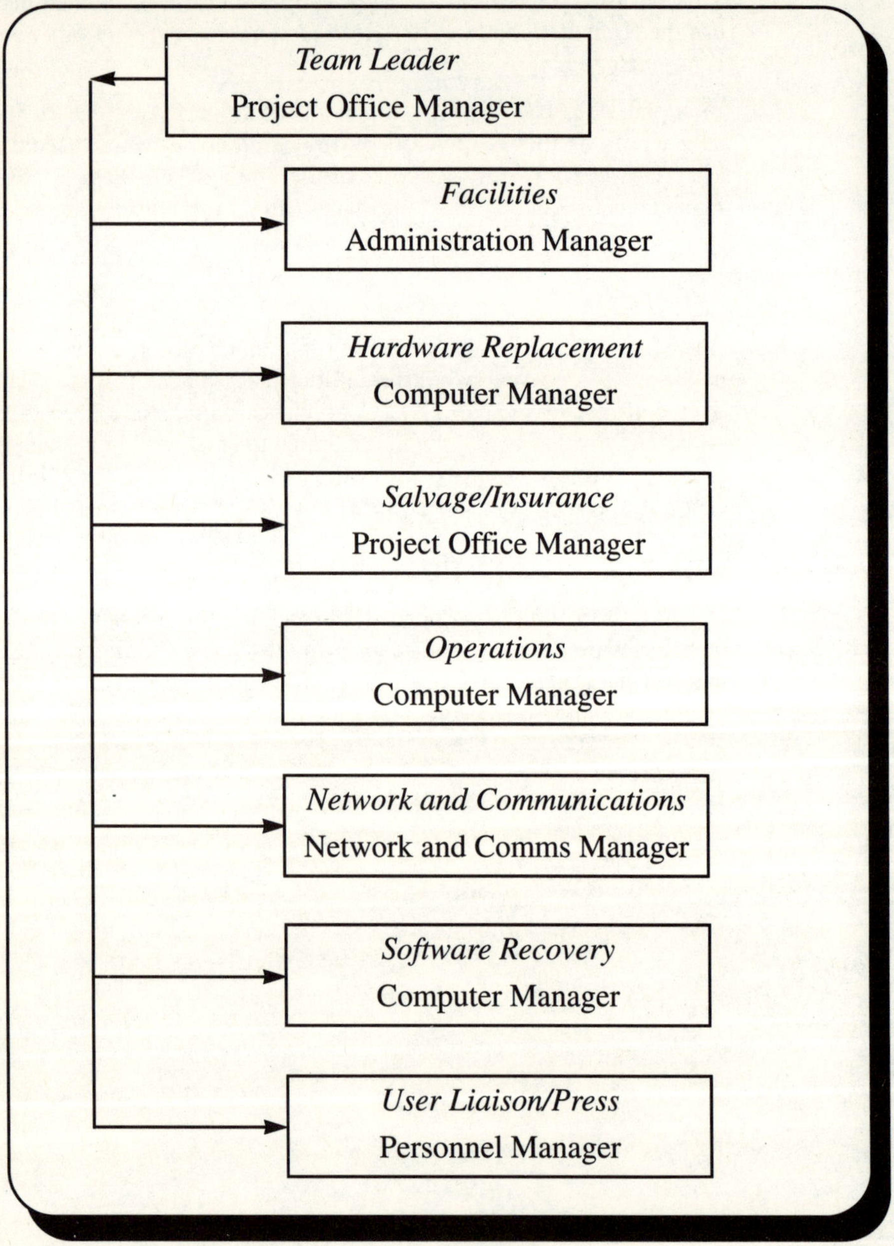

		Page No. 08
Standard Title:	*IT Disaster Recovery Plan*	
Std Ref. No.	*DR.94*	
Issue No.	*4.1*	Change No. 1
Issue Date:	*June 1994*	Change Date: June 1994

2. Recovery Phased Approach

For planning purposes four phases of recovery have been identified:

- Immediate
- Short Term
- Long Term
- Permanent Replacement

The interaction of the various phases of recovery is described below:

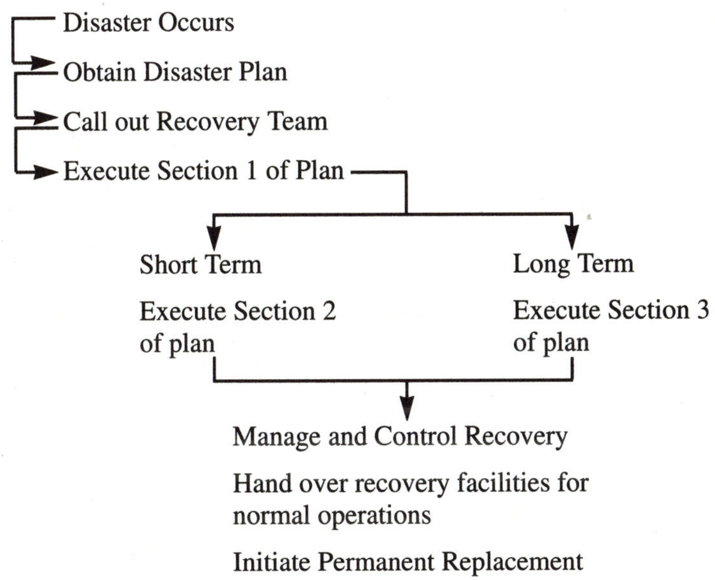

		Page No. 09
Standard Title:	*IT Disaster Recovery Plan*	
Std Ref. No.	*DR.94*	
Issue No.	*4.1*	Change No. 1
Issue Date:	*June 1994*	Change Date: June 1994

2.1 Disaster Team Leader Responsibilities

2.1.1 Ensure that all staff on duty are accounted for.

2.1.2 Call together the Recovery Team (home telephone numbers of the Recovery Team and other key members of staff are held in Appendix A of this Plan. Appoint immediate deputies for any members not available.

2.1.3 Make suitable arrangement for security and control of access to disaster area.

2.1.4 Establish working accommodation for the Recovery Team.

2.1.5 Assess damage to the computer centre (equipment, building, files, documentation, etc.).

2.1.6 If damage to the computer facility is serious, notify Teleinformatica S.A. (refer to 2.3).

2.1.7 If equipment is destroyed or damaged notify suppliers that immediate replacement or repair is needed.

2.1.8 Protect equipment and areas not damaged from further damage:

(a) If possible restrict the speed of fire and protect vital equipment, make sure the fire service are familiar with the installation;

(b) Close doors, shut down electrical equipment;

(c) Cover equipment affected by water from above, know where stop cocks and drains are situated;

(d) Extract smoke as quickly as possible;

(e) Dry out wet equipment as soon as possible;

(f) Secure the room and keep dry conditions;

(g) Do not power up until equipment is moisture free.

		Page No. 10
Standard Title:	*IT Disaster Recovery Plan*	
Std Ref. No.	*DR.94*	
Issue No.	*4.1*	Change No. 1
Issue Date:	*June 1994*	Change Date: June 1994

2.1.9 Establish recovery priorities.

2.1.10 Decide whether short term stand-by can be arranged.

2.1.11 Give team members a copy of the part of the plan for which they are responsible and instruct them to follow it.

2.1.12 Co-ordinate the activities of all team members, monitor progress and hold periodic team review meetings.

2.1.13 Ensure that statements on progress are issued to senior management and users and all IT Staff.

2.1.14 Ensure that immediate control is exercised over information passed to the press about the extent of the damage, the recovery timescales and impact on the business.

2.1.15 Ensure photographic records are obtained.

2.1.16 Determine the status of all jobs since the last update and establish the steps needed to bring databases and other files up to date.

		Page No. 11
Standard Title:	*IT Disaster Recovery Plan*	
Std Ref. No.	*DR.94*	
Issue No.	*4.1*	Change No. 1
Issue Date:	*June 1994*	Change Date: June 1994

2.2 Temporary Recovery Centre

2.2.1 Ibertalia has a contract with Teleinformatica S.A. which provides a portable computer centre of 1500 square metres erected and installed with electrical, air conditioning and communications equipment and lines in a seven day period, following a disaster.

2.2.2 In the event of a disaster it will be necessary to make one telephone call to initiate the Teleinformatica recovery procedure.

2.2.3 The Telephone numbers to call are:

01034 61 234 1349

or

01034 61 123 4567

2.2.4 These numbers are manned 24 hours a day, 7 days a week throughout the year. Give the operator the following information:

(a) Contract Number and Ibertalia's name and address;

(b) That a computer disaster has occurred;

(c) The scale of the disaster;

(d) Your name and title;

(e) Your telephone number.

2.2.5 A representative assessor from Teleinformatica will travel immediately to the disaster site and evaluate the situation.

2.2.6 The Disaster Situation will be assessed by the assessor who will determine whether a disaster has occurred. If this is confirmed then, provided that the intended site for the portable facility is still viable and that un-impeded access is given, Teleinformatica will supply, erect and install the facility.

2.2.7 If only partial damage has occurred but it is necessary to transfer or install replacement computer equipment in another environment in order to continue operations, the same emergency service will apply.

2.2.8 If damage has affected operations but is not sufficient to justify transferring to a portable facility the following applies:

(a) Air conditioning equipment, power distribution facilities and standby power can be attained from Teleinformatica.

or

(b) Portable accommodation units available for short term loan are available for ancillary operations (e.g., Data Preparation).

Page No. 13

Standard Title:	*IT Disaster Recovery Plan*	
Std Ref. No.	*DR.94*	
Issue No.	*4.1*	Change No. 1
Issue Date:	*June 1994*	Change Date: June 1994

2.3 Organization and Staff Support

2.3.1 Staff welfare: the stresses caused by working long hours in an emergency situation can quickly lead to staff problems. Good staff relations are vital if successful implementation of recovery arrangements are to be achieved. Monitor the hours worked by key staff and ensure rest periods are taken.

2.3.2 Transport arrangements: transport requirements for staff and equipment form an integral part of recovery planning. Various methods of transport should be considered so that prior authority can be obtained for the chosen method.

2.3.3 Office and storage space: it is important that suitable working office space is made available as close as possible to the recovery centre.

2.3.4 Telephones: priority will be given to establishing the data communications network but speech lines must also be provided quickly.

2.3.5 Hotel accommodation: during the recovery phase it may be necessary to accommodate, in a local hotel, key staff who live a long way from Alicante.

		Page No. 14
Standard Title:	*IT Disaster Recovery Plan*	
Std Ref. No.	*DR.94*	
Issue No.	*4.1*	Change No. 1
Issue Date:	*June 1994*	Change Date: June 1994

2.4 Plan Maintenance and Testing

2.4.1 Regular tests both of the long term procedures and short term recovery are essential if reasonable success is to be assured. Regular 'dry-runs' will be conducted, calling together the recovery team, both on a controlled and impromptu basis to ensure all the necessary recovery tasks can be achieved and all supporting details are in place.

2.4.2 For short-term recovery to be successful and implemented quickly in times of stress, frequent tests are essential.

2.4.3 Regular checks shall be made of the location of each copy of the Recovery Plan and that the correct issue is being held. Spot checks shall also be made to ensure at least one copy is held at a secure location away from the computer centre and that it is always readily accessible and up to date.

2.4.4 The team leader shall carry out periodic audits of the secure data stores and should be fully satisfied that all data and software can be recovered according to the standards.

		Page No. 15
Standard Title:	*IT Disaster Recovery Plan*	
Std Ref. No.	*DR.94*	
Issue No.	*4.1*	Change No. 1
Issue Date:	*June 1994*	Change Date: June 1994

3. Short Term Recovery

There is no short term standby computer arrangement planned. In the interim (before the computer service is resumed) support will be given to priority users either by:

- a switchable communications link to a remote standby computer;
- users will take key input data to a remote standby computer for input in the usual way;
- a limited batch processing service will be instigated;
- manual clerical procedures and the collection of input data will be initiated in readiness to the resumption of computing service.

		Page No. 16
Standard Title:	*IT Disaster Recovery Plan*	
Std Ref. No.	*DR.94*	
Issue No.	*4.1*	Change No. 1
Issue Date:	*June 1994*	Change Date: June 1994

4. Long Term Recovery

4.1 User Liaison/Press Responsibilities (Personnel Manager)

4.1.1 To assist the User Departments in implementing emergency procedures.

4.1.2 To act as liaison between Disaster Recovery Team and Users to ensure Users are kept informed of progress.

4.1.3 To act as liaison between Disaster Recovery Team and the Press to ensure that the right picture is presented to the Press.

4.1.4 To assist users where necessary to restore business systems to normal working as soon as possible after restoration of the computer facility.

4.1.5 Needs to:

- become familiar with Recovery Plan;
- be aware of all systems run on the computer;
- advice users on the necessity to maintain up to date clerical emergency procedures;
- assist users in preparing manual back-up procedures.

4.1.6 Act as user representative on the Recovery Team, reporting user problems when needed.

		Page No. 17
Standard Title:	*IT Disaster Recovery Plan*	
Std Ref. No.	*DR.94*	
Issue No.	*4.1*	Change No. 1
Issue Date:	*June 1994*	Change Date: June 1994

4.2 Facilities Responsibilities (Administration Manager)

4.2.1 To prepare the backup site for occupation and operation.

4.2.2 Ensure site is kept clear and is always available.

4.2.3 Hold any relevant information regarding standby power and details concerning reconnection of mains power. Re-establish mains power as soon as possible.

4.2.4 Establish minimum requirements for furniture and other office equipment. Procure and arrange delivery of furniture and other office equipment.

4.2.5 Set-up any catering and toilet arrangements.

4.2.6 Provide details of telephone requirements (speech lines) to Network Team.

4.2.7 Monitor completion of Temporary facility and agree formal handover.

4.2.8 Set up security arrangements for on-going operation of Temporary facility. Notify Security team if fence required.

4.2.9 Provide on-going cleaning, maintenance and support for the Temporary facility.

4.2.10 Keep records of expenditure and pass to Salvage/Insurance Team.

		Page No. 18
Standard Title:	*IT Disaster Recovery Plan*	
Std Ref. No.	*DR.94*	
Issue No.	*4.1*	Change No. 1
Issue Date:	*June 1994*	Change Date: June 1994

4.3 Hardware Replacement Responsibilities (Computer Manager)

4.3.1 To obtain new hardware to be combined with salvaged hardware to meet processing needs.

4.3.2 Define a target configuration to meet processing needs and liaise with Facilities, Software and Network Teams.

4.3.3 Establish contacts with manufacturers, leasing companies and brokers. Order new hardware and associated equipment.

4.3.4 Seek undertaking from suppliers about lead times for delivery in an emergency.

4.3.5 Keep schedule of all computer equipment up to date. Control delivery dates.

4.3.6 Liaise with Network Team, Operations Teams and Administration Support Team.

4.3.7 Supervise hardware installation and commissioning.

4.3.8 Hand over replacement site to Software Recovery Team to restore operating software.

4.3.9 Keep records of expenditure and pass to Salvage/Insurance Team.

		Page No. 19
Standard Title:	*IT Disaster Recovery Plan*	
Std Ref. No.	*DR.94*	
Issue No.	*4.1*	Change No. 1
Issue Date:	*June 1994*	Change Date: June 1994

4.4 Salvage and Insurance Responsibilities (Project Office Manager)

4.4.1 To appraise the damage, minimise further loss and salvage equipment which can be saved. Initiate insurance claims.

4.4.2 Conduct thorough and regular reviews of insurance cover for computer department.

4.4.3 Ensure schedules of all IT equipment are kept up to date and a current valuation is maintained.

4.4.4 Liaise with loss adjusters and insurers.

4.4.5 Collate records of losses and increased cost of working expenditure.

4.4.6 Assist in planning removal of salvaged equipment to new site.

		Page No. 20
Standard Title:	*IT Disaster Recovery Plan*	
Std Ref. No.	*DR.94*	
Issue No.	*4.1*	Change No. 1
Issue Date:	*June 1994*	Change Date: June 1994

4.5 Operations (Computer Manager)

4.5.1 To bring up the new installation and operate equipment to meet newly established schedules and restore the data control function.

4.5.2 Maintain operational documentation up to date and ensure one copy of key documentation held at Remote Store.

4.5.3 Keep control records in secure storage when not in use.

4.5.4 Draw up tentative floor plans with new hardware team and ensure temporary facility is adequate.

4.5.5 Ensure operations staff are aware of recovery plans and call out procedures.

4.5.6 Devise and monitor adequate software security procedures for all software. Ensure all software adequately backed up and stored off-site. Keep copies of essential documentation off-site or in fire proof safe.

4.5.7 Assist, wherever possible, with the unloading and installation of the replacement computer.

4.5.8 Check power, heating, air-conditioning, water cooling and weights with Teleinformatica.

4.5.9 Re-build control records, as required.

4.5.10 Inform users via user liaison team of any changes in procedures.

4.5.11 Supervise operation of equipment.

4.5.12 Resume normal operational routines as soon as possible.

4.5.13 Resume appropriate security procedures immediately.

4.6 Software Recovery Responsibilities (Computer Manager)

4.6.1 To install a working version of all Operating and Applications software.

4.6.2 Keep accurate records of software releases and details of patches, fixes applied.

4.6.3 Maintain 'standalone restore' recovery procedures and periodically test.

4.6.4 Obtain back-up tapes from the remote store at C/Valencia. The keys are obtainable from the purser at C/Calderon de la Barca.

4.6.5 Re-load all software. Carry out all control checks necessary to prove validity of software.

4.6.6 Ensure appropriate back-up procedures are re-introduced immediately.

4.6.7 Maintain records of expenditure and pass to Salvage/Insurance Team.

	Page No. 22	
Standard Title:	*IT Disaster Recovery Plan*	
Std Ref. No.	*DR.94*	
Issue No.	*4.1*	Change No. 1
Issue Date:	*June 1994*	Change Date: June 1994

4.7 Network Recovery Responsibilities (Network and Communications Manager)

4.7.1 To obtain new telecommunications hardware, to be combined with salvaged hardware to meet communications needs.

4.7.2 To re establish the teleprocessing network and supply communications facilities (both data and voice) at the backup site.

4.7.3 Discuss emergency telecommunications backup with Telefonica Orange, and Mercury. Hold any relevant reports, findings and associated plans etc.

4.7.4 Agree priorities for re-establishing the network.

4.7.5 Seek undertaking from suppliers regarding lead times for replacement equipment and service levels.

4.7.6 Review all network contingency plans on a regular basis.

4.7.7 Liaise with new hardware team to establish what equipment needs to be acquired.

4.7.8 Locate and order telecommunications equipment needed.

4.7.9 Supervise testing and commissioning of the network.

4.7.10 Liaise with Operations Team on network availability and hand over to Operations when commissioned.

4.7.11 Maintain records of expenditure and pass to Salvage/Insurance Team.

Appendix D

Glossary

Acceptable Quality Level (AQL)	Maximum number or percentage of defective items allowable under, for example, acceptable sampling.
Access Control	Covers those functions intended to control flows of information between, and use of resources by, users, processes and objects. Access control ensures that information or resources are only available to, or may only be created by, those with the correct authorization.
Access Control List	A list associated with an object specifying the access rights of users to that object.
Accountability (business)	Answerability for action carried out and performance achieved to other, e.g., by a manager to his superior or by the board of directors to its shareholders.
Accountability (security)	Covers those functions intended to record the exercising of rights to perform security-relevant actions. Functions may be required ensuring that actions by users and processes are recorded, subsequently making the users accountable for the consequences of their actions.
Act of God	An event due to natural causes (storms, earthquakes, floods, etc..) so exceptionally severe that no-one could reasonable be expected to anticipate or guard against it. In, law, an occurrence altogether beyond man's normal expectation or control.
Activities analysis	One of three techniques identified by Drucker to be used in deciding the organization structure appropriate for a company, the other techniques being decision analysis and relations analysis. Activities analysis is used to establish what the key activities in the company are, as distinct from generalized assumptions.
ANSI	American National Standards Institute - the US national standards body.
Appraisal	A word used interchangeably with evaluation, assessment, etc.
Architecture	A framework for a computer or communications system which defines its functions, interfaces and procedures.
Assertiveness	Management style based on maximizing positive impact and eliminating negative impact of key personal contacts with subordinates, peers and superiors, while also respecting and understanding other people's rights and opinions.

Assessment	The comparison of a company's management systems with the agreed requirements, e.g., BS5750 to determine likely subsequent compliance with it.
Assurance	A general term for 'confidence' meaning the specific measures that could be taken to establish confidence. *See also confidence.*
Audit	An independent review and examination of records and activities in order to test the adequacy of measures, to identify the degree of conformance with established policy or operational procedures and to recommend any indicated changes in measures, policy and/or procedures. In terms of security it covers those functions intended to detect and investigate events constituting a potential threat to security. In terms of quality refer to *Quality Review* in this glossary.
Audit Trail	The chronological record of transactions on a system that depicts all additions, deletions and alterations to both data and software. It enables the reconstruction, review and examination of a transaction from its start to finish.
Authenticated Identity	The identity of an individual that has been assured through authentication (*see authentication*).
Authentication (or Identification)	Provides the insurance that a participant does not provide a false identity, in other words it covers those functions which establish and verify the claimed identity of an individual. In order to control access to resources it must be possible to establish and verify user identities, add new users, remove former users, and amend the information required for the authentication of users.
Authentication Certificate	Authentication information in the form of a security certificate which may be used to assure the identity of an individual guaranteed by an authentication authority.
Authentication Method	A method for demonstrating knowledge of a secret, in which not all authentication information is shared by both parties.
Availability	The amount of time that a system/service is actually available for use by a user, within the agreed service times.
Average Outgoing Quality (AOQ)	Average number of defective items, usually expressed as a percentage of the total items, identified under acceptance sampling.

Average Outgoing Quality Limit	The maximum average number or percentage of defective items allowable under acceptance sampling.
Awareness Level	A measurement (low, medium, high) of the awareness needed by a particular audience of a particular subject.
B1 Security	Security assessment of IT systems by the US Department of Defence (also known as the Orange Book), related to how easily a system can be penetrated. Scaled from A1 – D2, where A1 is not penetrable. *See Chapter 5.*
Back-up	A copy of all data and software stored in machine readable form, for use if the main copies are lost/damaged.
Batch Production	Manufacture of a quality of a product but not in conditions of continuous or standardized production. Differs from the one off production or job production, the standardized production of mass production, and the continuous production – of process production or assembly line or flow line production.
BCS – British Computer Society	Founded in 1957 to promote knowledge and development of computers and computing techniques. It is now recognized as one of the major professional organizations in computing in the UK.
Benchmarking	A continuous process that measures an organization's operations, products and services against those of its competitors. It is a mechanism that can lead to competitive advantage.
Biometrics	The measurement of a physiological feature of an individual as a means of establishing identity for access control.
Bomb	Loss of computer program as a result of incorrect commands to the computer.
Brainstorming	A technique used to generate a large number of ideas quickly. Its main aim is to allow groups of people to make uninhibited suggestions whether outlandish or well informed, to various problems.
British Quality Awards Scheme	Introduced by the British Quality Association in 1984 to encourage total quality improvements. Awards are made in November each year to organizations with quantified and documented evidence of events or actions carried out to improve quality.

British Standard Institution (BSI) UK custodian of standards of measurement, nomenclature, safety, product performance, etc. in virtually all areas of industry.

BS5750 A British standard defining a basic set of rules by which quality systems can be developed, implemented and audited. BS5750 (1987) is equivalent to ISO 9001. Relevant parts are:

- Part 1 (ISO 9001) covering the supplier's capability to design and supply a product or service;
- Part 2 (ISO 9002) covering the supplier's capability to control the processes that determines the acceptability of a product or service;
- Part 3 (ISO 9003) covering the supplier's capability to detect and control the disposition of any product nonconformity during final inspection and test.

Bulletin Board A privately run nodal system offering information or recreational systems.

Business Planning The process of developing a Business Strategy and its associated plans.

Business Risk The risk inherent within any organization that occurs due to the uncertainty and variability in business activity which is influenced by day-to-day work and the economic climate.

Business Strategy A definition of an organization's future business direction, needs and objectives, and the resources required to meet them.

Capacity Planning Matching the level of operations to the forecast level of demand.

Cause and Effect Analysis Also known as the Ishikawa diagram (after its originator) or the fishbone diagram (after its appearance). This is a useful way of mapping inputs that affect quality. The effect or incident being investigated is shown at the end of a horizontal arrow. Potential causes are then shown as labelled arrows entering the main cause arrow.

CEN/CENELEC Comite Europeene de Normalization/Comite Europeene de Normalization Electrotechnique – two committees which have combined to address the harmonizing of standards amongst EC countries into European Standards and supporting ISO standards.

Certification Body	An impartial body, governmental or non-governmental, possessing the necessary competence and reliability to operate a certification system, and in which the interests of all parties concerned are represented.
Certification	The authoritative act of documenting compliance with agree requirements.
CESG	The Communications – Electronic Security Group, part of the UK Government Communications Headquarters (GCHQ), provides advice on the technical protection of nationally classified information.
Change Agent	Third person, acting as a catalyst, who assists in the achievement of the smooth introduction and implementation of change.
Checklist	Series of carefully prepared inter-related questions designed to aid analysis or appraisal of a specific subject, acting as an aide memoire.
Cipher	A method of cryptography by applying an algorithm to the letters or digits of a plain-text.
Cipher-text	Enciphered form of messages or data, for example, DES-encrypted information.
Closed-loop control	In quality control, where the objective is to control the process so that it does not produce sub-standard products. Any deviation in the required quality criteria signals an adjustment to be made immediately.
Cold Stand-by	This provides accommodation (either static or mobile) with electrical supply, environmental control and telecommunications connections. This accommodation is capable of supporting a computer, although one is not supplied.
Cold Start	A program, or system, is started from the normal starting point as if it had never been run before.
Compliance	An indication or judgement that the product or service meets the agreed requirements of the relevant specification; also the state of meeting the requirements.
Confidence	A measure of the security of a system as defined by a competent authority.
Confidentiality	Guarantees non-understanding of data during its transmission. It is normally carried by an encryption function.

Configuration	The requirements, design and implementation that define a particular version of a system.
Configuration Management	The procedure by which a system is managed throughout its life-cycle to ensure that modifications to the design and implementation are made in a controlled manner. It also identifies and defines the configuration items in an organization, recording and reporting the status of configuration items and requests for change, and verifying completeness and correctness of configuration items.
Conformance to Design	This is the extent to which the product or service achieves the quality of design, ie., what the customer actually receives should conform to the design, and operating costs are tied firmly to the level of conformance achieved.
Contingency Planning	Plans prepared in advance laying down action to be taken if abnormal incidents should occur. The aim is to minimize disruption to a business and possible financial loss as a result of loss or disruption to IT. (*See Appendix C*)
Continuous Improvements	Operating philosophy within an organization by which all staff seek to make systems and processes better on an ongoing basis.
Contract Review	Each customer order must be regarded as a contract. Within this a procedural dialogue must be established between the customer and the supplier that includes the specification interfaces and communications of changes.
Corporate Planning	The activity of planning and progressing the future business direction of the organization as a whole.
Corporate Culture	The beliefs, customs, relationships between individuals and functions, and accepted ways of working within an organization.
Corrective Action	This provides the means to never ending improvement of process operation. Consequently systematic planning is a basic requirement for effective corrective action programmes. The underlying purpose of this is to eliminate the causes of non-conformances by initiating investigations, analyses and preventative actions.
Cost of Quality	Includes prevention costs, appraisal costs and failure costs.
Counter measures	A check or restraint on a system, designed to enhance security.
CRAMM	CCTA's Risk Analysis and Management Method. For use in analysis of security aspects of information systems.

Cryptanalysis	The analytical branch of cryptology; the cryptanalyst's job is to breach ciphers.
Cryptography	The synthetic branch of cryptology; cryptographers create ciphers and codes.
Cryptology	The art of creating and breaking ciphers.
Data	Information recorded in a form in which it can be processed by a computer or other equipment operating automatically to instructions given for that purpose.
Database	A database is a structured collection of interrelated data that is independent of any applications accessing it. It is created and maintained by a database management system and a common controlled approach is used to add, delete or modify its contents.
Data Protection Act (UK)	Legislation concerned with information about individuals held on computers or other forms of electronic processing though not on dedicated word processors for the purpose of text preparation.
Data Security	Control of access to data within a database or computer system, usually by the use of passwords issued only to authorized personnel.
Decrypting	The process of restoring encrypted information to readability.
De facto standards	De facto standards are standards widely adopted by the industry usually by virtue of their widespread use. They often originate as products of a single manufacturer which are subsequently implemented by other companies for purposes of compatibility.
DES	Data Encryption Standard is a 'symmetrical key' algorithm which uses the same key for encryption and decryption. First published by the US National Institute for Standards and Technology in 1977. It uses a standard algorithm (Data Encryption Algorithm or DEA) with a restricted 64 bit cryptographic key.
Dial-up	The act of accessing a network by dialling an access telephone number or by initiating a computer to dial the number.

Digital Signature	The result of encrypting data by means of the signing party's secret key. This technique allows the sender of a message to attach additional data to that message which forms a unique and unforgeable identifier of the sender. The receiver can check the message to verify the message's authenticity.
DIN	Deutches Institut fur Normung - the German national standards institute.
Document Control	All documents relating to quality should be controlled, e.g., Quality Manual, procedures, standards, etc. Control is necessary to ensure that the most up to date issues are used and referred to.
Eavesdropping	Gaining access to computer information without having any control over what is displayed. Eavesdroppers may tap into telephone lines or even electromagnetic fields radiated by a computer screen.
EDI	Electronic Data Interchange is the electronic exchange of business data, avoiding the need for paper documentation of orders, invoices and payments.
Electronic Mail	The use of computer systems to 'mail' messages between users. Messages are usually held in a central store and retrieved at the recipient's convenience, this is known as 'store and forward'.
Employee Involvement	Involvement of individual, nonsupervisory staff in the improvement of the systems and processes of the organization.
Empowerment	This is basically being given the power to do something. This term denotes the kind of delegation in which a subordinate 'owns' a task and accepts full responsibility for it.
Encrypting	The process of rendering information unreadable to all except the holder of the key.
Failure	The termination of the ability of a hardware element to perform a required function (note, hardware can fail but software can only have faults).
Fault (hardware)	An accidental condition that causes a functional unit to fail to perform its required function.

Fault (software)	A manifestation of an error in software. A fault may cause a failure – synonymous with bug.
Financial Risk	The risk associated with debt.
Fraud	A false representation by means of a statement or conduct made in order to gain a material advantage.
Hacker	A person who breaks into a computer system dishonestly and probably illegally.
Hacking	Gaining unauthorized access to, and use of, a computer.
Hot Stand-by	This provides accommodation and equipment; a building, either static or mobile, with power, environmental services and telecommunications connections together with a computer and supporting peripherals.
House of Quality	Or Quality Function Deployment (QFD). System for designing a product or service based on customer demands with the participation of members of all functions of the supplier organization. It translates the customer's requirements into the appropriate technical requirements.
IEEE	The Institute of Electrical and Electronic Engineers. A professional body in the US that takes an active role in defining standards.
Impact	The result of an attack or accident on the system which may be due to destruction, unavailability, disclosure or modification of an information or physical asset.
Information	The meaning assigned to data by means of the convention and context used in its representation.
Information System	Any procedure or process, with or without IT support, which provides a way of acquiring, storing, processing or disseminating information. Information systems include applications and their supporting infrastructure components.
Integrity	Guarantees that data will not be corrupted during processing.
Internal Audit	Constant appraisal of the efficiency of management control systems in a company.

Information Systems Life Cycle	A collective term for the various stages that an information system goes through during its existence from its initial conception through to its final implementation.
ISO	The International Standards Organization is concerned with the development of international standards across a broad range of industrial products.
ISO 9000	See BS5750.
JIT	Just in Time – a stock control procedure for reducing high inventories (and long lead times).
LAN	A Local Area Network is a communications network connecting terminals and one or more computers over a limited geographic area, normally within a building.
Life-cycle	The phases of development and operation of a system from the initial concept to final disposal.
Machiavellian	Disowning any moral or ethical standards and holding that the end justifies the use of any means, however ruthless.
Modem	An acronym for modulator-demodulator. A device for interfacing communications equipment to the telecommunications network.
NACCB	The National Accreditation Council for Certification Bodies undertakes, on behalf of the UK Government, the impartial assessment of British certification bodies for the quality management system standards ISO 9000 and BS5750.
Network	An interconnected group of computers linked by a transmission facility.
Networking	The ability of two or more computers to communicate with each other through some form of data transmission channel. Networks can be within the same building (LANs) or spread over several geographic locations (WANs).
Non-repudiation	Giving undeniable proof that data has been sent or received.

Orange Book	Refers to the publication: 'Department of Defense Trusted Computer System Evaluation Criteria'. This defines criteria which constitute a uniform set of basic requirements and evaluation classes for assessing the effectiveness of security controls build into IT systems. The publication defines four divisions (A-D) of protection ranging minimal protection (D) to verified protection (A). Divisions C,B and A are further subdivided into classes.
Passwords	A protected string of characters that authenticates a computer user, specific response or an access type.
Pirated Software	Computer programs that have been copied and sold or given away in breach of copyright.
Plain Text	Readable, unencrypted data.
PRINCE	PRojects IN Controlled Environments, a standard methodology for project management used for IS projects in UK government departments.
Private Key	A key, used in an asymmetric algorithm, that is known to only one entity.
Public Key	The key, used in an asymmetric algorithm, that is publicly available.
Qualified audit report	If an auditor has reservations in relation to matters concerning the audit then he should qualify the report. All the reasons for the qualification should be given, together with a quantification of its effect. Audit reports are qualified where there is uncertainty which prevents the auditor from forming an opinion on a matter, or where the auditor's view conflicts with the view given in the management statement.
Quality	The totality of features and characteristics of a product or service that bear on its ability to satisfy a given need.
Quality Assurance	All activities and functions concerned with the attainment of quality.
Quality Circles	Groups of workers meet to discuss and attempt to solve problems in achieving quality and production targets.

Quality Control	The operational techniques and activities that sustain the product or service quality to specified requirements.
Quality Criteria	The characteristics of a product or service that determine whether it meets requirements.
Quality Management	Responsibility for application of quality – control and reliability.
Quality Manual	A document setting out the general quality policies, procedures and practices of an organization.
Quality Market	Market in which quality matters more than price.
Quality System	The organization, structure, responsibility, activities, resources and events that together provide organized procedures and methods of implementation to ensure an organization has the capability to meet quality requirements.
Reliability	The incidence of failure, expressed for example as the average of failures per month, or as the average interval between failures, often called 'mean time between failures'.
Reliability of Service	Covers those functions that ensure consistency and availability of service.
Repudiation	Denial of one of the entities involved in a communications of having participated in all or part of the communication or denial of the content of the communication.
Risk Analysis	A complex study of probability whose purpose is to evaluate risks and to analyse how far forecasts might go wrong and at what cost.
Risk	A measure of the exposure to which an organization may be subjected.
Risk Assessment	Process and procedures of identifying, characterising, quantifying and evaluating risks and their significance.
Risk Estimation	The process of qualification of the probabilities and consequence values for an identified risk.
Risk Management	Any technique used either to minimize the probability of an accident or to mitigate its consequences with, for instance, good engineering design, good operating practices or preventive maintenance.

RSA — Named after the investors, Rivest, Shamir and Adleman, as a public key algorithm which uses two different keys, one for encryption and the other for decryption.

SWOT — Analysis of the situation in terms of Strengths, Weaknesses, Opportunities and Threats.

Symmetric Authentication Method — Method of demonstrating knowledge of a secret, in which both parties share common authentication information.

Threat — An indication or possibility of an unwanted incident that could impinge on the system in some way.

Total Quality Control — Quality Control applied at all levels in an organization, including the most senior management.

Trapdoor — A secret method of entry into a system, which usually bypasses security controls.

Trusted Third Party — A security authority or its agent, trusted by other entities with respect to security-related activities.

User — Any person who usually uses a system.

Uncertainty — Measure of the limits of knowledge in a technical area, expressed as a distribution of probabilities around a point estimate. The four principle elements of uncertainty are statistical confidence, tolerance, incompleteness and inaccuracy of the input data, and ambiguity in modelling the problem.

Validation — The checking of a system for conformance with its requirements.

Vulnerability — Weakness which could be exploited to cause damage to the system or the assets it contains.

WAN	A Wide Area Network is a comprehensive communications network connecting a large number of terminals and computers spread over a wide geographic area.
Warm Start	A program, or system, is restarted following a stoppage without losing data from the previous run.

Appendix E

References

References

Analovi F and Kakabadse A, *Sabotage*, Mercury, 1991

Armstrong Clegg H, *The Changing System of Industrial Relations in GB*, Basil Blackwell, 1979

Berne Dr E, *Games People Play*, Penguin Books, 1964

British Computer Society, *Industry Structure Model,* BCS, 1991

British Standards Institute, *Code of Practice for Configuration Management of Computer-based Systems* (BS6488), BSI, 1993

British Standards Institute, *Code of Practice for Documentation of Computer-based Systems* (BS5515), BSI, 1984

British Standards Institute, *Guide to Quality Systems Auditing (BS7229 Parts 1 to 3),* BSI, 1991

British Standards Institute, *Quality Systems* (BS5750), BSI, 1987

British Standards Institute, *Quality Vocabulary* (BS4778), BSI, 1990

British Standards Institute, *Recommendation of Achievement Quality in Software (BS7165)*, BSI, 1991

British Standards Institute, *Total Quality Management (BS7850 Parts 1 to 2),* BSI, 1992

Clutterbuck D and Crainer S, *Makers of Management*, Macmillan, 1990

Crosby PB, *Quality is Free (The Art of Making Quality Certain)*, McGraw Hill, 1979

Crosby PB, *Quality Without Tears*, McGraw Hill, 1984

Department of Trade and Industry, *Guide to Software Quality Management System Construction and Certification Using EN29001,* DTI, 1990

Edwards Deming W, *Out of the Crisis*, Cambridge University Press, 1982

Gower, *Handbook of Quality Management*, Gower Publishing Co Ltd, 1990

Heller R, *Culture Shock — 'The Office Revolution'* Hodder and Stoughton, 1990

Ishikawa K, *What is Total Quality Control? The Japanese Way*, Prentice Hall, 1985

Jenkins M and Strugnell L, *Business Japanese*, Hodder and Stoughton, 1990

Juran JM, *Quality Control Handbook*, McGraw-Hill, 1988

Oakland JS, *Total Quality Management*, Butterworth-Heinemann Ltd, 1989

Plant R, *Managing Change and Making It Stick*, Fontana, 1987

Shingo S, *Zero Quality Control – 'Source Inspection and the Poka-Yoke System'*, Productivity Press, 1986

Sterling B, *The Hacker Crackdown*, Viking, 1992

Warman AR, *Computer Security within Organisations*, Macmillan, 1993

Waterman R jnr, *The Renewal Factor*, Transworld Publications Ltd, 1988

Whiteside T, *Computer Capers*, Siggwick and Jackson, 1978

Appendix F

Useful Addresses

Addresses	*Services*
4-Sight Consulting 51 Cowper Rd Harpenden Hertfordshire AL5 5NJ Tel: 0582 462324	Quality Consultancy
Admiral plc Admiral House 193–199 London Rd Camberley Surrey GU15 3JT Tel: 0276 692269	Risk Analysis Software
Airtech Computer Security Meadow View House Crendon Industrial Estate Long Crendon Buckinghamshire HP18 9GQ Tel: 0844 201800	Network Security
American Power Conversion 4 rue Sainte Claire Deville 77185 Lognes France Tel: 010 33 1 64 62 59 00	UPS Security Consultancy
Ampal Software White Haven 31a Church Rd Burton Joyce Nottingham Tel: 0602 314315	Access Control Software Encryption Software
BIS Information Systems Ltd Wimbledon Bridge House 1 Hartfield Rd London SW19 3RU Tel: 081 543 5353	CRAMM
British Standards Institution Linford Wood Milton Keynes MK14 6LE Tel: 0908 221166	Standards

Addresses	*Services*
CCTA HM Treasury Security and Infrastructure (SP3) Riverwalk House Millbank London SW1P 4RT Tel: 071 216 3136	CRAMM Security and Privacy Quality Management
Cheyenne Software Inc Airport House Purley Way Croydon Surrey CR0 0XE Tel: 081 781 1954/5	Back Up Services Network Security
CMG Computer Management Group Telford House Tothill St London SW1H 9NB Tel: 071 233 0288	Security Consultancy Quality Consultancy (BS5750)
Communications – Electronic Security Group (L7) Government Communications Headquarters Princess Elizabeth Way Cheltenham Gloucestershire GL52 5AJ	Security Standards and Guidelines
Computer Security Systems Inc. 1 Huntington Quadrangle Suite 1C07 Melville New York, 11747 USA Tel: (215) 569 1300	Data Encryption and authentication systems
Computer Associates plc Computer Associates House 183 / 187 Bath Rd Slough Berkshire SL1 4AA Tel: 0753 577733	Data Integrity Software Access Control Software Security Auditing Security Consultancy

Addresses	*Services*
Conner Storage Systems Kings Chase 107 King St Maidenhead Berkshire SL6 1DP Tel: 0628 777277	Back Up Services Network Security
Creative Insurance Services Ltd The Forum Station Rd Theale Reading Berkshire RG7 4RA Tel: 0734 323777	Insurance
Department of Trade and Industry IT Division 151 Buckingham Palace Rd London SW1W 9SS	Security and Quality Guidelines Watchdog
Digital Signature 5453 S. Woodland Chicago Illinois 60615 USA Tel: (312) 324 6533	Encryption Software (inc. RSA)
Galatrek International Ltd Scotland St Llanrwst Gwynedd LC26 OAL Tel: 0492 640311	Back Up Services UPS
Group 4 Systems Ltd Challenge House Northway Lane Tewkesbury Gloucestershire GL20 8JG Tel: 0684 850977	Access Control Software Offsite Storage
Hogg Robinson Group plc Lloyds Chambers Portsoken St London E1 Tel: 071 283 3100	Insurance Brokers

Addresses	*Services*
Home Office IT Systems Security Branch Clive House Petty France London SW1H 9HD	Security Standards and Guidelines
Hoskyns Group plc Hoskyns House 77-79 Cross St Sale Cheshire M33 1HF Tel: 061 969 3611	CRAMM Security Consultancy
Insight Computing Bridge House Bridge St Walton-on-Thames Surrey KT12 1AL Tel: 0932 222377	CRAMM
ISL Informer Systems Ltd ISL House Sugarbrook Court Aston Rd Bromsgrove Worcestershire B60 3EX Tel: 0527 576310	Security Consultancy
KPMG Management Consulting PO Box 695 8 Salisbury Square London EC4Y 8BB Tel: 071 236 8000	CRAM Security Consultancy
Logica Defence and Civil Government Ltd Cobham Park Downside Rd Cobham Surrey KT11 3LX Tel: 071 637 9111	CRAMM
Memory Technology Ltd Rubra 1, The Mulberry Business Park Wokingham Berkshire RG11 2QJ Tel: 0734 771588	Back Up Services Security Consultancy

Addresses	*Services*
Merck Hollander Ltd Alliance House 12A Baldwin St Bristol BS1 1RZ Tel: 0272 277208	PC Encryption Software
Merlin Gerin Orion House 171-177 High St Wealdstone Harrow Middlesex HA3 5EA Tel: 081 861 4040	Back Up Services UPS
Office of the Data Protection Registrar Springfield House Water Lane Wilmslow Cheshire SK9 5AX Tel: 0625 535777	Data Protection Act
Ontrack Data Recovery Surrey House 34 Eden St Kingston upon Thames Surrey KT1 1ER Tel: 081 974 5522	Security Consultancy
P & P Micro Distributors Ltd 1 Gleneagles Rd London SW16 6AY Tel: 071 769 1022	Data Encryption Software (DES)
Palindrome (UK) Ltd 2 Burlington Court Burlington Rd Slough Berkshire SL1 2JS Tel: 0753 810751	Back Up Services
PC Security Ltd The Old Court House Trinity Rd Marlow Bucks SL6 9DL Tel: 0628 890390	Access Control Software Security Consultancy Smart Cards Offsite Storage

Addresses	*Services*
Peter Norton 2210 Wiltshire Boulevard Santa Monica California 90403 USA	Norton Utilities Norton AntiVirus
Praxis Pl 20 Manvers St Bath Avon BA1 1PX Tel: 0225 444700	Quality Consultancy
Pronto Electronic Systems Ltd 466-478 Crambrook Rd Gants Hill Ilford Essex IG2 6LE Tel: 081 554 6222	Hardware encryption (DES)
Quality Methods Association (QMA) 6a St. Marys Bridge Plymouth Rd Plympton Plymouth PL7 4JR	Quality User Group
Rainbow Technologies Ltd Sentinel House 4 The Forum Hanworth Lane Chertsey Surrey KT16 9JX Tel: 0932 570066	Access Control Software Encryption Software
Reflex Magnetics Ltd 31-33 Priory Park Rd London NW6 7UP Tel: 071 372 6666	Training Security Consultancy
Safetynet plc 12-13 Bracknell Beeches Bracknell Berkshire RG12 7BW Tel: 0344 869933	Disaster Recovery Contingency Planning

Addresses	*Services*
Security Dynamics One Alewife Center Cambridge, MA USA Tel: 010 1 617 547 7820	Security Consultancy
Sophos Ltd 21 The Quadrant Abingdon Oxon OX14 3YS Tel: 0235 559933	Virus Prevention/Detection Security Consultancy
Survive! The Disaster Recovery Group Monadock International Ltd The Chapel Royal Victoria Patriotic Building Fitzhugh Grove London SW18 3SX Tel: 081 871 2546	Security Magazine/Publisher
Symantec Ltd Sygnus Court Market St Maidenhead Berkshire SL6 8AD Tel: 0628 592222	Virus Prevention/Detection
Systems Enhancement Corp Ltd Singleton Court Wonastow Rd Industrial Estate Monmouth Gwent NP5 3AH Tel: 0600 716400	Back Up Services UPS
TDS Ltd Axis Centre 3 Burlington Lane Chiswick London W4 2TH Tel: 081 994 3696	Security Auditing

Addresses	*Services*
Telematic Systems Ltd PO Box 54 Alban Park St Albans Hertfordshire AL4 OXY Tel: 0727 833147	Back Up Services UPS
The Association of Quality Management Consultants Ltd 4 Beyne Rd Olivers Battery Winchester Hampshire SO22 4JW Tel: 0962 864394	Quality Consultancy
The Institute of Quality Assurance PO Box 712 61 Southwark St London SE1 1SB Tel: 071 401 7227	Quality Consultancy
The National Computing Centre Ltd Oxford Rd Manchester M1 7ED Tel: 061 228 6333	Escrow Security Consultancy Offsite Storage
Topsoft Ltd 14 St. John St Bromsgrove Worcestershire B61 8QY	Smart Cards Virus Prevention/Detection
Touche Ross Management Consultants Computer Security and Audit Division Peterborough Court 133 Fleet St London EC4A 2TR Tel: 071 936 3000	CRAMM Security Consultancy Security Auditing
Trisys Ltd Langham House East 29-37 Mill St Luton Bedfordshire LU1 2NA Tel: 0582 33133	Back Up Services Consultancy

Footnotes

1 'Better' is a highly subjective term and depends on how an individual sees a particular service or product.

2 The US invested heavily in Japan in the 1950s to ensure that equipment and technology could be repaired quickly and sent back to the front war-lines in Korea and Vietnam.

3 **Corporate Culture:** This is defines as a set of behavioural and attitudinal norms, to which most or all employees subscribe, either consciously or subconsciously, and which exert a strong influence on the way employees resolve problems, make decisions and carry out their work.

4 One of the best General Computer Security books on the market to date is the one written by R.A. Elbra, *'Computer Security Handbook'* (published by NCC Blackwell). Mr Elbra describes in simple terms the basic principles of security — what are the risks, the vulnerabilities and threats to any IT system. It is a good readable introduction to the subject and should form part of any serious security conscious individual's reference library.

5 In National Security Survey (NCC Survey of IT Security Failures and Breaches (1991)) it was estimated that the immediate cost of physical breaches (with 43% being accidental) was as high as £580 million per year, while for logical breaches (with 33% being accidental) the estimated immediate cost was of £530 million per year.

Note: Physical security deals with the protection of resources from malicious or accidental physical damage or loss. Such physical breaches cause actual damage to or loss of the IT hardware, software and media and will probably result in loss of availability of the hardware, data or software. Logical security is concerned with the use of software mechanism for the provision of security. Such logical breaches affect data and software without physically damaging the hardware and will probably result in loss of confidentiality or integrity of data or software.

6 An IMPACT is defined as the effect on the system or environment or individual of the activation of the threat.

7 The British Standards Institute (BSI) is the UK custodian of standards of measurement, nomenclature, safety, product performance, etc.

8 Although I am only referring to eight Quality Experts within the pages of this book, this does not obviously mean that these are the only ones or that there are not others who have contributed towards the Quality ethos.

9 **JIT:** This is the process of production where each factory unit works to a lead-time, delivering to the next unit the **exact** quantity it needs without waste when it needs it to continue its work. In terms of quality the prime benefit of using JIT techniques is the elimination of waste. A JIT system tracks the following processes:

(i) Material movements;

(ii) Material accumulations (buffers);

(iii) Process flexibility.

It achieved notoriety in the 1950s when the Japanese developed it.

10 **Quality Control:** QC focuses on product defect detection through post production inspection. It is concerned with the adherence to standards and sorting out rejects. It is based on the theory of probability and hence is sometimes referred to as 'Statistical Quality Control'. The probability of a certain event occurring or not, e.g., a failure, in a given situation can be predicted with a degree of confidence by applying the appropriate reasoning and statistical theory. If x is the number of ways a specific event could occur and y is the total of equally likely results, the probability of this specific event occurring is given by the ratio $x{:}y$. For example, when you throw a die, what is the probability of it falling with an even number showing? The answer is the number of ways a specified event can occur ($x = 3$ even sides) divided by the total number of likely results ($y = 6$ sides). Therefore the probability is 0.5. This tool will assist on the control of quality in terms of managing the inspection of batches of work (acceptance sampling) and the inspection of parts from a running process (process control). Although this tool is still a very valuable mechanism in controlling quality it is divorced from the ethos of prevention as it is solely engaged in inspection after the event. For this reason it is now considered to be an unproductive method of maintaining Quality.

11 **Quality Assurance:** recognizes that 'inspection' is not the answer and that the entire production process must be committed to meeting the quality needs of the design via the prevention of quality problems through planned and systematic activities. The Japanese refer to this as hinshitsu hoshö.

12 **Total Quality Control:** attempts to expand the QA ethos beyond manufacturing by using many of the tools of variance analysis used in QA for long-term solution rather than short-term variations. Some of its main features are its relation to the reduction of direct costs and increase quality through the elimination of waste and maintaining continuous improvement through the refinement and expansion of quality control systems and procedures.

13 A Quality Circle is a team of four to twelve people, normally from the same job function who voluntarily meet on a regular basis to identify, investigate, analyse and solve their work related problems. In order to have effective QCs there are three fundamental elements it must have:

(i) Voluntary members who have basic problem solving and quality control knowledge and experience;

(ii) A leader that can guide the team towards a cost-effective solution;

(iii) Senior management support.

14 The Pareto Principle is named after the person who discovered it at the turn of this century: Wilfredo Pareto, an Italian economist. Pareto observed that 20% of the population in Italy controlled 80% of the material wealth. This proportion was later extended to other areas, for example:

— 20% of your clients account for 80% of your sales;

— 20% effort produces 80% effect (a very useful principle in Quality).

15 Deming in the 1990s and beyond: In 1980 Deming produced his fourteen points for management; here he postulates that in order for a company to stay in business it must adopt his suggestions. Briefly they cover the following areas:

1. create constancy of purpose for improvement in products and services;
2. adopt new philosophy;
3. cease dependence on mass inspection;
4. end awarding business on price;
5. improve constantly and forever the system of production and service;
6. establish training on the job;
7. institute leadership;
8. drive out fear;
9. break down barriers between departments;
10. eliminate slogans, exhortations and numerical targets;
11. eliminate quotas or work standards, and management by objectives or numerical goals;
12. remove barriers to pride of workmanship;
13. institute a vigorous education and self-improvement programme;
14. take action to accomplish the transformation.

These points were later revised to form his 'System of Profound Knowledge' which states

1. *Appreciation of a system* — understanding relationship between functions and activities;

2. *Knowledge of statistical theory* — including variation, process capability, control charts, interactions and loss function;
3. *Theory of knowledge* — predictions should be based on past experience;
4. *Knowledge of psychology* — understand human interactions.

16 Feigenbaum in the 1990s and beyond: Feigenbaum expanded his theories for the 1990s in the form of ten commandments:

Quality:

1. is a company wide process;
2. is what the customer says it is;
3. and cost are a sum, not a difference;
4. requires both individual and team zealotry;
5. is a way of managing;
6. and innovation are mutually dependent;
7. is an ethic;
8. requires continuous improvement;
9. is the most cost-effective, least capital-intensive route to productivity;
10. is implemented with a total system connect with customers and suppliers.

17 Taguchi in the 1990s and beyond: Taguchi expanded his theories of 'quality loss' in terms of various ratios that can suit manufacturing circumstances, for instance, how far is the average of any set of responses from the target? These ratios can be applied to the manufacturing of a product and services throughout the whole 'production life-cycle' enabling control factors to be identified that influence the averages and variances. Other types of averages included for example, the average outgoing quality (AOQ), this is the average number of defective parts identified during sampling and the average outgoing quality limit (AOQL) which is the maximum average number of defective parts allowable identified during acceptance sampling.

18 Juran in the 1990s and beyond: Juran's theories can be extrapolated to the 1990s in terms of his ten steps to improving quality. In his view, less than 20% of quality problems are due to the workforce with the remainder caused by management. management must take full responsibility for what happens in their company. The ten steps are:

(i) Build awareness of why the company needs to improve their performance and ultimately their product or service;

(ii) Set realistic goals for improvement;

(iii) Organize to reach the goals;

(iv) Provide training;

(v) Carry out projects to solve the problem;

(vi) Report progress;

(vii) Give recognition;

(viii) Communicate results;

(ix) Keep records;

(x) Maintain momentum by reviewing and improving annually.

19 **QFD:** is based on adhering to the 'voice of the customer' philosophy throughout all stages of production. For example, it could include product planning, parts deployment, process planning and production planning. It is mainly applied to the production of new products and services in terms of identifying the complex relationship between the new product to market timing, customer expectation, market share, product performance, costs, delivery, service and the profit margin. In order to come to terms with (and accept the trade-offs required, e.g., profits versus safety) these conflicting issues, the requirement of certain phases must be analysed and their relationship understood. The 'House of Quality' tables alias QFD, must be used to identify the requirement of different phases, where Phase 1 becomes the 'what is required' of Phase 2, and so on. The benefits of using the 'House of Quality' include:

- Marketing advantage since the product produced adheres closely to customer needs and hence increases profits;
- Reduction in development time and costs since there should be fewer re-engineering tasks;
- Critical items identified at an early stage leading to a significant reduction in start-up problems and costs.

20 **Goals:** A goal is a statement of results to be achieved with a predetermined time frame. They describe conditions that will exist when the desired result is achieved.

21 **SWOT** stands for Strengths, Weaknesses, Opportunities and Threats. A SWOT analysis is mainly undertaken to determine strategic objectives. A SWOT exercise would try to analyse, for example, the following questions:

(i) What business are we in?

(ii) What economic or other factors affect our business?

(iii) What is our competition?

(iv) What are our strength and weaknesses?

(v) What business do we want to be in?

(vi) What constraints will affect our development?

(vii) What are the most important problem opportunities?

22 Intuition is essentially arriving at decisions or conclusions without explicit or conscious processes of reasoned thinking. Within the work environment and especially in long standing teams, each member develops subliminal cues from gestures, casual remarks and knowledge of behaviours patterns and motives of other members. This can sometimes avert disaster in work-flows (e.g., member A 'feels' that member B is ill and not performing to his/her full potential).

23 A brainstorming session is a get together by a group of like-minded individuals who try to identify where a problem is occurring and also suggest solutions to various problems, no matter how outlandish it may seem. True brainstorming meetings are rare, as people tend to concentrate on current small problems with no intuitive, free-flowing ideas emerging. Barriers must be broken down, encouraging ideas and participation.

24 **Synectics:** This a method of problem solving and ideas generation developed by William JJ Gordon in 1961. It encompasses five principles:

(i) Deferment — look first for viewpoints rather than solutions;

(ii) Autonomy of object — let the problem take on a life of its own;

(iii) Use of the commonplace — taking advantage of the familiar as a spring board to the strange;

(iv) Involvement /Detachment — alternate between getting close to the problem and divorcing yourself from the problem;

(v) Use of metaphors — let emotional irrelevant things suggest analogues that can be used as new ideas.

25 Best Practice Benchmarking is a method of investigating in quantifiable terms how other similar companies have succeeded and learning from their experience. It is essentially the investigation of how the best companies meet their challenges and how to apply this knowledge and experience to meet and exceed your goals. The gains from doing this could be a better understanding of your customers and competitors, fewer complaints and more satisfied customers and a reduction in waste, quality problems and reworking.

26 Demings described that in general 94% of defects or faults occurred die to a design error calling them common cause defects.

27 Service Level Agreements (SLA): The SLA is the formal contract of service between the service provider and the user and can contain the following information:

- Service Provider Identification;
- User Identification;
- Contact Names;
- Period of Agreement;
- Service level time, e.g., 24 hours, 6 days a week;
- Level of service (includes percentage availability, maximum occurrences of failures allowed, time to restore service, standard downtime and routine maintenance);

- Escalation of problems;
- Procedures for changing the SLA and the schedule;
- Charges and payments;
- Limitation of liability;
- Termination conditions;
- Dispute Handling procedures;
- etc.

28 Software Production Life Cycle: This is sometimes referred to as Software Development Life Cycle. It charts the development of software from conception to maturity and back within project management structures. A normal life cycle has eight stages, ie., initial study and user request and specification; system design; program design; coding; testing; installation and release; live running and maintenance; review.

The importance of the life cycle is that software development is broken down into workable modules, each dependent on the previous one and within established time-scales and budgets.

29 **Software Engineering:** This is the application of structured and systematic methods by which the capabilities of IT are made useful to users via programs, procedures and associated documentation. This means that the production of good quality software is developed using optimum resources that meet requirements, on-time and within budgets, plus is maintainable.

30 Planning can be defined as the setting of aims and objectives. In order to reach these aims and objectives you need to select the necessary course of action while determining and allocating the required resources.

31 The term hacker can mean different things to different people. Sometimes it refers to the obsessive programmer who is eager to spend all his/her time with a computer, peeking and poking through a piece of complicated code. This type of activity is not necessarily illegal — it could be simply selfless devotion to work. Normally hacking denotes a criminal offence, where an individual uses their knowledge and skill to perpetrate illegal acts. This is the type of hacking that the computer-naive public are aware of and is normally publicised by the media.

32 A countermeasure is a mechanism or procedure which protects system assets by reducing one or more element of risk, detecting an activation of a threat or recovering from the activation of a threat.

33 An impact is defined as the effect on the system or environment or individual of the activation of a threat.

34 There is no formal definition of authentication, however, in order to help the reader, we can define authentication as requiring '.. the presentation of information, which, by its private or personal nature, uniquely identifies a given party ..'. Within CCITT's X.509 recommendation it states '... virtually all security services are dependent upon the identities of the communicating parties being reliably known, ie., authentication ..'. In the business sense, this means the assurance that the communicating parties are who they claim to be. In order to satisfy this definition, we can define authentication of anything as basically the identification of any (or a combination) of four human features:

- What a person uniquely knows, for example, his bank PIN number;
- What a person uniquely has in their possession, for example, the bank card itself;
- What a person is in a physiological sense, for example, a person's fingerprint;
- What characteristics a person has developed or learned, for example, when a person is required to write their signature.

35 Passwords are one of the most primitive forms of electronic authentication, even though they may be used to good effect in most IT systems. When used properly they can provide adequate authentication to support access control procedures, especially when used as part of a dynamic access control mechanism — where the actual password only forms part of the rules of access. However, the problems with passwords are well known and documented and are generally regarded as unsafe because there are so many ways that they can be abused, for example, the classic mistake with passwords is writing them down by the terminal or in a desk diary. They are then easily found by an intruder.

36 Physical Security deals with the protection of resources from malicious or accidental physical damage or loss. Such physical breaches cause actual damage to or loss of the IT hardware, software and media and will probably result in loss of availability of the hardware, data or software.

37 Logical Security is concerned with the use of software mechanisms for the provision of security. Such logical breaches affect data and software without physically damaging the hardware and will probably result in loss of confidentiality or integrity of data or software.

38 Remember that information is the most valuable asset a company has in its possession. The loss or compromise of this asset could effectively place the whole company in a very vulnerable position, possibly putting the company out of business.

39 **Security Kernel**: Security Kernels refer to the definition of a secure core or 'kernel' prior to any definition of the system (hence is basically used within 'new' systems development) and that the entire system must adhere to in its totality. The security kernel controls all aspects of security (for instance, within it will be defined the levels of data and its associated classification in terms of 'unclassified', 'restricted', 'confidential', etc.). The use of Security Kernels are widely regarding as an effective method of implementing the highest possible level of confidence in the security of a system.

40 **Postive Law**: Postive law is referred to all legislative rules imposed by the state, which is distinguished from natural law. Natural law (originated by ancient Greek philosophers) is the permanent underlying basis of all law. It was considered that there was a kind of perfect justice given to man by nature and that man's laws should conform to this as closely as possible, This theory has had a great influence on jurisprudence.

41 **Acts**: These are normally Acts of Parliament (statute) that set out legal rules and have (normally) been passed by the governing body of the time

42 **Legislation**: When referring to Legislation, we mean the whole or any part of a country's written law. In the UK the term is normally confined to Acts of Parliament, but in its broadest sense it also includes law made under powers conferred by Act of Parliament, law made by virtue of the royal prerogative, and Measures.

43 **Bill**: A draft of a proposed Act of Parliament, which must (normally) be passed by both Houses before becoming an Act.

44 **Code**: A complete written formulation of a body of law.

45 **Convention**: A treaty, usually of multilateral nature. The International Law Commission prepares draft conventions on various issues for the progressive development of international law.

46 **Notary Public**: A legal practitioner, usually a solicitor, who attests or certifies deeds and other documents and notes or protests dishonoured bills of exchange.

47 CCTA Risk Analysis and Management Methodology (CRAMM). CRAMM is a methodology for IT security, developed by CCTA with assistance from a leading software house. This methodology was commissioned by a senior Government IT Security Committee as a way of identifying thirteen mandatory requirements, which included the ability to encompass all technical (ie., hardware, software, communications) and non-technical (ie., physical, personnel) aspects of security.

CRAMM comprises three stages, the first two of which address the analysis of risk. The third determines how the identified security need can be met, ie., countermeasure selection.

48 The IT Security Awareness Programme is a detailed plan to develop, implement and maintain the IT Security Policy. It must also include translation of policy principles into detailed standards, procedures and other actions, such as training for all staff.

49 A disaster is anything that disrupts normal IT and communications usage, whether it is due to flood, fire or any other natural/accidental occurrence, or more typically programmer/operator error.

50 Recovery is described as being the organized method of getting the system back online again to its normal day-to-day state.

51 These attacks can be identified in terms of:

Unintentional Threats:

- equipment, power or environmental failure;
- fire;
- flood;
- natural disaster (gas explosion, storm damage, lightning, aircraft/vehicle impact);

- static electricity discharge;
- communications malfunctions;
- staff shortage;
- errors by operators, programmers, engineers or users;
- accidental corruption of data.

Intentional Threats:

- wilful damage (vandalism);
- theft;
- system infiltration (e.g., hacking or viruses);
- misuse of resources;
- arson;
- deliberate corruption of data;
- disclosure of proprietary information;
- eavesdropping;
- unauthorized use of hardware/software;
- violation of software licensing agreements;
- terrorist attacks;
- etc.

52 **Repudiation**: A user may deny sending or receiving a transaction or message. This can be of prime importance, for example, within a system where the transactions that are being transmitted across the network have a monetary value. For example, Electronic Data Interchange (EDI) can be used for transferring funds across different banks and accounts. Hence, any transmitted EDI transactions that moves £1,000,000 across from one account to another must maintain its CIA and of course must not allow repudiation of the messages once received/sent.

53 **Masquerading**: This is when hackers masquerade as legitimate users by obtaining a legitimate ID and password illicitly and accessing the system. As has already been alluded to, passwords are not 100% effective in authenticating the user, since it only identifies the individual as 'knowing' the ID and password.

54 **Escrow Agreements**: Escrow is an ancient legal term referring to a deed which only becomes effective on the operation of a future event. In the computer industry escrow agreement are agreements which deal with the deposit of source codes with a third party by the licensor or owner of the software. The third party, the escrow agent, holds the source code on terms that allow him to release it to the user of the software in certain circumstances which are usually the bankruptcy or liquidation of the owner of the software or the failure by the owner to carry out any specific obligation in the licence to the user such as the provision of maintenance.

Escrow agreements balance the rights of the owner of the software, who will have a considerable investment in the secret program routines in his source code, and the user, whose whole business may be dependent on being able to use the software.

55 The TCB uses Access Control Lists (ACLs) to authenticate the users.

56 Access permissions can only be granted by the individual authorized to access that object or file.

57 The audit trail as defined by Class C2 must identify: date and time of the event; the user concerned; the type of event; success or failure of the event; the origin of the request; the name of the object concerned; the ability for the systems administrator to selectively query the log.

58 A mandatory control system is defined in the Orange Book as '... a subject can read an object only if the hierarchical classification in the subject's security level is greater than or equal to the hierarchical classification in the object's security level and the non-hierarchical categories in the subject's security level include all the non-hierarchical categories in the object's security level. A subject can write an object only if the hierarchical classification in the subject's security level is less than or equal to the hierarchical classification in the object's security level and all the non-hierarchical categories in the subject's security level are included in the non-hierarchical categories in the object's security level.'

59 Sensitivity labels are a combination of hierarchical classification levels and non-hierarchical categories. Under the Orange Book it is recommended that there should be at least 8 hierarchical levels and 29 non-hierarchical levels. The hierarchical levels are normally 'Eyes-only, Top-secret, Secret or Classified' while the non-hierarchical categories are based on a need to know basis and therefore could be 'personnel, accounts, etc.'.

60 Subjects within the Orange Book are defined as any active entity, generally a person, process or device that causes information to flow among objects or changes the system state.

61 Objects within the Orange Book are defined as any passive entity that contains or receives information. Access to an object potentially implies access to the information it contains.

62 A trusted communications path is a mechanism by which a user can communicate directly with the TCB in a secure manner. Furthermore this mechanism can only be activated by the TCB or user.

63 ITSEC defines Identification and Authentication as '..covers those functions intended to establish and verify the claimed identity of a user. In order to control accesess to resources, it must be possible to establish and verify user identities, add new users, remove former users, and amend the information required for the authentication of users'.

64 ITSEC defines Access Control as '..covers those functions intended to control flows of information between, and use of resources by, users, processes, and objects. Access control ensures that information or resources are only available to, or may only be created by, those with the correct authorization. This will include functions controlling the setting and maintenance of lists and rules concerning access rights'.

65 ITSEC defines Accountability as '..covers those functions intended to record the exercising of rights to perform security-relevant actions. Functions may be required ensuring that actions by users and processes are recorded, allowing users later to be held to account for the consequences of their actions'.

66 ITSEC defines Audit as '..covers those functions intended to detect and investigate events constituting a potential threat to security. It will often be required that system events are recorded so that later investigation will reveal any security violations and their consequences'.

67 ITSEC defines Object Reuse as '.. covers those functions intended to control the reuse of data objects. There may be requirements that system resources are open to reuse, without the allowing of improper information flows through those resources. Functions for the initialization or clearing of unallocated or reallocated data objects may be included'.

68 ITSEC defines Reliability of Services as '.. covers those functions intended to ensure consistency and availability of service. This may include functions to guarantee the timely performance of time critical tasks, to prohibit non-time critical tasks from becoming time critical, to ensure availability of resource when required, and prevent unnecessary supply and retention of resources'.

69 ITSEC defines Data Exchange as '.. covers those functions intended to ensure the security of data during transmission over communications channels. Such functions may be covered by other generic headings, but different types of mechanisms are often required to secure communications with external systems'.

70 Refer to Appendix B.

Index

Index

access control 52, 70, 77, 101, 116, 138, 140-143, 148, 201, 205, 232, 252-254, 256, 257, 268, 271

accountability 67, 83, 136, 137, 139, 141-144, 232, 271

Alderfer 58

assurance 67, 117, 126, 136, 137, 139, 141, 148, 151, 152, 166, 233

audit 52, 64, 66, 69, 70, 71, 78, 80, 94, 96-99, 105, 106, 109, 116, 123, 125, 130, 132, 136, 138-140, 142-144, 146-160, 185, 192, 204, 205, 233, 253, 258, 259, 272

audit trails 52, 67, 71, 72, 99, 117, 125, 137, 148, 205, 233, 271

authentication 67, 101, 116, 137-139, 141, 143, 144, 233, 253, 267-268, 271

authorisation 67, 142

availability vii, 4, 16, 44, 67, 71, 73, 79, 81, 92, 100, 101, 127, 135, 141, 188, 198, 233, 261

backup 70, 71, 91, 93, 96, 97, 101, 117, 129, 234, 253-256, 258, 259

Belbin, Dr. Meridith 23

benchmarking 40, 234, 266

brainstorming 34-36, 234, 266

British Standards Institute (BSI) 5, 9, 10, 103, 128, 235, 249, 262

BS4778 105, 107, 249

BS4891 9

BS5179 10

BS5750 vii, 1-2, 10-11, 63, 64, 71, 79, 104-126, 128, 142, 150, 157, 235, 249

BS7229 149, 249

business impact 100

business impact analysis 93-94

calibration 118, 122, 125

CASE 71

cause and effect 34-36, 235

certification levels 136-138

Churchill, Winston Spencer 160

classification of information 82

CoI - Cost of Inspection 50-52

Companies Act (1985) UK 72, 195

computer misuse 73, 76, 77, 86, 87, 148, 195, 204, 237

confidentiality vii, 4, 16, 67, 78, 81, 86, 92, 100, 101, 117, 135, 141, 188, 193, 198, 202, 203, 261

configuration management 114, 118, 122, 123, 131, 132, 237

Consumer Protection Act (1989) UK 72

contingency planning 52, 70, 78, 80, 81, 87-89, 91, 93-99, 101, 110, 117, 148 ,192, 203, 205, 213, 237

contract review 110-111, 131, 165, 170, 237, 257

control of non-conforming products 123, 125, 142, 165, 177

CoP - Cost of Prevention 49-52, 148

CoQ - Cost of Quality 42, 48-53, 237

CoR - Cost of Rework 50-52

corrective action 124, 125, 131, 132, 165, 178, 237

CoS - Cost of Security 52, 79

counter measures 52, 66, 82, 88-100, 137, 237, 267

CRAMM 79, 88, 89, 91, 123, 203, 237, 252, 253, 255, 269

Crosby, Philip B. 8, 11, 18, 46, 249

cryptography 101, 114, 119, 129, 238

customer / supplier chain 18, 19

data protection 70, 73-76

Data Protection Act (UK) 70, 195, 203, 238

DEF STANS 9

delegation 28, 60

Deming, W. Edwards 6, 8, 50, 249, 263, 266

DES 122, 150, 238, 256, 257

design control 111-112, 165, 170-171

disaster recovery 66, 79, 87, 88, 96, 207-229, 257, 269

disciplinary measures 86-87

discretionary protection (C-Orange Book) 137-138

document control 71, 109, 113-114, 131, 165, 172, 239

eavesdropping 77, 101, 239, 270

Elbra, R.A. 261

electronic document interchange (EDI) 79, 117, 126, 129, 150-152, 239, 270

empowerment 20, 23, 28, 59, 239

encryption 52, 92,143,148, 151, 202, 239, 252-254, 256, 257

ESCROW 111, 259, 270

Fagan, Michael E. 127

Fayol, Henri 5

Feigenbaum, Armand V. 6-8, 264

final inspection 106

financial audits 147

Fineman 58

fire 53, 69, 87, 90, 91, 269

fish-bone analysis 34-36, 235

flood 53, 269

Frankfurther, Felix 103

fraud 53, 76, 77, 90, 98, 99, 117, 148, 240

goals 23, 27-28, 265

Goldthorpe 58

hacking 53, 65, 72, 73, 76, 77, 79, 135, 240, 267
handling, storage, packaging & delivery 124, 165, 178
Health & Safety at Work Act (1974) UK 72, 192
Herzberg 58
Hoshin 21

impact 53, 66, 82, 84, 90-95, 100, 187, 240, 261, 267
information security 67
inspection & test status 123, 165, 177
inspection 49, 120-123, 127, 128, 262
inspection and testing 120-122, 165, 175-176
inspection, measuring & test equipment 122, 165, 177
integrity vii, 4, 16, 67, 71, 73, 81, 92, 100, 101, 105, 135, 137, 141, 188, 198, 240, 253, 261
internal quality audits 125, 131, 151, 165, 169, 179, 240
International Business Machines (IBM) 6, 127
Ishikawa diagram 7, 35-36, 235
Ishikawa, Kaoru 7, 249
IS08402 107
ISO9000 1-2, 63, 104-126, 128, 165, 241
ISO9001 79, 104-126, 128, 149, 152, 164-182
IT security awareness 81, 83-86, 269
IT security manual 84, 183-206
IT security policy 52, 67-81, 109, 119, 123, 124, 136, 138, 139, 141, 183-206
IT Security Evaluation Criteria (ITSEC) 135, 140-146, 271-272

Japan 3, 5, 6, 261, 262
Jones, Carole L. 127
Juran, Joseph M. 6-8, 11, 249, 264
Just in Time (JIT) 5, 8, 20, 152, 241, 262

Kanter, Rosabeth Moss 6
kernel (Security) 71

Kipling, R 156

Kirk, Captain James T. 29

leadership 21, 28, 40, 48, 53-62

legislation 72-79, 81, 85-87, 185, 195, 268-269

Lincoln, Abraham 147

Logical Security 67, 71, 103, 185, 261, 268

Machiavelli, Niccolo dei 5, 241

management of change 59-61, 79

management responsibility 53-62, 79, 108, 109, 131, 132, 165-167, 264

Mancera, Antonio vii

mandatory access control (MAC) 138, 142, 271

mandatory protection (B-Orange Book) 138

manufacturing 41-43

MARION 79, 91

Maslow 58

masquerading 101, 270

Mays, Robert 127

metrics 45-47, 122, 126

minimal protection (D-Orange Book) 137

mission 12, 13, 40, 44

motivation 56-59

Nietzsche, Friedrich 5, 135

non-repudiation 67, 101, 241

notay Public 79, 269

Ohmac, Kenidi 6

open systems 103

orange book 135-140, 242, 271

pareto 7, 12, 263

passwords 4, 67, 70, 137, 139, 196, 201, 242, 268

Personal Quality Critieria (PQC) 1-2

personnel security 194-196

Peters, Tom 8

physical security 67, 70, 71, 77, 101, 103, 125, 185, 192-193, 261, 268

pioneers, quality 5-9

planning 27, 32, 49, 50, 62, 78, 81-88, 96, 112, 149, 152, 267

Pope 58

prevention 21, 49, 51, 81, 100

PRINCE 71, 148, 171, 242

problem solving 21, 32-41, 263

procedural security 67, 70, 185, 196-199

process control 118-120, 165, 175, 262

process maturity levels (PMLs) 46

process quality measures (PQM) 41-43

product identification & traceability 117-118, 165, 174-175

purchaser supplied product 116-117, 165, 174

purchasing 114-116, 131, 165, 173-174

Quality Assurance Criteria (QAC) 41, 42, 242

Quality Assurance (QA) vii, 5-64, 151, 152, 154, 164, 165, 242, 262

- awareness 20, 81, 83-86, 164
- chain 18-20, 66
- circles 7, 21, 32, 242, 263
- control 7, 21, 40-41, 126, 243, 262, 263
- cup 10-11
- Functional Deployment (QFD) 21, 240, 265
- management system 105, 108-110, 125, 129, 130, 132, 149, 243
- manual 62-64, 105, 113, 136, 151, 153, 161-182, 243
- policy 21, 12, 16, 63, 105, 108, 109, 167
- Policy Deployment (QPD) 21
- records 125, 131, 165, 179

Quality standards vii, 20, 21, 49, 62, 103-134, 153
    system 62-64, 104-106, 109, 110, 125, 130-132, 150, 153, 165, 169, 243

reliability 44, 79, 103, 127, 137, 143, 243, 272
repudiation 101, 152, 243, 270
responsibility (Security) 81-82, 142
Revans, Reg 29
rework 49
risk analysis 52, 70, 78, 79, 81, 87, 89, 90, 93, 99, 100, 146, 148, 203, 243, 252
risks 35, 66, 69, 71, 72, 79, 81, 82, 84, 85, 87-93, 100, 110, 134, 136, 191, 212, 243, 267

security awareness 52
service 41-43
service level agreement 44, 117, 266
servicing 126, 165, 179
Shingo, Shigeo 7, 249
smart cards 52, 92, 151, 201, 202, 256, 259
sensitivity divisions 136-138
software copyright 73
    engineering 44-45
    Performance Engineering (SPE) 44-45
    piracy 73
    quality 44
SSADM 71
stastistical techniques 126, 165, 180
statistical quality control 6, 51, 127, 262
SWOT 27, 49, 244, 265
synetics 34, 36-38, 266

Taguchi, Genichi 7, 8, 21, 264
tapping 53

teamwork 21-32, 40, 52, 61
technical security 185, 201-202
theft 53, 84, 87, 90, 98,125
threat 66, 67, 69, 79, 84, 88-92, 98, 100, 102, 117, 134, 136, 141, 187, 191, 244, 267, 269, 270, 272
TickIT 79, 112, 128-134
total quality control 7, 262
Total Quality Management (TQM) vii, 2, 12, 18, 21-41, 46, 48, 51, 53, 59-62, 66, 84, 99, 100, 125, 131, 132, 152
training 28-31, 40, 49, 62, 70, 78, 80, 83, 85, 91, 92, 104, 109, 125, 131, 132, 148, 165, 179, 194, 257
Trusted Computer System Evaluation Critieria (TCSEC) 135-140
Trusted Computing Base (TCB) 137, 138, 271
Twist, Oliver 29

United States of America (USA) 6-7

verified protection (A-Orange Book) 138
vetting (staff) 79
viruses 53, 65, 76, 77, 84, 90, 91, 135, 197, 198, 257-259
vulnerabilities 79, 80, 84, 87, 89, 99, 117, 144, 244

Watson Jnr, Thomas 6
Wells, H.G. 1
White Book 135
Whitman, Walt 65

zero defect 8, 32, 43, 66, 81, 92, 127